Le Flambeau
School of Driving

by Peggy Senger Morrison

Published by Unction Press

710 Thompson Ave NE, Salem OR, 97301

Copyright Peggy Senger Morrison

First Printing June 2016

ISBN: 978-0-9819989-6-1

Portions of this book have been previously published by Peggy
Senger Morrison under this name and Peggy Senger Parsons.
This title contains some material from So There I Was ... (June
2009), So There I was ...In Africa (November 2009). Portions have
also been published on Peggy's blog, sillypoorgospel.blogspot.
com, unction.org, and ReligionandSpirituality.com a publication
of United Press International. All scripture quotes are from the
King James Version or are a translation by the author.

Book design and artwork by Brandon Buerkle

www.quakercreative.com

Dedicated to my Departed Parents,
Bernice and Orville, who get smarter every year.

Table of Contents

Foreword

There are four recognized branches of Quakerism in America today. All trace their roots to the same person, an itinerant 17th-century preacher named George Fox who began wandering about England around 1645, exhorting everyone he met to leave the established churches and their clergy and scriptures to follow what he called the "Light of Christ" within them. He entered churches, which he called "steeple-houses," and stood up during the sermons of the pastors, whom he called "hireling priests," to dispute theology with them. Dressing in leather, he wore his hair unfashionably long beneath a broad brimmed hat which he refused to take off before priests, magistrates, nobles, or anyone, in fact, but God; this refusal to do "hat honor" to his social betters regularly landed him in courts of law, and often in jail.

Though he was not above lecturing or sermonizing when the situation called for it, Fox and those who began to attend the self-referentially titled "Meetings for Worship" which grew in his wake, primarily practiced something they called "waiting worship" or "waiting upon the Lord"- sitting in silence until and unless they felt led by the Light within them to speak. Women and children were considered perfectly valid vessels for such a leading, and spoke as equals with the men; this did not help Fox's standing with the civil and church authorities. The followers he gathered about him called themselves first "Children of Light," then "Friends of the Truth," and finally "The Religious Society of Friends," which is still the sect's official name today. The nickname "Quakers" has been with them almost from the beginning: originally an epithet bestowed derisively around 1650 by a magistrate whom Fox had ordered to "quake before the Lord," it rapidly became a badge of honor. "Quake before the Lord" the Friends certainly did in their Meetings for Worship – quake till their chairs shook – so Quakers they would happily be called.

Like any institution more than 300 years old, the Society of Friends has had its share of schisms – which is how the four varieties I mentioned earlier have come to be. They cover a broad spectrum. At the right end are the Programmed, or Evangelical, Friends: they call their buildings "churches" and have pastors and hymns and an order of service, though their pastors are "recorded" rather than ordained and their orders of services often have a great deal of waiting worship built into them. On the left are the Unprogrammed Friends: they call their buildings "meeting houses" and have no pastors and no hymns and no order of service, only waiting worship. They sometimes wait an entire meeting in silence. Evangelical Friends are very Christian ("Christ-centered," in Quakerese); Unprogrammed Friends may be Christian, but they may also be Universalist or Buddhist or agnostic or even atheist. Someplace between those extremes are the Quakers who belong to Friends United Meeting, who call their buildings either churches or meeting houses and may or may not have pastors and hymns and sermons and may or may not be strongly Christian. Off to one side are the Conservative Friends; their theology is like that of the Evangelical Friends, but their Meetings for Worship are like those of the Unprogrammed Friends. They are a very small group, but if George Fox came back to life in America today, it is the Conservative Friends whom he would be most likely to hang out with.

And then there is Peggy. Peggy has been called, not inappropriately, "God's very own loose cannon." Beginning as a member of the Evangelical Friends, she remains grounded there theologically but has moved far to the left to embrace the social-gospel politics of the Unprogrammed Friends. Worship in the Quaker body she founded and long pastored, Freedom Friends Church in Salem, Oregon, is neither programmed nor unprogrammed, but a hybrid of the two. There are two almost completely contiguous Yearly Meetings – the name Quakers give to their regional associations – covering Oregon and its neighboring Pacific Northwest states – North Pacific Yearly Meeting for the Unprogrammed Friends, and Northwest Yearly Meeting for the Evangelicals. Freedom Friends Church belongs to neither of them. It is a Quaker remix, a throwback to the early days of the Society of Friends. I said earlier that George Fox, should he come back, would be most comfortable with the Conservative Friends. That is actually incorrect. He would be most comfortable – he would be downright *down* – with Freedom Friends Church.

I first met Peggy Senger Morrison in the summer of 2002. The Annual Session of North Pacific Yearly Meeting (Unprogrammed) was held that year on the campus of Oregon State University in Corvallis, and Peggy – she was Peggy Senger Parsons, then, and still associated with the Evangelicals – had been called to be our Friend in Residence (translation from the Quakerese: keynote speaker). An Evangelical Friends' pastor, from one of the most conservative Yearly Meetings in the United States, chosen to keynote the annual gathering of a group of fiercely pastorless Unprogrammed Friends from one of the most liberal Yearly Meetings on the planet? I was very curious to see what would transpire.

I was not disappointed. Striding into view in red python-skinned boots, long hair flying behind her – think Vicki the Biker from the "Rose is Rose" comic strip – she roamed the stage like a caged panther while presenting a thoroughly Biblically-based, Christian message to those thoroughly non-scriptural, Universalist Friends. Speaking without notes, as the Spirit moved her, she was nevertheless concise, organized, erudite, and challenging. She spoke of hope, using as her example the Disciple Peter, who denied his Lord three times and yet was chosen by the resurrected Christ to be the Rock on which he would build his church. She spoke of trust, using the same Peter, who could walk on water – as long as he didn't look down. ("Then he sank. Like a Rock.") And she spoke of Love. Here's how she closed:

> So this I do know. When I am stuck in my certainty, I am lost. And when I am stuck in my uncertainty, I am equally lost. But when I surrender to the possibility of Love, and do what Love asks of me – then all things are possible. I have hope – not because of anything I know. I have hope because I am known completely, and because the One who knows me completely, loves me completely.

Rumor had it that she had arrived on campus riding a motorcycle. Rumor was correct.

It was shortly after this that Peggy – unstuck, from both certainty and uncertainty – took her own leap of hope and trust and Love, and left the Evangelical Friends to found Freedom Friends Church. That is, I suspect, when the seed was planted which has now become this book. It began life as a series of columns for

United Press International. In 2009, she put a number of those columns between two covers and titled the resulting book "So There I Was..." I picked up a copy at North Pacific Yearly Meeting's bookstore the next summer and was blown away. Here was a book that truly "spoke to my condition." The language was pithy, sassy, often self-deprecating ("I've been to seminary; I am perplexed at a much higher level than when I was a child"), and so true it was positively painful. The first section, "Spiritual Disciplines for the 21st Century" became my personal guide. I began buying copies of the book in bulk to distribute among my relatives and friends.

Then came the news that "So There I Was..." would cease publication.

I understood Peggy's reasons. She had a new book coming out, "Miracle Motors," which contained some of the same material; she had become dissatisfied with the older book's look and production quality. Most of all, there was the matter of how she was identified on the cover. She had recently gone through a difficult divorce and the name "Parsons" had become a painful reminder, a drag anchor that hindered her forward progress. "So There I Was..." was something she could sacrifice to set that anchor loose. I was disappointed but withheld judgment.

Peggy came to the 2014 Annual Session of North Pacific Yearly Meeting – on her motorcycle again – to do a book signing for "Miracle Motors." I bought a copy and read it. A good book. It contained a lot of my favorite stories from "So There I was..." It contained much of value and interest beyond those. It did *not* contain "Spiritual Disciplines for the 21st Century."

I emailed Peggy, offering to edit a new edition of the older book for free if she would bring it out again. She accepted. And that is how the volume you now hold came to be.

It is not, strictly speaking, a new edition; it is more like a new book. It has a new title. Nearly all of the material that went into "Miracle Motors" has been excised; much new has been added. Some of the new material comes from blog posts; some of it comes from a later companion book to "So There I Was...." entitled "So There

I Was... In Africa;" and some of it was written especially for this volume. The Spiritual Disciplines are here, intact but reordered. So are the sections on Quaker thought; on lessons from Peggy's life (expanded and retitled); and on theological reflections from current events (also expanded and retitled). New sections cover Peggy's thoughts on sexual minorities and on theological myths. And there is a very large, occasionally harrowing, often humorous, always intense and interesting new section on her work as a trauma healer in East Africa following the genocidal civil wars in that region. The African section, unlike the rest of the book, brings no remarkable theological insights; it offers, instead, the remarkable *experiences* of one who, having had those insights, is determined to live them – unflinchingly, unremittingly, and wherever in the world they require her to go.

If you haven't read "So There I Was...," by all means read this book. If you *have* read "So There I Was...," read this one anyway; in computer terms, this is version 3.0 to the earlier book's beta. If you have read and loved "Miracle Motors," read this for the insights it will give you into the roots of that book; if you are a Quaker, read it for the insights it will give you into your own faith. If you have never read either "So There I Was..." or Miracle Motors," have never heard of Peggy Senger Morrison, and think Quakers died out in the 19th century or live on only as oatmeal and motor oil, read this book and prepare to have your head explode.

And if you are one of my relatives and/or friends, beware. I am going to start handing out copies again.

—William Ashworth

Critically acclaimed environmental author William Ashworth holds an Oregon Book Award for Creative Nonfiction (1999) and a Kansas Notable Book Award (2007). A committed Quaker, he has held numerous positions in both his home meeting and in North Pacific Yearly Meeting.

Pray for me. If I perish, I perish

—Queen Esther

The world has edges. Not the kind that mariners used to worry about, but hard, sharp drop-offs none the less. They are cut by economics and culture, religion and mental health, gender, race, and status. Some people get pushed to the edges, some people seek them, and some are born there. I have come to believe that God does God's best work at the edges. It took me a while to figure it out, but I now know why I am here. I am here for the edge people.

Frontiers are dangerous. You better grow some spiritual cojones if you want to spend much time there. You better have some skills. You better go deep or you won't get far. We are all enrolled in a cosmic Driver's Ed class. Some of us never show up the first day. Some stay in the classroom. Some kidnap the instructor and head for the horizon during the practicum. I know I need better skills. I practice. I fail. I remember. I apply. I drive too fast. It could all go up in flames at any moment.

I am an explorer following the faded maps of previous explorers, and charting new territory. I move in a Christward direction with some edgewise theology. I'll never catch up with Jesus. But sometimes I find the bread crumbs and wine drops that he leaves me as a trail. Sometimes I catch a bit of his whistling around the next bend. Always, we are heading to the places where many say God cannot be found. They wouldn't know God if God bit them on the nose. Godless places do not exist. But there are places forsaken by God's people. I know, I've been there. I've pulled people out of ditches in those places. I have fallen in those ditches. Ditches are sneaky.

This is a collection of spiritual exploration stories. These are the stories of a student driver.

Now, Bring me that horizon!

—Captain Jack Sparrow

7

Spiritual Disciplines for the 21st Century

Matteo Ricci was a fine example of a Jesuit. Members of the Society of Jesus are scholars, but they are not scholars ensconced in an academic hermitage. They study for the purpose of engaging the world on the world's terms. Grounded in spiritual discipline, they go out into the world. They often end up as adventurers.

Ricci was born in 1552 in Italy, to a wealthy merchant family. He entered a Jesuit school at the age of nine. He immediately went deep into scholarly pursuits. At sixteen he was off to Rome to study law, but by nineteen he had joined the Society of Jesus. After six years of studying classic philosophy, theology, astronomy, and cartography, he asked to be assigned to the mission to the Far East. On the shores of the Indian Ocean he studied four years for the priesthood. He landed in Portuguese Macau, the gate to China, in 1582. There he studied Chinese, becoming one of the first westerners to become fluent in word and script.

The Ming Dynasty was deeply suspicious of outsiders, and it was rare to receive permission to visit. If you wanted to stay, it was understood that you would not ever leave. Ricci took the name Li-Mateu and immersed himself in Chinese culture. He dressed as a mandarin – a bureaucrat scholar. He brought with him clocks, musical instruments and scientific instruments as conversation starters. He completed a remarkably accurate world map, annotated in Chinese. He not only translated Western and Catholic classics into Chinese, he translated Chinese classics into Latin. He taught Galileo's sun-centered astronomy. His repute soared when precisely predicted a solar eclipse. In 1601, he was granted patronage of the reclusive Ming Emperor, Wan Li. He never met the emperor, but he was allowed unheard-of access to the Forbidden City, and entry into the highest levels of the Emperor's advisors.

He was a missionary and a priest. He baptized converts to Catholicism, but did not require conversion to European culture. He held that it did not diminished Christ to accommodate Christianity to cultural wisdom. He affirmed the veneration of ancestors. Back in Rome, the

Ricci method of evangelism was both applauded and condemned. Ricci did not know or care.

When he died in 1610 at the age of 57, the emperor dedicated a Buddhist temple to be his burying place and shrine.

Adventure

So there I was, halfway across the state of Texas. I was working on a spiritual discipline.

I am mildly allergic to the entire concept of discipline. It smacks of work. It stinks of tedium. These things do not call to me. But I do desire to be a deeply spiritual person, not the kind of pop-faith consumer who has a new guru or path with every season. I am ready to settle down: to choose one path and stick to it, and spend the rest of my life mastering it. To do this, I am afraid that I must practice a spiritual discipline or two.

The purpose of practicing any spiritual discipline is twofold: to aerobically exercise the soul, and to increase awareness of the Divine. The traditional practices of prayer, fasting, simplicity, and so on, have great merit, and I occasionally work at them. But I have found a new discipline that suits me, and stretches me in ways I never thought possible. It is the Spiritual Discipline of Adventure.

The Spiritual Discipline of Adventure is not simple thrill seeking, but is the intentional choosing of the less certain way in order to allow the Divine maximum room to move. When we are outside our comfort zone, when we are on an unknown path, our senses are heightened, including the spiritual senses that so often lay dormant as we proceed through life on autopilot. On an adventure we pay more attention to detail. We are aware of, and communicate our thoughts and desires more diligently to, our Designer. We listen better.

Choice is an essential piece of any spiritual adventure. We must acknowledge, embrace, and take responsibility for the freedom we are given as eternal children of a Divine Creator. An adventure that is not freely chosen is a detour at best, and is sometimes a nightmare. Many of us use our freedom to so fill our lives with busyness, structure, and control that there is no room for adventure. We do this almost without thinking, unconsciously barricading our lives against the unknown. But I tell you, it is still choice; it is intentional, and intention counts.

It is not a spiritual adventure if you are treading a well-worn path. Fresh road is required: you must navigate not by memory, but by a combination of reason and trust. You must become aware of crossroads when you come to them. Often they are not marked or obvious. Daily we make decisions that will change our entire future; often it is only in hindsight that we see it. The discipline of spiritual adventure says that we can develop foresight, and a present awareness that allows us to be fully conscious participants in our choices. Beyond that, it tells us that the universe is trustworthy: that we can renounce fear, and trust our Creator and our own spiritual senses to keep us away from disaster when on uncertain paths. A crossroads is a pivotal place where fear wrestles with obedience. It is one of the best places I know of to develop discernment, or wisdom listening.

But we do not seek this discipline without purpose; we seek it with the desire – the craving – to see with our own eyes the movement, influence, and evidence of the Divine. We can only see this when we get our plans, our agendas, and ourselves out of the way. There are no preplanned spaces in my Calendar for miracles.

Spiritual adventure can be fun, but often it isn't. It is always stretching. Even a genuine miracle can be scary at the time – just ask Jonah. It doesn't always feel safe, but practiced properly, it *is* safe. In fact, it is much safer than living a spiritually unaware, unawakened life.

Simple risk-taking is betting on your luck, or your skill; like any bet, the odds can be good, or the shot can be a long one. Spiritual adventure presumes that there is another player, and that the Other has your true best interests as its goal and guiding principle. This is an essential truth: yes, the house always wins, but you and the house have intimate connections.

When we walk in expectant, holy boldness, we are alive to the moment, holding only the ground we stand on, ceding all else to possibility. Divinity loves this. It makes excellent dance partners of us, and Divinity loves to dance. Often Divinity leads, but It enjoys just being with us, and lets us lead if we wish. Divinity loves to protect and to play. At times, Divinity loves to party.

So that is how I got to a spiritual crossroads in the middle of Texas. I was on a cross-country motorcycle ride, and it was a spiritual adventure. I had planned my trip as carefully as a human can plan. But I also had learned to trust the unexpected, and to listen for the voice of the Divine coming from strange quarters.

It was a day that the weatherman had predicted to be clear and warm for the entire state. I had stopped for gas at a town aptly named "Junction." Sitting on the porch of the gas station was an old lady, nursing a soda in the afternoon heat. She watched me pump gas, she watched me pay for gas, and just as I was getting ready to leave she said:

"Where y'all goin'?"

"Up to Sweetwater via Abilene."

"Fixin' to take the highway?"

"Yes ma'am, straight north from here."

"Don't."

"Excuse me?"

"You don't want to go that way – you want to go up the back way, through Eden and San Angelo."

(Generally speaking, I don't care for people telling me what I want and don't want.)

"But my map shows the road through Abilene to be shorter."

"You deef? Or are you just not listenin', girl?"

"Is there construction, or something I don't know about, on the road to Abilene?"

"You're kinda stubborn, ain'tcha? Or maybe you're just not a bright chile? You do as I tell you, ya hear?"

"Yes Ma'am – Thank you."

She just wasn't the kind of lady that you argued with and expected to win. I decided to follow her advice. The roads she put me on were smaller, and longer, but all went well. About halfway north I did notice some black storm clouds off to my right, but the sun shone on me the whole way. At last I pulled into Sweetwater and got a room. I turned the TV on in time to see a news report. Abilene had gotten hit by a freak thunderstorm that afternoon; they had six

inches of rain, flash flooding, golf-ball sized hail, and two tornado cells. All of this directly on the route I had planned, and because of "Our Lady of Junction," all precisely one county east of me.

When you have choices to make, does it seem at times that Wisdom is silent? Does this frustrate you? Cause you to be afraid? Confuse you? I would have you ask, first, if you have had a time in the past when the right choice and the true path were clear. If you have, then you can rest confidently in the knowledge that, if it is important for you to choose one way over the other, Wisdom will show up. If you do not feel that clear direction, then be happy! You may be facing the prospect of Spiritual Adventure. Choose the less certain way this time. Listen to the crazy stranger. Make it the expressed intention of your heart to make the most room for the Divine to move. Then proceed, with alert attention, listening ears, and a light step. Watch and see the handiwork of the Sacred. Miracles will happen, strangers will speak truth, and angels will become your comrades. And you will grow – I guarantee it.

Attendance

I was driving away from my house on a busy Monday morning. My "To Do" list was stacked like planes coming into O'Hare. My head was in air traffic control mode, oblivious to everything but the blips on my personal radar.

I slowed to a not-quite-full-legal stop at the corner of My Street and Major Arterial. The bank was cleared for landing and the post-office was on final approach. Then that still small voice I have learned to listen to piped up with an urgent request

"Peggy, could you please attend to the train coming into Grand Central Station on track number Four? – it's coming in a little fast."

"Whaaa?"

I applied full brake and looked about. All seemed normal in the sleepy residential neighborhood. Then I saw her: the little choo-choo on track number Four. She was about two years old (maybe), riding a Big Wheel along Major Arterial. She was blonde, female (probably), and peddling along at good speed, about a block and a half away. With no adult anywhere in sight.

I parked. She peddled toward me, crossed the next side street at below bumper height, and kept coming. She never looked sideways or back. I got out and met her on the sidewalk. She applied her Fred Flintstones and came to a stop at my toes.

"Hi, baby."

She looked up at me and put her thumb in her mouth.

"Baby, where's Mommy?"

Tot unplugged thumb and looked over her shoulder.

"Let's go find Mommy, okay?"

"Otay," she chirped.

Executing a crisp three-point Big Wheel turn, Cindy Lou Who applied speed and proceeded in the direction of her origin. I followed at a brisk walking pace. We went three full city blocks, crossing two side streets, this time with me as crossing guard, and then she made a right turn. I was about to call 911 when a door opened at the end of the block and a blonde woman popped out her head and called, "Haley?"

I continued to Haley's house. I informed Mom of where I had contacted Haley. Mom thanked me and appeared to be ready to start scolding Haley. As a card-carrying member and journeywoman of the International Union of Mothers, I felt the need to interrupt and make the lesson explicit.

"I could have as easily picked her up and put her in my car," I said gently.

Mom looked a little stunned.

"It's not Haley's job to keep Haley safe," I said, even more gently.

Mom scooped up Haley in her arms and nodded.

"Have a good day. Bye, Haley."

"Bye-Bye." chirped the tot.

I returned to my car and to my radar.

This was not an unusual occurrence in my life. My children could tell you how young they were when they noticed that their mother seemed to be "on call" to the universe. My therapist might tell you that I have rescuing tendencies. I prefer to say that I practice the Spiritual Discipline of Attendance. The Biblical mandate for this is the story Jesus told about the guy in the ditch. Of course, it is more formally known as "The Story of the Guy Who Helped the Guy in the Ditch," but you know the story. It's all about looking off your own radar and showing up where you are needed, when you are needed, and then taking action.

Here are the requirements of the Spiritual Discipline of Attendance:

You must attend.

You must be able to be present and mindful; aware of your surroundings. You must be able to observe without seeking to simply fit what you observe into your ready-made boxes.

You must attend at two levels. You must be able to have one ear and eye on the world and one ear and eye on the Divine. You must be willing to take input from the Divine. This is what makes it a spiritual discipline, and not merely paying attention – which is not a bad thing – but is different.

You must attend with the expectation of use.

You must show up for life willing to take action. You accept the fact that in any given situation you may be the person most capable of attendance.

You must attend with minimum fear. Sometimes all you have to offer is a non-anxious presence. Sometimes you may be called upon to be resilient in the face of actual threat. Fear kills love and a lot of other things.

You must attend with hope. Ditch people can't always dredge up their own. You must carry a supply of this at all times.

You must attend with Faith. (See above.) Sometimes people have to be able to believe in you before they can believe in anything else. It takes courage and integrity to put yourself out there. If you try to attend without faith in yourself, and in a power greater than yourself, you will incinerate quickly.

You must attend with Love. (See above.) It is advisable to carry as much of this as possible, and to stock up at every opportunity by letting others love you. You cannot top the tank too often.

You must attend without entanglement. You must have a healthy sense of self in order to keep yourself out of the ditch. Never think that you are too cool to fall into a ditch. Ditches are sneaky. You must not attempt to do for people what they can and should do for themselves. The guy who helped the guy in the ditch was able to do some very personal attendance, and then he delegated.

Now, finally – to make the lesson explicit – *this is not an optional discipline.* Evil also attends, with diligence and willingness. Evil carries a stockpile of strife, malice, and despair. Evil wants you to think that it is bold and fearless, but evil is actually reckless out of necessity, because evil is afraid – very, very afraid. Afraid, among other things, that we will all learn to attend.

The Story of the Guy Who Helped the Guy in the Ditch is found in the book of Luke, the 10th chapter, in the Christian New Testament.

Gratitude

It was time for my weekly clock-cleaning.

I was training to be a counselor. I was in my last term. I had 18 months of clinical practicum in my backpack. End of tunnel in sight – I didn't expect that light to be an oncoming train.

I had a new supervisor, and she did not appreciate me. I don't think that there was anything about me that she liked. Her disdain of all things Peggy was apparent from the first session. Our meetings focused on listening to, and critiquing, tapes of my counseling sessions – my clients signed up for this by getting a cheap student-driver counselor. From the get-go it was apparent that she thought I could do nothing right. I remember her criticizing the tonal pitch of one of the sounds that counselors make to show empathetic listening. She didn't like it when I spoke; she didn't like it when I was silent. Realizing, of course, that a good supervisor would never give *only* criticism, she occasionally faintly praised ridiculously small things; as in "Well, Peggy at least you called your client by her proper name – that was adequate."

I never did figure out if there was anything I did to precipitate her treatment of me, but I do know the moment that I sealed the deal.

After weeks of listening to her tear apart my work, I looked up at her shelf of books by feminist theologians and psychologists and said, "Gee, you know, I would have thought that feminist supervision would have been a little more nurturing than this."

It wasn't a clever thing to say. After that, she called the school I was about to graduate from, and the clinic where I was doing my practicum, and tried to get me held back and fired. It's pretty rare to get held back a grade in graduate school, but she tried.

At that point, I was starting to wonder if, despite lots of evidence to the contrary, I really sucked at counseling – and if I did not, how I was going to get through the last couple of months of this ordeal.

I hired an independent person, another clinical supervisor, to give me some perspective. He listened to my tapes and told me that I was doing fine. I asked him for advice on surviving an upcoming exit interview, when my supervisor would meet with me and the director of the clinic where I was working. The one I was hoping would hire me after my graduation. I was certain that she was going to try to make sure I did not get that job.

His advice: "Thank her."

"For what? – abusing me?"

"Yes. Call it diligence and thank her for it. Make a list of everything you can possibly think of, and thank her for it. Thank her for providing you with a chair to sit in, thank her for agreeing to see you, thank her for her attention to detail. Start with that list, and take up as much time as possible. Then when she gets her say, argue with nothing and thank her again, in detail. Gratitude is your only option; any other response will look like defense or offense, and they will both fail. But Peggy – you have to thank her sincerely. You can't sound facetious when you do it."

I didn't like his advice, but I took it. It was nasty hard to do, but I did it. The look on her face was pretty precious, but the bottom line was that I graduated, got the job, and that woman has become an unnamed footnote in my story.

That was my first awareness of Gratitude as a spiritual discipline. I am grateful to her for that. Really.

My mom taught me to say "Thank you" – but that was usually for things that were good, and that I liked. She gave me a way to express my natural gratitude. The discipline of being grateful when things are going to hell in a hand basket came harder and later.

But I have come to believe that it is a foundational spiritual discipline. It is the discipline that frees you to learn all the others. It completely circumvents resentment. It takes anger and divides it into that which requires action and that which can be released. Eliminating resentment and reducing anger allows you much more time for attendance. It makes failure bearable. It sweetens everything that is already sweet. If I start and end my day with gratitude, nothing that happens in between has the power to ruin tomorrow.

A couple of years back I received, second-hand, a prayer from a Benedictine nun. It was shared with me by a friend, and it dropped immediately into that hole in my soul that is truth-shaped. She said, "Pray this prayer daily: *Thank you for everything – I have no complaint.*"

I have tried to do this, not just daily but hourly, and moment-by-moment. It is not easy. Some things, like interruptions and thwartings, do not fall easily into the gratitude basket. I wrestled for a while with thanking God for things that I did not really believe God was sending me. I do not believe it is God's explicit intention for me to be sick or stupid or in harm's way. But then I came to believe that these things were part of the global package, and that – for all its faults – I choose to believe that the package is good.

Most of my problems are the consequences of my own foolish actions. I have come to realize that having painful consequences for stupidity is indeed a gift from God; how else am I going to know when to change?

A smaller percentage of the things I hate are the consequences of other people's stupid actions. But I have learned to thank God for these, too, because they give me a chance to be perfected in my own reactions, and to step up to the plate for things like justice and peace.

The smallest percentage of my grief is in response to things that are not in human control, like death and sickness. This *is* God's deal – it is part of the set-up. I do not like it very often. But I have come to accept even these things, and to trust God in them.

The hardest part of this prayer is the "choosing not to complain" bit. For years I have used God as my unedited sounding board. If I have to yell at somebody, why not God? I mean, God's a tough mother and can take it, right? God has always seemed patient about this, and after I rant a bit, I always feel better. So to give up complaints seemed to be giving up one of my favorite coping mechanisms. It also seemed at odds with justice. There is a lot of bad stuff going down on this planet; don't we need to make an issue of certain things? Shouldn't we complain?

What I have discovered is that forsaking complaint and moving into gratitude has zero effect on the truth. In fact, it makes truth clearer, and you can move straight into action.

"Dear God, thanks for this mess – I have no complaint – please get my back as I step into the middle of it."

Sometimes I need to do something. Sometimes I need to be something. I have found that gratitude is the fast track to the place where God needs me most, and where I most need God.

Release

I was getting on a plane – returning home, but leaving a huge chunk of my heart behind. I had just dropped my firstborn child off at college, half-way across the country, and every bit of 18 years of mommy conditioning told me I was being bad – very bad.

You do not dump your children off among strangers, hoping that they will figure out how to live in a foreign environment. You do not abdicate your responsibility for keeping the worst of the world at bay while they learn and grow. You do not suddenly cease your constant, if often unwelcome, teaching commentary on their life.

You do not just walk away. You just don't.

Except that we all do – eventually. Every successful parent does, eventually, just walk away. So there I was. It didn't help that this was an extremely competent child, and that my mothering had mostly been consultative for the last year or two. The problem with competent children is that they often think that they can do all sorts of grown-up things – whether they can or not.

And it *really* didn't help that when I got home the family dog "yelled" at me for weeks. He would go into her room, bark, and then come in to me and bark at me.

"Stupid woman! You've lost your puppy!"

"I know, Alex, I know."

When his Lassie imitation failed, he fell into a depression that lasted until Christmas.

The girl, of course, was fine. I, however, was just starting my work in the Spiritual Discipline of Release. Some of the spiritual disciplines are optional; elective courses for the spiritually motivated and inquisitive. Others are mandatory. Release is one of the mandatory ones, a core requisite. You can do it badly or you can master it, but you are going to take this class.

You will release. If you are lucky enough to live so long, you will release your parents, your children, and your lovers. You will eventually release your strength, and whatever mental superiority you ever had. The more you are blessed, the more you will release, until the day comes when you release your very life. It may be ripped from your clinging grasp, or it may float away like the fall leaves, but you will let go of it. Fortunately, Life, in its kindness, offers you many opportunities for practice before that day.

I have learned a few things that help. I have learned to breathe and relax my body on command, especially under stress. I have learned to pray. I have learned to trust God to be God, and to run the universe, with or without me. I have learned how to discern if something is my problem or somebody else's problem, and I don't usually try to fix other people's problems. I have learned that control is an illusion, and that when I cease trying to control, my influence actually increases. I have learned to trust people; most of the time, they do an adequate job with decent intent. All of these things help me let go.

Which is good, because the course comes with a mid-term exam. Mine asked me to walk away from my life for a few months.

This is a thing that competent, professional, middle-aged, middle-class American women rarely do. Like most of my peers, I spin plates, and I spin with the best of them. I lose a saucer every now and then, but nothing major.

At exam time I had hearth and home, two part-time professions, and a handful of odd gigs on the side. Plus a dangerous hobby or two. Being me, I had a leadership role in most parts of my life. Much easier to lead than to follow – less frustration, usually turns out pretty well. My kudos cabinet was well stocked.

But there are some things that are so focus-consuming that you have to lay everything else down to have a chance of doing them right. I was about to go to an unstable, dangerous, alien part of the world, to do complicated assessment and training. It was a one-plate, one-pole spin.

So I let go of everything else for a bit. My counseling clients had to take care of themselves or find other help. My fledgling church flew without me. My family ran the house without my help. My second daughter packed away the 120-year-old Christmas ornaments that I never let anyone else touch. My motorcycles sat cold, with batteries draining and oil sludging. The plants in my late father's greenhouse prayed for mild weather. And the 101 unforeseen mini-crises that occurred during my absence were handled, or not, by someone who was not me.

That same first daughter that I abandoned to her college life had a favorite Sesame Street bit when she was tiny. It was a musical number where Ernie wanted to play the saxophone but was having problems because it took two hands to play and one of his hands was occupied by holding his beloved rubber ducky. A conundrum. A series of famous cameo singers sang this advice to the orange everytoddler: "You gotta put down the ducky, yes, put down the ducky; you gotta put down the ducky if you wanna play the saxophone."

So I put down my life, and I blew.

Failure

The Department of Motor Vehicles is not a fun place to fail.

I was taking the motorcycle endorsement test for the first time. As a permitted learner, but not a licensed rider, I had arrived accompanied. Just as with cars, you can practice riding on the streets with an experienced friend. Unlike practice driving in a car, if you make a big mistake, all that your friend on the other bike can do is scream and then call 9-1-1.

My friend Owen had not only taught me how to ride, he had financed my first bike. He is that sort of a friend. That day, he stood on the sidelines and watched as I went through my paces on my shiny new Honda Rebel. At 250 cc's and a mere 300 lbs., she was just the sort of light, nimble bike that you want for the test.

They do this test off road, in a parking lot that is painted with a test course. The tester that day was a serious looking young man with a clipboard. He inspected my bike and my gear, gave me instructions, and then the go-ahead. I did great at the slalom cones. I braked from speed without skidding. I demonstrated the ability to use turn signals and horns without problem, downshifted on a corner. I passed all his tasks with ease until the last one. This was the "tight turn trick." Painted on the pavement is a three-sided bay, precisely the size of two parking spaces. You are required to enter on the left side going at least 15 mph; you must then execute a turn inside this bay and exit on the right side without touching the white lines. There is a dot painted at the apex for reference.

I had practiced a U-turn on a two-lane road, but this was considerably tighter. I gave it my best shot. Gassed to 15. Entered the bay. Braked. Turned at the apex, and made a critical mistake. I looked down at the dot on the pavement, and then the bike was down and I was standing over her. I looked up. Owen had his eyes covered, cringing. The clipboard boy was shaking his head and walking toward me.

I was furious and humiliated.

I don't remember picking up my bike. The next thing I do remember was putting the front wheel back down on the ground from somewhere in midair. Apparently I was pumping a bit of adrenaline. I remember the front tire bouncing as I set it back down. I looked up again at the clipboard guy. He stopped, took one step backward, and made a "settle down" gesture with his free hand – eyes wide open.

"Ma'am, you okay?"

"Grrr – I flunked – right?"

"You are going to have to wait three days to take the test again – but you can take it again – I am sure you will pass next time – ma'am."

"Grrr."

(To Owen) "Make sure she takes a few minutes to calm down before you guys ride home, okay?"

I did calm down, a bit. The fury wore off with the stress hormones. But I was in complete freak-out about flunking. I just could not believe it. I called a sympathetic friend.

"I flunked! I can't believe it. I flunked!"

"Peggy, chill. It's just like flunking a quiz at school, only with infinite do-overs."

"Excuse *me*! I have *never* flunked a quiz."

"Never? Never in 20 years of school?"

"Of course not!"

"Um, okay – it's like getting fired from a job. You get another job."

"Oh, give me a break – *no one* has ever fired *me*."

"Man ... then it is like getting dumped."

"What!? Dumped? I don't think so!"

"You know what, Peggy? You needed this. God decided it was your turn."

My friend was right. I was in a failure deficit situation, and that is not good. I was 35 years old, and I had never learned the Spiritual Discipline of Failure. This is not an optional discipline. As it turned out, in the next decade of my life I was going to be in a couple of big situations where success by any normal standard of success was not going to be possible, and God needed me to be fit for the task. So I started a series of practicums in the art of not getting it anything close to right.

It's a tough class.

The core truth of this discipline is that you must learn to take your focus off of "outcome" and put it onto "process." I had been hung up on flunking and not looking at how I flunked. This is a killer of a mistake. It not only can get you killed in certain situations, it kills learning and joy the rest of the time. It drastically increases fear, because there is always a dreaded outcome and never a preventative within your control. I needed to forget about the test and learn the crucial lesson that motorcycles will go wherever you put your eyes. In a tight turn you look out to your exit, not down at the pavement. When you learn this lesson, tight turns cease to be scary. And friends, Life offers many opportunities for the quick U-turn.

I don't really see God as some sort of cosmic tester with a clipboard, but I have learned to leave grading to the Teacher. The work is mine, but the grade, if any, is not my job or my problem. When faced with an experience that looks like failure, I take a deep breath, calm down, and look at the process of my work; inevitably, there is a part of the situation that I am trying to control that is really not in my power, and part of the situation that actually is in my control that I am ignoring. Then I let go of the former, focus on the latter, and sign up for do-overs.

Fortunately for me, I worship a God of infinite do-overs.

Generosity

On every Saturday night of my childhood I got paid. Freshly scrubbed out of the tub; my Sunday school lesson book had no empty blanks. Sunday school came with homework back then. Mother was in the kitchen, cranking off the church bulletins on the mimeograph machine – kachunk, kachunk, kachunk. Dad was in the living room, ready to hand out weekly allowances to his progeny.

My allotment was one US dollar, and I got it whether I was naughty or nice – it was grace. But I received this allowance on Saturday evening for a specific purpose, and in a specific form. I was given ten shiny dimes, after the candy store at the corner closed, when there was no other opportunity to spend my riches until Monday. I received it in dimes, not quarters, because my father believed in a ten percent tithe. That was off the gross, not the net. When the basket came around the next morning, it was expected that I would put in one of my dimes. We belonged to a church that preached tithing, but did not make it mandatory for membership or good standing, and I do not think that my dad checked up on us to see if we had put our tenth in. He didn't need to; he set us the example, and trusted us to follow his lead. He was a good leader.

When I was twelve I became apostate. I did not, of course, tell my parents this; but in unspoken protest, I withheld from the church the tithe of my considerable babysitting revenues. I decided instead to send my riches to a group that was saving baby harp seals in Nova Scotia. It never occurred to me to stop tithing just because I happened to be apostate. When I told my dad about this – the harp seals, not the apostasy – he was concerned, but asked only, "Is that what you think God would have you do?" I told him that I thought Jesus really loved the baby harp seals, and that yes, it was what I felt led to do. He accepted my decision.

I have been a religious and philanthropic donor for as long as I can remember. I believe in it. I believe it is good for the giver and good for the world. I believe in giving locally, nationally, and internationally.

I support my local church. (My apostasy did not last much into my twenties.) This is where the ancient practice of tithing comes in. If you have ten families, and everybody gives ten percent off the gross, then the rabbi eats as well as the average member. This has worked for millennia, and there is no reason to challenge it now. I happen to believe that for all their problems, religious organizations have done more good than harm. Sitting in a pew is optional, but if you sit in a pew, you should support the work of that group or find another seat you can support. Hopefully, they are doing more than dusting pews.

I believe in doing some giving in secret. After my father left this planet to pursue other interests, I discovered that he was giving regularly to many organizations. Some of them I knew about;

some I did not. There was a group on the north side of Chicago that helps male prostitutes; my dad was a regular and generous supporter of their work. I got a phone call from their director when I sent a last check and a note to them. He choked up on the phone talking to me, telling me about the notes of encouragement that my dad would send with his checks. He said to me "I can find other money, but where am I going to find those good words?" Yeah, me too.

I believe in doing some giving spontaneously. Mostly, I like to know where my money is going. I like to see annual reports, and I like to see low overhead costs. I like accountability. But sometimes, the Spirit just says "Here, now" and I try to respond. I like to help the person in the grocery line in front of me when they cannot find that last buck they are looking for in the bottom of their purse. Nobody ever has to send an item back, if I am standing in the line behind them. Freaks people out – but it's a lot of fun.

However, I have heard a lot of lousy preaching about giving in my life. A lot of shameless hooey. Let me debunk a bit of it.

Giving to the church is *not* the same as giving to God. This silly notion gets put out there all the time. I heard Saint Bono say once, "My God does not need your cash!" It is just so obviously true. God owns it all. Did before you came along and will after you are long gone. Because it tickles God's cosmic fancy, the Divine lets us push stuff around, but don't kid yourself – God is not a beggar. People who tell you that giving to them or their organization is the same as giving to God have ego, or possibly blasphemy, issues going on. Shame on them.

From which follows the corollary: giving does not make you acceptable to God. God finds you acceptable already. Face it, God's crazy about you – indulgent as all get out. This does not mean that God does not have issues with some of the stuff that you are doing, but you can't fix that by writing a check.

Giving is not a get-rich formula. Giving to that which purports to be, or even is God's work, does not force God to give to you. It doesn't sway the Divine opinion of you in a way that makes

29

God want to bless you. There is no magic here except this: when you give away some of your stuff, you are freed from the slavery to stuff. You place your bet on the kindness of the universe. You trust. And that changes you, and frees you from the terrible lie that says there is not enough to go around, and then you find that you have plenty. And you feel a lot richer. People who are not fearful and mistrustful are more productive.

Here is what I have found to be true about giving: it does not matter how much you have or how much you give. If you have ten dimes, you can part with one. It is good for you to part with one. It is good to develop the Spiritual Discipline of Generosity. It is good to start when you are young. It is good to start with your first job. It is good to revisit your giving when you have a change in fortunes. It is fun to split a windfall. It is especially important to give when you don't feel like it, when it seems risky. It changes you, and you change your world.

My dad was never a wealthy man. He did not have a professional job or a college degree. We lived in a rented flat for most of my childhood. But he left his children a nice little bit, and when I took over his books at the very end, I discovered that he was giving 40% of his retirement income away. And that was off the gross, not the net.

Forgiveness

My new house came with an unusual neighbor. This fellow was 96 years old, in relatively good health, living independently in his home. Besides always hoping to be a good neighbor, I am a collector of stories, and I saw him as a potential treasure house of material.

I made a few advances, brought over leftovers, and started engaging in over-the-fence conversation. This was a man who should have remembered the turn of the 20th century – should have remembered not only the First World War, but also the Spanish American War. He should have remembered Shoeless Joe Jackson and the Black Socks scandal. But I soon found out that this old gent had only one story – a list of nine decades of offenses the world had dealt him. If you listened long enough, the story always came back to a beating with a buggy whip that his father had given him as a boy for a bit of petty larceny that he did not commit. That was the injustice that started a life of injustice-list keeping. He had no other stories; it took too much energy to keep his list.

After failing to draw out any other story, I attempted to talk to him about a Galilean I knew who was also whipped for crimes uncommitted, but who managed to ask his father to forgive the abusers. When I used the word forgiveness, he gave me an odd look, as if it was a word he hadn't heard for a long time. He fell silent for a moment and then, with sudden passion, said:

"Forgiveness, huh? When my old man was dying, he asked me to forgive him so he could die in peace. And I spat in his face and said "You can rot in Hell for all eternity if my forgiveness is what you need!" I will never forgive that old man!

My neighbor died just before his 100th birthday – unchanged, as far as I knew. I think it was as sad a situation as I have ever known – and completely preventable. I wonder if he knew the old proverb, "He who seeks revenge should dig two graves."

The Apostle Paul says this, in his letter to the Ephesians:

> Let all bitterness, anger, uproar, and blasphemy with all their evil, be removed from you. Instead, become kind and tenderhearted to each other, forgiving each other in the same way that God through Christ forgave you. Then you will be imitators of God, acting like beloved children. (Ephesians 4:25)

Here's what I notice about this counsel. First, that anger is a given. Paul wastes no time figuring out why it is there; it just is. Second, that there is a process, not an event that is clearly injurious to the soul: anger turns to bitterness, which turns to uproar, which leads to blasphemy. Then there is another process described that is soul-nourishing, where anger leads to right choices, which leads to compassion, which leads to forgiveness. It looks like the question is not how quick you forgive, or even if you get to the end of the process, but which road you are on. It seems that the essential key to resolution is direction.

Some people want forgiveness to be a simple choice; a decision. Some want it to be an emotion – if you feel like forgiving, great but, if not, don't worry – there are no bad feelings. Some want it to be an action you can take, whether or not you believe it or feel like it – act like you forgive, and maybe the other things will come along. I think that each of these is inadequate.

So what is it, then? What is this thing we call forgiveness? I may not be able to name it, I may have to settle for just calling it a mystery, but I can recognize another member of its genus. It is like Love, which is also purported to be choice, feeling or behavior, but is in fact, in its pure form, a perfect integration of the three. Forgiveness is like this, a passionate, decisive course of action. Passionate, because it clearly requires an emotional capacity. If you aren't ready, you just aren't ready. Decisive, because it is a choice available to a free soul: it is not a commandment. And a course of action, because it has to be lived out.

It's like driving a car to a certain destination. The cognitive part is deciding to make the trip and choosing the destination. This requires that you have knowledge of where you are going or the ability to consult a map. And like any destination, if you have been there a few times it gets easy to find again. It also requires that you look out of the windshield and assess information as you go. You must think all the way.

The emotional part is like the dashboard full of little lights that tell you if you are running hot or cold, if you have enough fuel, etc. We all have emotional warning lights within us if we learn to pay attention to them.

The behavioral part is expressed by the fact that you have to actually do things – start the car, steer, brake, etc. – if you want to get to your destination.

Any of these parts can cause problems if you try to do without them. If you try to drive without gas or oil, and ignore the lights, you will fail. If you gas up but never look at a map, or even look out the windshield, you will certainly not arrive at your destination. And if you plan, map, and gas up, but just sit there, you will fail again. All systems must be go; all systems must cooperate together to get you to your destination.

So it is with forgiveness. If you decide to forgive, but ignore your emotional responses, your journey will be short. If you run entirely on emotions, and do not think or choose, your journey will be even shorter. And if you plan for the destination, and care for yourself, but do not enact your plan, it will be futile.

You must decide that you want to be on the road to forgiveness, even if it takes your whole life to pursue it. You must know what it looks like, and what it will require of you. Then you must assess your own emotional capability, filling as many deficits as you can, and doing careful self-nourishment along the way. You can ask others who are skilled in the journey to offer guidance and care. It is also important to note that you need Divine help in this. Paul stated that we were to let these things be removed from us. We choose to be helped on this journey. Forgiveness must come from a position of strength.

The journey will take as long as it takes. I believe the length of time will be proportionate to the hurt. For small hurts, this process can be as short as a thought, a feeling, and an action in short succession, almost automatic. For the great injuries of life, this may be a long road, but it is infinitely better than the road of bitterness.

I read a quote in a book by Joan Chittister, a prayer which she says was found by the body of a dead child at the Ravensbruck Concentration camp. I look at it now and then, not as a standard to be measured against, but as an inspiration:

> O Lord, remember not only the men and women of good will, but also those of ill will. But do not remember the suffering that they have inflicted upon us; remember rather the fruits that we have borne, thanks to the suffering – our comradeship, our loyalty, our humility, our courage, our generosity, the greatness of heart, which has grown out of all this, and when they come to judgment, let all the fruits we have borne be their forgiveness.
> —Joan Chittister, *In Search of Belief*

Retreat

I was in the convent chapel, listening to the Sisters of the Queen of Angels Monastery singing the evening praise.

I was just listening. This is hard to pull off, because the sisters are so hospitable that, if you do not take a book of prayer out of the rack, they will assume that you don't know where they are and will get you one. If you have a book and do not open it, they will assume that you cannot find the right page and they will try to help you find it. As a Quaker – a severely unliturgical heathen – I do have trouble with the book. Sometimes the seasons, the days, the songs, Psalms and Magnificats, can get a little overwhelming. I do okay with the "Our Father;" I have even picked up the "Hail Mary," although they don't seem to use that one so much in group worship. But sometimes I just like to close my eyes and listen. The sisters read a piece of the Book of Psalms out loud every day. The service has a brief reading from somewhere in the New Testament, but a big chunk of King David's lyrics daily. I wonder what he thinks of their rendition. I wonder if he wishes he was getting residuals – well, maybe he is.

There is something eerie about the voices of a few dozen gentle, kind, often elderly women, intoning the imprecatory Psalms. They put very little emotion into the words. David used many of his words to curse his enemies: swords in their hearts, destruction, wrath, revenge. The sisters give voice to these sentiments rather unsentimentally. I have never seen them flinch at even the most embarrassing parts – smashing the heads of the enemies' babies on rocks, etc. To their credit, they do not seem very inflated when they read David's words making the tenuous case for his own righteousness, either. They just speak these words out into the air, a display of the best and worst of the human condition, as if to say, "Hey, God, look at us – this is what we are – what are you going to do with us?"

Due to a trip to Africa, an illness, and a few other things, I had not been out to the monastery for six months before this trip. It had been the longest lapse in ten years of mostly monthly visits. I usually tried to get out for a 24-hour retreat. I spent an hour or two with a spiritual director, trying to take an honest look at my own spiritual condition and whatever notion God was attempting to squeeze into my feeble heart, brain, and soul at any given time. Then I spent the rest of the time resting, or praying, or doing anything except my normal work and worry. It was good for me.

They didn't like to let me work, although there is work to do out there--they all work, as part of the Benedictine Rule. My spiritual directors all think that I am rather bad at Sabbath, and it is true, so I rest. I don't take many silent retreats. As a Quaker, I am supposed to be good at this – which is not quite so true. But some of the sisters enjoyed my dinner table tales of modest adventure, so I served in my own way.

That trip out, after such a long break, I was itchy. The American allergy to stillness and disconnect had me all but in hives. No iPod, no computer, no phone, no TV. No to-do lists, no calendar, no demands on my time or attention. It was exactly what I wanted and needed and it drove me crazy. What happened next was predictable: I crashed. Right after dinner, I laid down on my bed for a minute and fell asleep, in my clothes, on top of the bedcovers. I slept like that for fourteen hours. I was not sleep deprived – I am a good sleeper – but my brain just couldn't stay conscious and do nothing. It was a shock to my system. My dreams were vivid and many, confused and mildly disturbing. I woke up, had coffee, and did some praying and writing. Then, with my spiritual director's blessing, I took off a couple of hours early. I got back on my motorcycle and tripled the miles between the monastery and home.

The sisters like it when I bring the bike. They get a kick out of seeing it parked in front of their home. Makes people wonder, I guess.

I left so much better than I came. It is kind of a Roto-Rooter for my soul. Sometimes I flew out there desperate for the break. Sometimes I had to pull myself away and make myself go. It is a discipline: the Spiritual Discipline of Retreat. I have found that no matter how good I get at listening to God's Spirit in everyday life, I regularly need to completely disconnect in order to reboot my hard drive. Stuff just runs better.

I recommend disengagement. You cannot spiritually advance without some kind of regular retreat. It may seem counter-intuitive, but it is true. It can take many forms, and you don't need the vocational religious types, fun though they are. But you need it. Ask your soul.

Supplication

Talking to Annabelle was not easy. I had known Annabelle for about fifteen minutes. It was my first day, on my first trip out of the USA, in Burundi – the least developed country in Africa. Annabelle was to be my household helper. I knew this because I had been dropped off to an empty house and introduced to her.

My host knew that I had no Kirundi, Annabelle's first language, and he believed that she had none of mine. I was trying to learn Kiswahili, and though my helper had not had much school, she had plenty of Kiswahili, so my host commanded her to speak nothing else to me. Then he left.

I was to run my own household. Annabelle had no clue what I wanted, but she understood the basics of what I needed. I needed to know when she would be coming and what services she would provide, and we needed to negotiate her pay. Our attempts to communicate in Kiswahili lasted about fifteen minutes, until we were both good and frustrated, and then fell into our native tongues and a bit of prayer. We discovered that we both had some French vocabulary, and that Annabelle had a lot more English than she advertised. We started communicating in a badly mixed mess of four languages.

Annabelle's best sentence was "Give money moi." She said it with authority – almost a demanding tone.

I had "Kwa nini?" ("Why?" in Kiswahili.)

"Chakula, market," she said. ("Food, market.") Okay, money to go to the market to buy food.

We worked on the currency and she left me.

After she left, I felt flustered. She seemed awfully bossy. I wondered if we were going to get along. It was only later that I found out an important fact. Kirundi has no word for "please," so Annabelle had no concept of "please," no way to ask nicely, no word to indicate supplication. She had the simple imperative, and nothing else. I started to think about a society with no verbal way to implore. The educated classes had picked up the French "S'il vou plait", if you please, but Annabelle did not observe the French niceties.

At that point, I needed Annabelle a lot more than she needed me. She did need a job. She was twenty-one years old and functionally an orphan, taking care of seven younger siblings. She lived in the ghetto called Kamenge, and at that time they were being chased out of their house at gunpoint three or four times a month. She was resilient, and resourceful, but a little cash was going to help.

I was in more need. I had no idea what I was doing. I had no way to feed myself. I didn't know what water was safe. Some of the insects in my house were harmless and a few turned out to be deadly. I didn't know one from the other. I didn't know how to get a taxi. I didn't know if it was safe to walk anywhere. I didn't know what to do when the electricity company came around and threatened to turn me off unless I paid them off. Annabelle was my key.

I was relieved to see her arrive the next morning with coffee, pineapple, and bread. I knew I needed her help and I knew I needed to learn to communicate with her. So I started learning, and by example teaching, the art and Spiritual Discipline of Supplication.

"Annabelle, please, s'il vous plait, tell me..." and we started around the house naming things. After things, we started working on behaviors, then higher concepts. She asked me questions. We still mixed four languages.

You cannot know how important supplication is until you recognize your need. I think everybody should be dropped on the equivalent of another planet once or twice to make this real. Another way to learn this is to develop a nice raging addiction and let it mess up your life. Then you get to do the First Step that every recovering alcoholic knows so well: "I came to realize that my life was unmanageable." Recognizing that you cannot make it on your own is a foundation for spiritual growth.

Americans are just so blessedly arrogant about this. We think we can manage anything: our lives, our country, your country. And it is just so obvious to everyone else that we are not any good at it. Spiritually, a lot of people have to hit bottom before they recognize that they have a need for a God. There are a lot more atheists in the middle and upper classes than among the poor. The poor and the sick will tell you that they know they need help.

After you recognize your need, you have to ask for help. Stop and ask for directions? How good are we at that? Not very. Let somebody else see our un-manageability, our need, and our weakness? Not our long suit – by a long shot. Welcome to Step Two – "I came to believe that a force greater than myself could help." You have to believe help is possible. You have to recognize it. You have to approach it – willing to be seen for what you are, and where you are.

Then you have to actually accept the help that comes your way. Step Three – "I made a decision to turn my will over to that power." This means that you ask, and you lay down your personal preferences and take the help that is given, not necessarily the help you asked for, or the help you thought you needed. They call this, "Taking Life on Life's terms."

Then you "Let go and Let God."

You can sum this process up thusly:

"Oh Crap! Oh Look! Oh Help! Okay."

This is actually an optional spiritual discipline. God will love you just as much if you never ask for help, or fail to recognize and accept the help that comes your way. But ignoring this discipline may shorten your life exceedingly. I guarantee it will impoverish your life tremendously.

I learned to ask Annabelle for many things. I didn't worry about looking like a Mzungu Ujinga – (Stupid white person) – because I *was* a Mzungu Ujinga. Annabelle learned to take risks, and ask me for things other than the necessary things. She learned to ask for what she really needed.

"Paygy -" (That's how she said my name.)

"Paygy – pleeze – mange chakula moi?" ("Peggy, please can I eat food?")

"Annabelle – Vous (kir: wewe) mange today, Ijumaa?) ("Have you eaten today, Friday?")

"Oya." ("No.")

"Ayya! Annabelle, Vous mange chakula nyumbani moi, ego?" ("You eat food here at my house, yes?")

"Oya, never." ("No, never.")

I discovered that this girl came hungry to my house each morning and never touched a bite for the six to eight hours she was there, as she cooked three meals for me, because she believed that eating my food was forbidden. Thieves lose their jobs. I had no clue. I was sick.

"Annabelle! – Chakula Moi – Chakula Vous!" I said it with authority. ("My food is your food.")

The next day, my host came in and found Annabelle sitting at my table having her breakfast with me. I had gotten up for the coffee pot and topped off both our cups, and offered him some. He looked surprised.

"Why are you serving Annabelle?"

"Why not?"

Courage

I was teaching trauma healing to my first group of African students. They were women and men, old and young, Catholic and Quaker, highly or barely educated. The one thing they had in common was a deep desire to learn how to bring healing from the horror that was all around them in Burundi, a country that had survived ten years of war and genocide.

I had the latest theory and methods on treating Post-Traumatic Stress Disorder in my back pocket. I was an experienced teacher, but I had precious few words in common with them. I was to teach six hours a day, five days a week, for two weeks. I thought I was brave to come all this way and give it a try.

I was assigned a team of two translators. I worked them in tag team fashion, and they worked with half the team and at three times the length that they would in the US. Sometimes one translator would be working into Kirundi while the other worked into French. Kirundi is not a language conducive to psychobabble, so I was working at simplifying my language, and I tried to jettison the jargon unless it was critical. Still, my translator would often hold up a hand to stop me, and there would be an animated discussion in Kirundi and sometimes French until they coined a new word – at which point my translator would say "Voila!", and we would proceed. We had one aide de camp assigned to write these words down, and we generated a Kirundi glossary of psychological terms. I felt very successful.

On our second morning, there was what my Burundian friends euphemistically call "activity," outside the compound. All I heard was a small thump and a tapping noise. I thought someone was moving furniture and hanging pictures until I noticed that every one of my fourteen students had a stiff body and glazed eyes and did not appear to be breathing. A few seconds of silence later, my translator whispered "Mambo sawa" (Kiswahili for "things are okay") and, as one, they shuddered and came back to the here and now. It turns out that the noise I heard was a hand grenade and some automatic rifle fire, at a not-far-enough distance. That was when I decided to administer a PTSD checklist to my students, and found out that all my healers were in need of healing.

By the third morning, I was relaxing enough in my teaching to start noticing details about individual students. Innocent had only one ear. At break, I put my hand to his head and made universal female clucking sounds of sympathy. "Machete" he said, with a smile on his face.

Filbert had one hand in a large bandage. I noticed something else about Filbert. He often started taking notes in the space between my speaking and the translator's. I suspected he had more English than he was letting on. I was sure of it when I made a lame attempt at a joke, and he laughed at the tag of my punch line, and all the other students looked at him and then looked expectantly at the translator for their funny. At lunch I got him aside without an intermediary and said, "Filbert, you are such a bright student – where did you get your English?"

He looked at me, sized me up, and made a decision. Out came the story of Filbert Nahimana, Greatheart.

Filbert hailed from the town of Makamba, almost on the border of Tanzania. Several long, awful, bus rides from the capital. He had always been a studious child, eager for learning. He got a start on English in secondary school, but the war interrupted his studies. His town was squarely in the middle of rebel control. Life was hard. The rebels were suspicious of education, and extremely suspicious of outsiders.

Filbert had a long-standing habit of attempting to speak with anyone who had English, in order to improve his own. He came to the attention of the local leaders for doing just that, speaking English to someone from the outside. They hauled him in and interrogated him, and when that produced nothing, they tortured him by bending his thumbs back and burning him between his fingers with a cigarette. This also got them nothing, so they tossed him in the street and figured they had taught him a lesson.

Filbert bandaged his hand, and a few days later he met with someone from the local Trauma Healing Center. They recognized promise in him and recommended him for the classes that were about to be held in Bujumbura. So Filbert the Brave and his tortured hand left to go and learn from an English-speaking teacher in the enemy capital.

He was my best student of that batch. He studied at night and asked me tough questions by day. He was curious, skeptical, and eager. When we finished, the director of the Trauma Healing Organization asked me whom I thought he should hire for the Makamba center. I had no trouble nominating Filbert.

Filbert the Courageous went back to the rebel-held town. He worked to heal others. His courage, giftedness, and diligence did not go unnoticed. When the war was over, he ran for local office and was eventually elected Chief of Zone – something like Mayor. I have every reason to hope and believe that they do not torture people there on his watch.

Thus did I learn the Spiritual Discipline of Courage from one of its masters. Courage knows fear and walks right through it. Courage is friends with hard work. Courage has a purpose that reckless, and thrill-seeking will never know. Courage does not step out from great riches to risk the tithe; courage pays the price up front, with a promise made from faith and hope. Courage walks the path of righteousness and counts on the vouchsafe of God. Courage counts coup before the battle begins, and accepts its own wounds as the proof of honor. Courage can never be foresworn.

I pray that someday I will be honored enough of God to be given the chance to be courageous. I pray that the teacher is worthy of her students.

Compassion

The airport concourse was so long I could see the curvature of the Earth. Gate B-95, no kidding. Deep winter, northern Europe, holiday season – Delay Central.

I was still pretty fresh when she caught my eye. Mid-twenties, with a baby at her breast, four pieces of luggage, a half-crazed two-year-old boy, and a compelling look of desperation. I had about three seconds to make a decision; look the other way, or be drawn into a vortex of need.

Compassion struck, and I surrendered to it. There are Union rules about these things. I engaged the toddler, then took the well-fed babe for a sleep in my arms while the mother changed the boy's diaper and rearranged herself and her luggage. She was on her way to Copenhagen from Vancouver, British Columbia – she had experienced two delays already. She wanted to see her parents. Women will do crazy things for love.

The most important thing I did was make sane adult conversation with an intelligent young woman at her wit's end. You can give people some of your wits when they have exhausted theirs. Wits transfer. Wits R Us. This is good.

She needed to see a ticket agent. She looked at me, took a deep breath, and made a huge decision. She decided to trust. It was a stunning act of beauty in an airport, our high temples of fear-driven security. A wave of warmth spread out from her and the anxious people around her shuddered a bit as the scent of Heaven massaged their tight spots. Angels whistled low and long.

"I am going to take the boy and see the agent; can I leave the luggage and the baby with you?"

I looked her in the soul and spoke with what I hoped was gentle authority:

"She is safe here – All is well – do what you need to do."

"You have no idea how I appreciate this."

"Actually, I do; been here, done this."

An hour later, I walked them to their gate and saw them on their way.

Compassion is a mystery. It is like unto its sisters, Love and Forgiveness. It has a big emotional component; sometimes it just falls upon you.

Compassion also requires action. Without action, the feeling is called pity, and there are really good reasons that everyone disdains pity.

Compassion is a decision; you always have the choice to look the other way. Some days you assess the need of the other, and of yourself, and realize that you have to take care of yourself. You may determine that your resources and the need at hand are not a good match. You may realize that the need is too big, and that the best you can do is report the situation to the switchboard at Higher Power Inc. They dispatch 24/7.

Compassion is an emotional, decisive course of action. Thank God, it is as common as dirt. And it is also one of the most powerful agents working in our world. It is an essential, but optional spiritual discipline.

Which makes it precious.

Mix it with a little trust and the gates of Hell get rattled.

Surrender

I was twelve years old, it was springtime, I was out in the back-yard in the evening, and I had just decided to become apostate.

One of the problems with this picture is that I was twelve and knew what apostasy was; willing, full-knowing revolution against God and God's faith. A change of loyalty – defection. This was the choice of Lucifer, the fallen one. Another problem was that it was precisely what I wanted.

At that age I looked a lot like Pippy Longstockings: skinny, strag-gly hair in two messy braids, tall for my age, pale, and weak. But I had left the Sunday evening class that was supposed to be my preparation for baptism and made a big decision: No, thanks. I'll work for any team but yours.

My rebellion was supported by three pillars: God's people, God's teaching, and God.

Despite the fact that I had loving parents who walked their talk, they seemed to be an anomaly. The guy teaching my baptism class preached love and beat his kids. The big deal youth preacher down at Moody Bible Institute thought that the most important thing we could do as young Christians was to smash all our rock music. There were people telling me that I should simultaneously worry about college and the end of the world, which was going to happen any minute. These people seemed bad or nuts – take your pick.

Doctrine-wise, I had picked up this: "Hey little girl, the best per-son who ever lived was brutally murdered and it was *your* fault." Nobody in our church ever debated whether to blame the Jews or the Romans; those nails were meant for your hands, and the guy with the hammer is just part of the plan. This was a bit heavy for a child.

Then there was my personal observation of God. He apparently stood by while the world was in a severe mess. His supposed cure on the cross did not seem to have had much effect. And I did not buy the notion that this was also our fault for not accepting Jesus as our Lord and Savior, because many of the people who did profess this acceptance were doing a lot of the bad stuff. I was twelve, but I understood racism, and the Christians who supported it. I understood and even approved of human free will, but I didn't like what God was doing with God's will. I didn't like how things were set up. I blamed God.

So I stood there and looked at the sky and said this:

"I know you are there. I know you want me, but I refuse you. I want nothing to do with you or your church. Go away and leave me alone. I will be just fine."

And then I went in and put on my PJ's, asked my mom for milk and cookies, read some Tolkien, and slept peacefully.

I may have been apostate, and courageous enough to tell God, but I wasn't stupid enough to tell my mom. So I started my life of closet apostasy and ironically, serious hypocrisy. I did decline baptism. I told my parents that I did not feel ready and that surely they wouldn't want me to be baptized until it felt right. They looked worried, but they agreed.

I eventually taught Sunday school, because it was easier than sitting in Sunday school. I was president of the youth group because somebody had to do it. I went to camp. I sang, because it pleased my mother. I did precisely whatever pleased me the rest of the time, and I counted the days until my escape. I had some close scrapes running my own life, but I was making it. Sure I was scared, hiding a lot, faking a lot, but it was only temporary.

At eighteen, by a narrow margin, I achieved the velocity required to get out of the black hole suction of the nearby Christian College. I was accepted at a prestigious liberal arts school with no tests, texts, or lectures. It followed Mortimer Adler's regimen of the Great Books. I read Sophocles in Greek. Did science with Archimedes and contemplated Plato, and then worked my way through history. Nobody told you what to think, they just asked questions and put up with know-it-all eighteen year olds like me. All this in the lovely city of Santa Fe, New Mexico – 1,500 miles from home – paid for, of course, by my mother. Freedom.

I drank beer. I rode horses. I got myself a guy. It was great. Until sophomore year.

They only had three questions at this school. You applied them to every text. What is the author saying? Is it true? And if it is true, how does it change your life? I should have smelled a trap.

Because sophomore year we read the Bible. Cover to cover. And asking the questions were these two guys, our academic midwives and nursemaids. At one end of the seminar table was Michael Ossorgin, conceived in Russia, born in Paris just after the revolution, graduate of the Sorbonne. A Russian Orthodox Bishop – he chain-smoked and drank hard and glowed with holiness – this worried me a bit. At the other end of the table was Robert Sacks, Jew, slight of frame and fettered by cerebral palsy. He occasionally shouted, and often laughed, and was a planetary expert on the Book of Genesis. He scared me a bit. They were absolutely nothing like anything I had ever seen before, only they were like everything I knew was true.

The Old Testament wasn't too bad. All those years of Sunday school helped me sound pretty smart – at least I thought so. Then we read the New Testament – in Greek – slowly. And there was that pesky Jesus – purported God. And those dirty questions. And the holy guys at the ends of the table.

> In the beginning was the Word (reason, ratio, relationship, everything that ever made sense) and the Word was God. And this Word lights up everyone who ever came into the world. So often they do not recognize it. But if they do recognize it they become completely alive. (Paraphrase of John I)

And I found that the truth wasn't in the book, or in other people – glowing or not – and it wasn't in the discussion, or the dogma, or the reading. It was inside me, and I recognized it, and I began to live. I walked out of the seminar hall into the foothills of the Sangre de Cristo Mountains and I looked at the sky and I said:

"I know you are there/here. I know you want me/have me. I surrender."

Nothing changed and everything changed. But a conversation started that night that has never stopped. I accepted Life on Life's terms. God is God. The deal is what it is. Huge pieces of the deal hurt. A lot of the people are unmitigated screw-ups, including me. But I am awake, alive, connected, and real. I fake less. I am scared less.

And I have to surrender every day. It is not a one-time conversion sort of thing. I am asked to accept things as they are, not as I would have them be. It is the hard path to peace. It is the hardest of all the disciplines, and the most important.

This is what I know.

If that riptide tugging at your knees is God, dive for the undertow and drown.

Origins

It was the first day of June in the year 1880, and winter had finally let loose of Marinette, Wisconsin. Marinette sits on the western border of the Upper Peninsula of Michigan, hugging the spot where the Menominee River pours into Lake Michigan. Well, sometimes pours; in 1880, the river and the lake froze over for more than half the year. But while the water was liquid, logs flowed so thick down the Menominee that you could walk across it, and a dozen sawmills cut those logs up and shipped them off by water and by rail.

The census worker was given the task of counting up the workmen and their families. This day, he was in the company housing of the Chicago and Northwestern Railroad. Scots and Irishmen mostly, many of them immigrants who had come through Sault St. Marie. The housing was hardly better than shacks; he was glad he did not have to winter over in any of them. His script was beautiful, and he prided himself on a neat page. Since he was counting the railroad yards, he had pre-written "R. R. Labor" down the page to save time. Door by door, he took the names of the men and their wives and children.

The Scotsman sat by his door enjoying the late-day sun. He was still filthy from shoveling coal. His wife stood in the doorway, a toddler on her hip. Name? "Alexander Morrison" he said, deeply burring the r's. The wife was Mary, the child called Bess.

"Occupation, railroad worker," the census taker supplied. "Birthplaces?"

Mary named her birthplace.

"Nae!" boomed the man.

"I was too born there!" said Mary.

"Nae, I'm not a Railroad man."

"What?" cried the worker. "You're livin' here, and you're covered with coal. What am I to think you are?"

"I am an Explorer. Scrive it doon right, now. That's what I be."

Mary sighed and rolled her eyes. And the census worker smudged his page, in several places, due to irritation. But he put in the record that Alexander Morrison was his own man, and an explorer.

That Scotsman was my great-granddaddy. And I am also an explorer.

The Beauty in Darkness

My family took a summer vacation in a cabin by Devil's Lake in Wisconsin. I was six, and tucked into a warm bed on a back sleeping porch. It had been a warm August day, but the summer night air was decidedly cool. I had played myself into righteous childhood exhaustion. My parents were sleeping in another room – my brothers were nearby. There were no locks on the doors. All was quiet, and with no moon that night, stunningly dark.

Because I was sleeping deeply, at first I was not even aware as the strong male hands folded the blankets under me, and lifted me from the bed. Groggy – when a voice whispered "Shush, don't wake anyone," I obeyed.

It was only when I was carried out the back porch door, and slipped out into the dark woods, that I realized what a strange thing was going on. I looked up into the face of the man carrying me.

"Daddy, why are we out in the woods?"

"I've got something important to show you, Peg."

Good enough for me. I think I snoozed some more as he walked on. Up a hill and into a clearing.

"Daddy, it's cold!" I whimpered.

"I know, Honey. Look up."

He cradled me in his arms and I looked up into the night sky. There was a meteor shower going on – the Perseid meteor shower, to be exact – and it was a good show that year. Stars rocketed like fireworks across the heavens.

"Wow, the stars are running around!"

"Peggy, I want you always to remember this. Sometimes you have to go out into the dark and the cold to see the really beautiful things that God has to show you."

I remember.

Being as we are – human, mortal, fragile, stuck in time and space – we tend to have human, fragile, and stuck values. Pain is bad – pleasure is good. Life is good – death is bad. Wealth is good – poverty is bad, and so on. Unable to do much in the way of comprehending the actuality of God, we tend to project upon the Divine our own values. Surely God agrees with us, wants for us what we want, right?

I think perhaps not.

Here's what I have observed about God's apparent values:

I think God cares more about beauty than comfort.
I think God cares more about courage than safety.
I think God cares more about freedom than good behavior.
I think God cares more about sacrifice than suffering.
I think God cares more about generosity than wealth.
I think God cares more about honor than position.
I think God cares more about truth than harmony.
I think God cares more about harmony than purity
I think God cares more about grace than rewards or punishment.

I think the list goes on.

To see the things that God cares about, you have to go into some pretty cold, dark places of human behavior. War is evil – in every case – but in the dark, joyless, airless mineshafts of war there are sometimes found diamonds of human nobility, honor, and sacrifice that stand out more brilliantly for the despicable background.

In the midst of our cold, harsh treatment of the homeless and the mentally ill, I have seen kindness and courage. I have camped out in the Valley of the Shadow of Death, and while the amenities are nothing to write home about, there is a little restaurant there called "In the Presence of My Enemies", where the Maître d' is Jesus and the kitchen is full of cooking angels. You can always get a table there. No reservations are required.

I have seen sick and suffering children preach sermons of simple hope and truth that Charles Spurgeon and Dr. Martin Luther King could not touch. If it were up to me, no children would ever suffer. It appears that God wants to hear them preach.

I hear people say, "I don't want a God who claims to be loving but allows this stuff to happen!" I get this. I sympathize. But I honestly don't think we get to pick our God. I think we get to pick our response to God. I think we get to spend our lives aligning our values (or not) to a cosmic set of values in which death and pain are no longer relevant. Old father Job expressed this when he said, "Though you slay me, yet shall I trust you." (13:15)

I choose to believe that God's values are better than mine, because I have seen the beauty in the darkness.

I remember, Dad.

The Green Mile

I was walking the green mile.

Okay, it wasn't a mile, it just seemed like it. And I wasn't actually condemned to death, though as a second grader, I might as well have been. But the long corridor was a sort of turquoise green. Dead little girl walking, and worst of all, I had to do it every Tuesday afternoon for all of second grade.

The call came at 2 PM every week, just before all the other kids went to recess. My teacher, Miss Cartier, tried to be as subtle as possible, sidling up to my desk and whispering, "Peggy, it's time." But it didn't matter, because all the kids knew where I was going. They snickered behind their hands and giggled as I got up from my seat and left the room. I was nervous and often managed to kick something or bump into something on the way out. Kids would stick their foot out and try to trip me if the teacher took her eyes off me. Miss Cartier didn't let them get away with any words, but that didn't matter either, because there was after school, and before school, and other recesses to get the taunts in. I was labeled for the rest of grade school.

I was walking down to what the kids at school called the "retard room." Even in 1965, nobody was allowed to call it that in front of teachers or staff; it was officially the classroom for the "handicapped" children. But on the playground that is what they called it, and they called me a "retard."

I actually got to know the kids in that classroom. Some of them spent their whole days there. Some kids assigned to that class spent part of their days in a regular classroom. It was a pretty progressive school district. Some of them had physical difficulties, some had developmental difficulties, and some of them didn't seem all that different from the kids in the regular classes. I was there because I was pigeon-toed. Seriously pigeon-toed. I tripped over my own feet all the time. I scuffed my Mary Janes all to death. They tried making me wear those special stiff high shoes, but that didn't help. So I got sent to Miss Belknap, the physical rehab teacher.

Here's what the other kids didn't know. The long walk down the green hall was hell, but heaven was just on the other side of the door to Miss Belknap's room. The room was full of giant toys and gymnastics equipment. She wore sneakers and shorts while all the other teachers were in heels and dresses. She was kinda loud, and funny, and she was pretty masculine for a lady. She called me "Girly." I didn't know anybody else like her. But she liked me. I think she liked all her kids. When I walked in the door, she welcomed me, like a beloved lost lamb. As if she was surprised to see me. As if I was the best part of her day. She was the best part of my week.

She taught me how to walk. How to turn my hips so that my toes would go straight. How to tuck in my tiny little butt so that my hips would open out. We practiced many walks. We walked like ducks; we walked like cowboys. She would have me put my hands behind my back as if they were tied, and I would pretend to walk the plank – with plenty of pirate talk to go with it. We laughed a lot. Wednesday mornings during second grade, I was always a little sore. I remember one day in the spring when she was pretty pleased with me, and she said, "Well, we could quit now, Girly, but as long as we've taught you to walk straight, we might as well teach you how to walk pretty." I did not object. Then I spent a few weeks walking like Miss America with a crown on my head. If they would have let me stay with Miss Belknap for the three R's, I would have stayed. Miss Belknap was my secret treasure.

There is a stanza in the Serenity Prayer attributed to Reinhold Niebuhr that goes:

> Living one day at a time;
> Enjoying one moment at a time;
> Accepting hardship
> As the pathway to peace.

I learned the truth of that every Tuesday in second grade. After the mocking, there was grace. After the loneliness, there was kind attention. After the pain came fun. I could have let the humiliation ruin the joy, but I didn't. In my memory, the grace is huge and lively and the persecution is ghostly and pale.

Perspective is a choice.

So there I was ten years later, 1975, in the grocery on an errand for my mother. I whizzed around a corner in my three-inch platform sandals and miniskirt. I heard a loud voice from the back of the store yell,

"Stop right there! – Is that you Peggy? Peggy Senger?"

I executed a perfect pivot turn and faced Miss Belknap, now a retired teacher. I grinned. She whistled a loud wolf whistle as all the patrons of the store turned and looked.

"Look at that walk! Look at that pretty, humdinger of a walk! Give me a bit more, Girly!"

So I gave her my best strut and then a hug and we laughed. And she said,

"Well, Girly, when you walk that plank they are gonna remember the last thing they see! Go get 'em."

So I did.

My Worst Nightmare

I was lying in a motel bed, contemplating my demise. Staring at the ceiling at midnight. Sleep would not come. At eight in the morning, I was scheduled to enter a hole in the ground and travel several miles underground, guided only by a kerosene lamp. I didn't want to do it, but pride kept me from saying so. It hadn't been my idea. I wasn't at all sure that I would come out alive. I was praying for a way out of going in.

I held my Raggedy Ann doll tight – possibly our last night together. I wasn't planning to take her in – at least *she* would survive. I was eight years old.

Like many childhood nightmares, this one happened on a family vacation. We were bivouacked near Mammoth Cave National Park in Kentucky. My dad was a great amateur scientist with an interest in geology, and he was excited about the trip. My mother had worked all year at a part-time job to pay for the vacation, and this was the highlight. I knew I couldn't let her down. My brothers seemed to be sleeping peacefully. I hadn't told anyone that I was claustrophobic. Not even when dad signed us up for the multiple miles, lantern-only walk. But I was terrified. I had figured we would look into a big cavern; I would keep my eye on the door, and leave as soon as possible. But no, we were going in deep, and walking through narrow corridors connecting cave after cave, and coming out miles away from the entrance. It was pretty much the worst thing I could think of.

The saving grace was that I knew I could hold my dad's hand the whole way. I was pretty sure that he would get me out alive if he could. He was invincible, resilient, courageous, and ingenious. My plan was to stick to him like glue and if a brother or two fell into a hole, then that was just collateral damage we would have to take.

I survived, of course. Even though it didn't help that the guide enjoyed playing up the danger and drama. Telling of historical accidents. People who got lost and never came out. Occasionally, he would drop stones into holes so deep that you never heard them hit bottom. About three quarters of the way in, we encountered the mummified remains of an ancient native gypsum miner, perfectly preserved by the cool temperatures and the minerals. A boulder had fallen and crushed him, and he had lain there, hand sticking out from under the rock, for millennia. The guide told the story with great relish, emphasizing that the boulders all around us could move at any time, "Perhaps we had better move along, folks..."

I have been to some interesting places since then, including active war zones, but I do not ever remember being so thoroughly afraid. If not for my father's hand, I do not believe that an army could have taken me into that cave, or gotten me out. But I think I could go there now. Even without my father. A cave is no longer my greatest fear.

Not by a long stretch.

We are told that the Vatican is releasing the confessional papers of Mother, now Saint, Theresa of Calcutta. I guess the confidentiality rights of the confessional stop at death, at least if you are on the path to canonization.

We are told of the stunning testimony of these papers. How she had deep, vital, visceral experiences of God early in her life, and begged of Him a vocation to the poor. How certain she felt of this vocation. And then, after starting her work with the sickest of the poorest of the most oppressed, she never again experienced the perception of the presence of God. Though this tormented her, she continued the work; doubts and fears overcome by memory and determination. She believed she was doing the right thing. She believed she was following a true call. She believed. But she did not experience the intimacy of her Lord, through a decades-long walk through darkness and pain and suffering.

She didn't know why. Her confessors did not blame her faith, or her practice. Was it because she had agreed to descend into the hell of Calcutta? Had she signed up to suffer with them, and the worst suffering was this silence? She did not know. They did not know. She never found a satisfactory answer. We can only presume that the answer came with the sweet embrace of death.

Before she died, she asked them to destroy the letters and they would not, because they saw them – not as evidence of a lack of faith, but as proof of fidelity, determination, obedience, and submission of a nearly supernatural order.

I agree.

I agree that the physical, emotional, and spiritual perception of a real and intimate God is near to heaven on earth. But I also agree that these feelings, these perceptions, are not the substance of faith. I know many faithful people who do not seem to be wired for these perceptions, yet who believe, who act as disciples, who act as the hands and feet of God. Who simply live righteous lives, with or without belief. They are blessed.

But I get the perceptions. Often. I feel God. I sense God. I hear God. Occasionally, I see God. I have learned to wait for the sense, to listen for the sense. I don't think it makes me a better disciple. But it makes it easier to be a disciple.

And now, my worst nightmare: It could stop. It could stop even if I am a faithful servant. It might stop *because* I am a faithful servant.

It might stop.

Would I continue to believe, to act, to pray, to serve, if it stopped? Could I continue that way for decades, without despair? Honestly, I don't think I would last a week. I have not the courage for the long, dark walk without the hand of my strength, my hope. All I can do is hope that He understands and indulges my weakness.

It was Mother Theresa who said "I know God will not give me anything I cannot handle. I just wish he didn't trust me so much."

It is the scariest thing I know.

Protection

I was selling insurance door to door. Which was odd, because I was only fourteen years old.

It was about a week before Halloween. I was the president of the church youth group. This was not a powerful or prestigious position, since it was a small church and there were only about six teenagers. I was technically apostate at the time, but mostly no one knew it. I had really good parents, and I not only didn't want to break their hearts with my apostasy, I was also hoping they would pay for college. Being in charge of the youth group meant that I had some influence over the level of religiosity, and could keep it to forms my hypocrisy could tolerate. A kind of theological détente.

Everybody knows that youth groups can only have fun if they have some cash to spend. It was part of my job to think up fund-raisers. I wanted to do something fresh. Something that actually provided a useful service to the community. Something that didn't involve too much manual labor. Then the light bulb went on. We would sell window-egg insurance.

Some bad kids (not us) used the "trick" part of "trick or treat" to throw eggs at houses. It was common enough that local grocers would watch out for any kid trying to buy eggs in bulk in late October. My brilliant idea was to go door-to-door selling an insurance policy for a One dollar premium. If your house got egged, you call our hotline and we send a nice kid out immediately to wash your windows. I figured that most housewives would think it was a good deal and that most houses wouldn't get egged, and that we would clean up (so to speak). I didn't bother to run the idea past any adults. I printed up the flyers and coupons and the group of us set out to sell.

To our great disappointment, we made no sales – none. Some ladies just stared at us. Some ladies yelled at us like we were hooligans. "No. Ma'am, we are here to *protect* you from the hooligans!" We regrouped – confused.

I went to my afternoon job as a soda jerk in the local ice cream parlor. I sat in the back room with Robert, the old man who washed dishes for the restaurant. I told him my troubles. He laughed himself off his chair – he laughed so hard he cried. Then he carefully explained to me the concept of a protection racket. See, we lived in a neighborhood heavily populated by the higher levels of the Chicago mob. Robert asked me if I had tried to sell my insurance at the home of Tony Accardo – a few blocks away. "Jeez, Robert, I'm not a *moron*, nobody would egg Tony Accardo's house!" At fourteen I knew about the mob, I just didn't understand the finer points of their day-to-day business.

So here is what Robert taught me: "protection" was a process whereby the wise guys in the area "watched" your home, business, or auto, in exchange for money that you paid them so that they would refrain from vandalizing your home, business, or auto.

We did a bake sale instead.

Oddly, this is pretty much what I got out of my early theological education. If you did enough stuff for God (the preferred currency), God would refrain from blasting you. I am not saying that my parents taught me this – they didn't – but it was a fairly common theme in the church culture I lived in.

Then I noticed that this God was a pretty crummy wise guy. He often appeared to blast good people anyway. A God less honorable than the Mob was not a God I wanted. Hence the apostasy.

Eventually, a truly weird thing happened. I met the Lover of my soul, the present Christ, and I found out that some really malicious slander and libel had been committed against Him, but that He was way too gentle to blast anybody over it, although the power to do so seemed to be there.

Jesus is not a racketeer. I came to understand His protection as a state of being in which, surrounded by His love, other things, including some pretty major hurts, begin to heal and rapidly lose their power over me. Some things that ought to hurt don't even bother me anymore. His Love has become my armor.

We started to travel together, and sometimes, (just to mess with my head, I think), He started to provide some pretty amazing incidents of physical protection. Most of these events have happened when I was participating with Him in His hobbies (life transformation, wound healing, captive freeing, etc.). So there I was again, back at the beginning, doing cool stuff, for and with Him, and there He is protecting me from blasts. But from the inside, it had none of the feel of a scam.

It is also a mystery to me, unexplainable, because sometimes the protection does not seem to be there, and many people have never experienced it at all. Yet He assures me, it is there all the same. We argue about this a bit.

Being a wee bit of a risk taker, I occasionally test the limits of this protection. I have not yet succeeded in outrunning it. Mostly I just take it for granted, because I have way too much other stuff to do. But none of what I do is attempting to sell theological insurance – door-to-door, retail, or wholesale.

Poll watching

Poll watching in the 44th Ward of the City of Chicago, 1975: I was a youthful volunteer in the office of Alderman Richard Simpson. I wasn't old enough to vote, but I was bright enough to poll watch. Poll watching was a tradition necessitated by corruption.

The voting machines were those big mechanical monsters with the levers that clicked and the Las-Vegas-style side arms that swept your vote into the count with that satisfying "ka-chunk." At the end of the day, a human had to open up the machine and look in the back and call out the numbers. Another human wrote the numbers down as they were called out, and another human carried the book downtown where more humans tallied the numbers from the books.

At each step of the way, we assigned a human to watch the official human. Did he call out the number that was there? Did he write down the number that was called out? Did that book stop anywhere between the precinct and city hall? At each step, corruption had its chance, and at each step we watched them. It worked pretty well as long as you had an army of volunteers. This was quite an education for a young, optimistic kid interested in politics.

City hall was a trip in those days. All the aldermen were men, and they were all white. Few of the staffers were female, and fewer still were youngsters, but somehow I had the occasional run of the place. The rooms of city hall were blue and brown with cigarette and cigar haze; the former tended to float above the latter. They had a thirty-gallon coffee urn; they made the coffee on Monday and re-heated it all week. Friday coffee dissolved metal. You got tough or croaked.

The guy I worked for lost almost every vote 48-2, but he knew he was right, so it didn't matter. Wrigley Field was in the 44th, and on a sunny summer day (pre-lights at Wrigley) nobody cared if you took the afternoon off and took in a game. All in all, it was a sweet deal.

I learned to take corruption as part of the package. There was a precinct in the city that was nothing but a mom and pop store and a cemetery, but that precinct turned out a large vote every time the Mayor was up for election. The bums loved Election Day; voting for whiskey kept them busy all day long.

But I also learned that you could deal with corruption – you could witness to it – you could moderate it. Some days you could even talk to it and get stuff done.

The ironic truth was that while Dick Simpson may have needed poll watchers to get his votes counted, the Mayor never needed corruption to get his. Cook County, Illinois may have stolen the 1960 election for JFK, but the people of the City of Chicago loved Mayor Daley; he won by an honest landslide every time. The garbage got picked up, the snow got plowed, and everybody knew the rules. You were taught the rules.

My high school driver's education teacher stood before our class and showed us how to fold a ten-dollar bill behind our driver's license in just the right way and then to present the whole wallet to the cop.

"Never, I mean never, offer a cop a bribe." He said.

"That's wrong and it's stupid – cops don't like to have their integrity questioned. Put the bill behind your license like this. If he wants it, he will take it, if he doesn't, he will take your license and hand you back the wallet. Nobody wants some snot-nosed kid calling you crooked."

I also learned about political delusion, a thing running rampant in our nation's capital these days. Daley was getting old when I was there. He was fat. He was Irish. He smoked. He was red in the face all the time. It was only a matter of time until he fell over from a heart attack. And this city of millions had absolutely no plan for succession.

One day, an alderman stood up in city council and said, with great respect and humility, "Meanin' no disrespect to da mare, may he live to be a hunnert, but don'cha suppose we need ta, maybe, just in case, have a plan, you know, if, God forbid, something should happen ta him, a long, long time from now?"

Stunned silence ensued.

And then, Vito Marzullo, 25th ward, rose to his feet, and shouted at the top of his lungs;

"Our Mare, Richard J. Daley, mare of the great city of Chicago, WILL NEVER DIE!"

And that ended that discussion. Alderman Marzullo was, of course, incorrect in his assertion: Daley died a few years later, and it was a mess.

I have been thinking a lot about the oligarchy that was Chicago, and how much they loved voting. They loved it like they loved baseball. They loved it like they loved food and beer. Politics was the religion of the city as much as Catholicism. Looking back, both the politics and the Catholicism were probably corrupt, but back then nobody cared. People came from places where their grandparents' votes and prayers weren't counted.

I have been thinking about my friends in the Democratic Republic of the Congo. They voted last week. For many citizens, this was their very first taste of democracy. They are still waiting for results. The United Nations poll watchers report that, despite incidents of violence and corruption, the election proceeded with enough integrity that it should count.

I am sure that they have relaxed their standards. But what people there are hoping for, dreaming for, is the kind of election that Chicago, America, takes for granted – one where the loser admits that he has lost, and does not immediately start an armed insurrection. Mr. Kabila and Mr. Bemba have both said they will respect the results, but they both have armies, and folks are worried.

What the people of the Congo need is for the loser to lose, and then for the winner to actually form a government that works, most of the time – well, some of the time would be a good start. They don't have any snow to shovel, but they need some roads, and some police. Police who would only sometimes take the bribe would be a great start. At the moment, they only sometimes have police, and the police sometimes rape and kill. A democratically elected, predictable, stable, oligarchy would be a great improvement for my friends – like it was for Chicago in the 20th century.

I respectfully submit that Chicago should send a delegation to help. Experience, a track record of success, and karmic debt should determine the members. I nominate Fast Eddie Vrdolyak, Vito Marzullo and Dan Rostenkowski for point men.

Out of gratitude, I am sure that the DRC would be glad to send us some great musicians, a thing Chicago also loves. Everybody benefits, everybody's happy.

Now go out and vote! Once!

PS: Please do not write and tell me that Vito and company are dead. This I know. This has never yet stopped a Chicago politician.

The Legal Tender Saloon

It did not occur to me that the Atchison, Topeka and Santa Fe Railroad would not actually stop in Santa Fe. The schedule of stops promised it. I was 18, and deemed responsible enough to travel across the country to a place that I had never seen before.

My first solo travel had been done at about the age of 10. Also by train, from Chicago to downstate Illinois. My parents put me and my little valise on the train. My mother introduced me to the conductor and told him that I would be getting off at Bloomington, and that my grandfather would be waiting for me at the station. I do not think that my father tipped him, because watching out for travelers was the definition of the man's job. Being well-behaved on the train was my job, and no one doubted that I would do it. I remember chatting with others passengers, and boldly walking up to the bar in the all-ages lounge car and ordering a 25-cent grape Nehi soda.

Eight years later, with a mostly successful adolescence behind me, my parents took me to the same Union Station and put me and a large, over-packed trunk on the same train south, this time heading for the prestigious St. John's College in Santa Fe, New Mexico. I had not visited the campus. My parents had barely achieved the bottom of the middle class, and scouting trips to far-flung colleges was just not part of their world. I had been holding a job since I was 14, and driving since 16. If I was smart enough to be accepted, then I was brave enough to get there.

I enjoyed the ride. I sprung for my meals in the dining car. The room did not have enough white linen-clothed tables to allow for solo diners, or even solo couples, so the stewards seated people together according to their own rules of social decorum. Solo young women were seated with the best available single gentleman, with a married couple for ballast. You cleaned up for dinner.

I still wasn't old enough to drink, but they warned us just before the Kansas border that we were entering a dry state, and the bar would close till Colorado. I was told by an older and wiser traveler that a thirsty gentleman could still get a beer below stairs with the stewards, for a generous tip. Ladies were not supposed to get thirsty.

After cutting off the corner of Colorado, we descended into New Mexico. The southern tip of the Rockies looked like every Western I had ever seen. Ponderosa pine and grasslands. Ranches and tiny towns. I hadn't laid eyes on anything my citified self would call a city since we crossed into Kansas. My only images of Santa Fe were from the college catalogue, which showed the stunning campus and the Plaza downtown. So I was watching for adobe and Indians. While I was thus engaged, at just about 30 hours out from home, on a bright August Sunday, we stopped at what I knew was to be my landing place.

We had come out of the mountains into the desert. According to my ticket, this was "Lamy (Santa Fe.)" I thought "Lamy" was the name of the station, like "Union." The conductor put the steps down for me, and a man had my trunk off the baggage car before my shoe touched down. I was the only disembarking passenger; no one was waiting to get on. The train headed off for Albuquerque immediately.

The station was, indeed, made of adobe, and it was about the size of a filling station. It was also closed. A sign said that inquiries could be made at the saloon. I laughed. Then I looked about more carefully. Desert in every direction, and you could see a long ways. Santa Fe should have been a good sized town. It was, after all the state capitol. Santa Fe was not there. I had taxi money in my pocket; it had not occurred to me that there would not be any taxis. There was a wooden building across the dirt road, the only other building in sight. And darned if it didn't say Legal Tender Saloon. It was about 3pm; hot, and windy, and dusty. I started dragging my trunk across the road. I have no idea why I thought it would not be safe alone on the platform.

I was slightly disappointed to find a regular door on the saloon, rather than the swinging type I knew from the westerns. But I scraped my way into the cool darkness. I was almost alone, except for a middle-aged guy behind the ornate bar. He looked long at me.

"I didn't know anyone was getting off today. Sorry, I would have opened the station. St. John's, then?"

It was good to have someone acknowledge something in my reality and my century.

"Yes. Excuse me, but, where is Santa Fe?"

" 'Bout 20 miles that way." He pointed. "Is the college sending a car for you? You called, and let them know when you were arriving, right?"

"I didn't know I was going to need that – I just thought I would get a taxi at the station."

"Where you from, kid?"

"Chicago."

"HA, well. Welcome to the Wild West. I'm Richard. Have a seat – I'll call up to the school."

He tried. No one answered the main number on a Sunday afternoon.

"Well, heck. I close up at five. I'll drive you up then. Want a burger? You don't look old enough to drink. Green chiles on the burger? No? Well, you have some things to learn, Missy."

"Thanks. Can I sit at the bar?"

"You thought I was coming out to a table for you?"

Bold as I was, and providential as Richard obviously was, I was still concerned about going off into the wilderness with some dude I had just met. My mother did have some rules. I still followed some of them.

Sipping from an icy coke bottle, I probed. I was having a hard time letting go of my plan.

"Mr. ... um Richard... I don't want to put you out; you sure there is no way I can call for a taxi?"

"Well, you could try Bustos. He's the only driver for hire around here, but it will cost you and he's not all that reliable. But here's the phone – I'll dial the number."

A woman answered. "Si?"

"Hello ma'am. I'm out at Lamy and I need a ride to St. John's. Is there a taxi available?"

"How old are you?"

"Um, 18, I'm a new student – is there an age limit? I have cash."

"You sound twelve. HEY! BUSTOS! Get your fat ass off the couch! Little girl needs a ride from Lamy."

There was some yelling in Spanish, and then she said, "Bustos says he has to put a tire from one car onto the other. He'll be there in about an hour. Have Richard make you a burger, have the Chiles – they're real good this year."

"Mr. Bustos is coming." I said, as Richard put down my burger and fries."

"Would've been faster to wait for me. But... all part of your education, I guess."

Just before five, Bustos rolled in; in a 1950's Chevy that was three-quarters yellow and one-quarter green. He was fat, and maybe not sober. He greeted Richard like the old friend he was, and ordered a beer. Richard put his hand out for two dollars. Bustos put his hand out to me. I gave him the money. Richard pulled a cold one for himself, as well.

"Dickie, you lazy bastard, you couldn't drive this girl up to the school?"

"I offered, she's from Chicago, wanted a real taxi. Thought it would be safer with a son-of-a bitch like you, I think."

They laughed, hard. I started dragging my trunk towards the car.

Quaker Not So Plain Dress

It was a busy day for my mother and me; I was being born, she being delivered of a child. We were at Presbyterian St. Luke's Hospital in Chicago, right off the Congress Expressway – which was six lanes in 1957, not the present eight, and had not yet been named for Mr. Eisenhower. It was snowing, which was not surprising, as it was New Year's Eve. My father was concerned for his beloved wife and excited about the prospect of his second child, and it would soon dawn on him that her two-weeks-early arrival would give him a tax deduction for the entire previous year. Everything went well.

About 20 blocks due east, at 325 West Jackson Boulevard – just off Upper Wacker Drive – a Mr. Jack Stern had a small but prestigious couture dress studio. He sold his dresses almost exclusively through Marshall Field's designer dress section. The holiday season was always a busy time. Even though he was in the middle of the Spring into Summer dresses, and planning for the 1958 fall season, his regular customers knew that they could come in for an emergency fitting or to ask for something special. That week, a very special order was filled for a simple but elegant black dress. Rayon crepe, simple on top, three-quarter-length sleeves, fitted at the waist; it was flattering to the figure that was planning to wear it to a society funeral. Its subtle glory was the large satin bow just above the fluted, knee length hem.

The dress was delivered to a North Shore address. I was delivered, and taken west, in due time, to the suburb of Oak Park and an apartment above a bakery.

I know how I ended up in Salem, Oregon. After 18 years in Oak Park, I went to college in Santa Fe, New Mexico, married an Oregonian, and followed him home. (The Quaker thing that came after that was a bit of a surprise to me.)

The dress has a more mysterious history. It was not worn often – many couture dresses suffer that fate. But somehow it found its way west across the continent and eventually to a Goodwill store in Salem, hanging on a rack with a tag that said $15. The prospect of an ignoble end as an Audrey Hepburn Halloween costume was very real.

Quaker preachers do not wear vestments. Our worship attire is not usually distinguishable from the other members of the meeting. This is one of our testimonies. Those of us who facilitate weddings and memorial services dress appropriate to the level of festivity of the occasion. For my brothers in the ministry, a suit and tie is almost always sufficient. Female ministers have to be a bit more creative. You want to look appropriate, but not call attention to yourself. I like elegant, when I can pull it off.

Being a Quaker preacher is not usually a high-remuneration gig, at least not materially. I shop at Goodwill. And so it came to pass that a baby girl of a certain vintage and a couture dress of the same vintage found each other, forty years and several thousand miles away from the neighborhood where they both started.

Odd that this sort of a dress would end up attending Quaker weddings and memorials. But no more odd than my own journey.

I am more sentimental about some inanimate objects than I probably ought to be. I tend to anthropomorphize certain things, like motorcycles. But I guess that I believe that the cosmos, animate and inanimate, is ordered in a way that the pull of a strong human pathway will sweep along other physical bodies like leaves on a wind-swept path.

Mr. Jack's dress and I have both had better endings than might have been.

We are grateful.

Cleaning and Gleaning Theology

Shortly after his 88th birthday, my father, Mr. Orville Senger – a good and righteous man – left this planet to pursue other opportunities. He was a simple man, and did not leave much in the way of possessions, at least not by the world's standards; but he had a small and interesting collection of junk. This collection was stored in various places around my house, which had been his home for the last twelve years: the greenhouse, the garage, the basement, the closet in his room. I went through them slowly, deciding what to keep, what to give away, what to throw away, and what to share with my brothers. It was slow work, because it was emotional work. One of my father's defining habits was labeling things and making signs. He had distinctive handwriting. It was pretty illegible; my mother said he should have been a doctor. When he wanted you to see something and pay attention, though, he wrote in big block letters. I have been finding these notes and signs around the house. I hear his voice every time I find one.

Just before Easter, I was in the corner of the basement where he kept his gardening supplies. I found a box with a small space heater in it, the kind he would have used to heat his greenhouse in winter. There was a sign attached to it:

THERE IS NOTHING WRONG WITH THIS – IT JUST NEEDS A NEW FAN MOTOR

This means that it was broken, but he couldn't bring himself to throw it away. It was an inexpensive appliance; the part probably would have cost more than a new one. I know that this habit of keeping things was part depression-era frugality, but it was also an attitude that he had about everything, including people. He was a "redeemer" – a person who gave a hand up – a fixer. He believed that anybody, given a choice and a chance, could start over. In his last years of life, he was supporting a ministry on the North side of Chicago that helps teenaged male prostitutes get off the streets. I can hear him say, "There's nothing wrong with those boys – they just need some help."

My parents raised me in a church that taught the doctrine of human depravity; that people were inherently bad, fallen, beyond the ability to change without massive cosmic intervention, which they clearly did not deserve. My dad taught me by example just the opposite; that people are basically good, worthwhile, and respectable. They mess up and make bad choices and need help, God's help and each other's help, but they are worth helping. Note to parents: what you teach by example will trump the doctrine of any church you attend – every time.

I felt very sad holding that heater. Its redeemer had left the planet. It was headed for the recycling bin. I was reminded of the words of ancient Job: "I know that my redeemer lives, and that one day He shall stand on this Earth." Job's friends kept trying to tell him that there was something wrong with him. Job knew better, and hoped. I am grateful that my redeemer, Christ, believes that there is nothing in me that cannot be made whole, and has indeed stood on this earth and does live, and does continue to work on me.

Today I was in the closet in Dad's room. I only got about half way through this most secret treasure trove before my heart gave out. Toys from his childhood; favorite music, on tape and vinyl; unfinished water color paintings; gizmos, gadgets, and widgets galore. And a package with a label that read:

DO NOT DISCARD – DISCUSS WITH ME.

This was a bit mysterious; who did he think he was writing this to, and under what conditions? I did not make it a habit of going through his things. I am not a reckless trasher. If someone were going through his things, it would be under the present conditions, and he would be gone. Now, how am I supposed to discuss this with him?

I opened the package. It contained about a dozen issues of *The Saturday Evening Post*, from 1948 through 1952. One of them had a lead article entitled, "What kind of president will Dewey make?" Seriously, who would throw these things out? I will keep the magazines – there are enough for all of his kids and grandkids to have one.

I will also keep the sign. I may have it framed. It is another example of my dad teaching theology through everyday events. It isn't about magazines; it's about life.

When something or someone seems useless, antiquated, beyond repair – talk to your cosmic parent about it. Talk to the Maker. There is value there. Treasure is found in surprising places. Everything and everyone is redeemable.

Quakers, Not Just For Breakfast Anymore

He was one of us – a Quaker – a member of the Religious Society of Friends. Tom Fox embodied the testimonies we hold dear. He was a man changed by timeless truth and, being changed himself, he changed the world around him. Not content to just know the truth, he acted upon it.

Tom went to Iraq to be present to the civilian victims of a war his country perpetrated – to join them physically in their trouble. He lived and worked for two years in a regular Baghdad neighborhood without guards or guns. I saw news celebrity, Anderson Cooper, react on camera, as he interviewed the clerk of Tom's Quaker meeting. "He lived *outside* the green zone without a guard!?" Yes, Anderson, he did. He taught peacemaking. He acted as an intermediary between incarcerated Iraqis and their families. He made friends. He was a non-anxious presence to occupier, insurgent, and the people caught in the middle. In 2005 he was kidnapped and killed while doing this work.

> This is why the Father loves me, because I lay down my life – and I will take it back again. No one takes it away from me. On the contrary, I lay it down voluntarily. I have set it aside.
>
> —Jesus, The Gospel of John

Tom Fox's life was not taken from him. Tom Fox laid his life down a long time ago. He surrendered it into the hands of the Divine. Because he knew it was safe there, he was able to walk unbound by fear, letting the Light within him control and impel him forward into the work of peace. Tom's life was safe in the hands of God before he went to Baghdad, it was safe in Baghdad, it was safe in captivity, and it is safe now. The loss is ours to bear. But it is a temporary, perceptual loss, for we have also put our lives into the hands of the Divine, and so our lives and his remain together.

Tom did not fail in his task. I am sure that many of the tears shed for him were Iraqi tears. I am sure that many of the prayers that have been spoken for him have been spoken in languages other than English. I am certain that Tom had some effect on his captors, even if we do not see it. I am certain that his life will inspire a hundred others to pick up his work around the world. Task completed. Mission accomplished.

"Thee was faithful."

Proselyphobia

I was supposed to be going door-to-door selling religion. What I was actually doing was sitting under a tree lying about going door-to-door.

Youth camp was not going well. Despite the fact that many of us were showing clear signs of spiritual doubt, confusion, and obvious natural and spiritual immaturity, the powers-that-be decided that they should send us out into the neighboring community as representatives of the faith.

I do not know what they were thinking.

As it was the only way to get to the Saturday night watermelon feed and hayride, I decided to play along. But when it came down to it – time to knock on a door and ask somebody if they wanted to meet Jesus – I just couldn't do it. I didn't have any Jesus to introduce them to. Even as a backslider I had more integrity than that.

But there was a form to fill out, reporting on the result at each house on my assignment. So I ditched my partner on the pretense that this would go quicker if we split up, and then I bought a soda, sat down under a tree, and made up responses. Lying to my youth leaders seemed like a better idea than lying to unbelievers. I had another choice, of course – lie to nobody, and "come out" as the apostate I was – but that would have certainly gotten back to my mother, and I was not up to that.

I think this experience was the genesis of my proselyphobia.

Yes, that's right, proselyphobia – the fear of recruitment – especially religious recruitment. I have this fear, and perhaps so do you. It is common among religious people, even people whose religion teaches that recruitment is critical and mandatory. It is equally common among people who think their faith is a good one among equals. It is common.

The problem for me is that I am called to be an evangelist. It is an inconvenient phobia for me to have. These days I don't think respectful religious recruitment is inherently bad. I have something authentic to talk about. I actually think that I carry the following wonderful truth around in my back pocket:

There is a God. This God loves you. You can have immediate, constant access to this God. This God will show up and teach you. This God became human in the person of Jesus of Nazareth. You do not have to live in captivity to, or fear of, anything.

I carry this around, I know it experientially, and I believe that people around me are literally dying for the want of it. They die from addiction, from loneliness, from despair, from idolatry. I think that what I carry around would save lives. And still, I am at times afraid to talk about it.

I think part of my fear comes from really, seriously, not wanting to be associated with people who have done nasty, coercive, sometimes violent recruitment. The proselytizing that they attempted to train me in as a youth was merely annoying in comparison, but I don't want to be associated with that either.

If you divided the whole world up into the teams by belief, I would have to choose the team that includes Johnny Cash, Joseph Shabalala, Bono, and Mother Theresa, even if I have to have Jim Dobson and the Spanish Inquisition. Any other team is just not my home. But the point is not to divide up into teams, it is to be able to talk to anyone on any team and teach and learn from each other. And this is hard.

I am pretty sure that the sub-group I hang out with now, the Quakers, would never, under any circumstances, use violence to force people to convert. The worst behavior that I have witnessed among them is emotional manipulation designed to provoke a cathartic convincement, and even that has gone out of style. And even the most ardent promoters of using emotion to get at faith would admit that it is a useless endeavor unless the soul is ready for God. Yet this overly-emotional approach has left many Friends proselyphobic.

At the other end of the Quaker spectrum, some Friends think that it is offensive to even say to somebody that you think they should consider a life of faith lived the way we live it. These same folks often have no trouble loudly proclaiming their political beliefs in the streets, but they would never carry a picket for Jesus or Quakerism. It would just seem gauche. So they talk about peace, and justice, but not about God. And because they don't like to promote what they have, they are hard to find sometimes.

I have parked my buggy between these two ends. I believe that people are free – that they are grown-ups, mostly. We live in a society teeming with ideas and experiences. I am not offended when someone offers an idea or an experience to me. Why should I be afraid to offer mine? I know which times and places are appropriate and which are not. If I offer a description of the source of my hope, it is okay with me if you say "No thanks." When I meet a person who has a deep, practical, working faith unlike my own, I usually want to learn from them. I feel no need to try to talk them out of what is obviously working, however they name it. This is true even if that deep, practical, working belief is agnostic or non-theistic. But the reality is that many people around me don't seem to have something that works. And some are interested in an intimate connection to the Divine. I have that. I know how I got it. I don't think that it is hard to get. Yet I often say little or nothing about what I know.

I know that I am afraid of false advertising. People promise stupid stuff in the name of religion, like "This faith path will solve all your problems, or automatically make you rich and healthy." These are lies, but faith does have its benefits. You never need to feel truly alone. You can seek and find meaning. I have learned to talk about faith honestly, but still I hesitate.

I know that I am afraid of hypocrisy. I mean, I am a screw-up, always have been, always will be. I used to be afraid of being a public minister. It felt like the gateway drug to becoming a TV evangelist with the resultant inevitable fall. I don't even like people taking my picture, let alone videotaping me. I have an uncanny ability to cause videotaping systems to malfunction. But actually, faith has made me less of a hypocrite, not more of one. There are parts of my life I can let you see and imitate. There are parts where you might want to find a better model, but I know one from the other. I will tell you if you ask. Yet at times, I hesitate to make plain even the good parts.

I know that I am plagued by occasional deep doubt. What if I am a lot more delusional than I think I am? What if I have dedicated my life to the playing of a pretend game, and am encouraging others to join me? What if the present Christ is just an elaborate imaginary friend? These moments come, yes they do. But they never stay, because it takes much more energy to sustain the doubts than to sustain the belief. I always relax back into faith. I love better from faith. I laugh better from faith. Everything that is good about me is better from the place of faith. My doubts don't disqualify my testimony; they make it stand out in clarity.

Like all phobias, proselyphobia does not evaporate in the face of logical argument. It can only be conquered by learning to relax in the face of that which you fear. I am working on my proselyphobia. I have made up my mind to speak and write what I know. I am learning to take responsibility only for my testimony, not the effect my testimony has on the world – that is God's job, not mine. I am choosing to speak from my own experience, flawed example though I am, or perhaps especially because I am a flawed example.

I am getting over it.

Dangerous Quakers

Somedays I just feel dangerous.

I was tired of my government, my society. I could have taken my great big motorcycle out for a fast run, but that didn't feel dangerous enough. I could have joined the large rally at the State Capitol a few blocks from my house, "Si, Se Puede!" but they seemed to have things under control and did not need me. I whipped a few e-mails off to my congressional representatives about torture and detainment without legal recourse and rendition, but it did not cool the fire in my belly. I needed to do something way outside the bell curve, something so radical that if everyone followed my lead, it would shake foundations, topple governments, create societal chaos – I was in that kind of mood.

So this is what I did. First, I took a chunk of money that I was planning to use for a nice shopping excursion and sent it to a group in the third world. I thereby robbed the US economy of that money, and I robbed the US government of the taxes on that money. Then I went out and put into the hands of a young person a piece of paper that they could use to make sure that the US military could not aim its recruitment lies in their direction. Then, to cap the day, I went to meeting for worship, and I, the preacher, did not preach. I did not tell them what to think, I did not tell them what to believe. We sat silently and let God talk to the folks completely without theological middlemen.

You see, I am a dangerous Quaker. You have heard about us, I am sure. Senator Patrick Leahy (D-Vermont) was recently asking the FBI why they were spying on groups like the Quakers and the Raging Grannies. Apparently there were about a hundred anti-war groups that were spied on that could have been mentioned. I suspect that the Quakers and the Raging Grannies got named because they seemed so patently and ridiculously undangerous. With all due respect, Mr. Senator, if you think that an enraged grandmother is not a dangerous thing, you have never seen one. And please do not count the Quakers out. Not yet.

In addition to the FBI, the Department of Defense and the NSA have been spying on us. Apparently they haven't found anything worthy of detention or harassment yet. I feel kind of sorry for these guys. They have fallen on hard times. Their info is all swiss-cheesy. So as an act of charity, I am going to make it a little easier on them. Tune in your web data miners to this station and stay tuned. I cannot and *do not* speak for all Quakers. But I can speak for me. I am about to give you some solid intelligence. Listen up!

The Top Ten Reasons why I am a dangerous Quaker and should be watched carefully:

1- I believe that there is a seed of God and goodness in everyone. It may be small, starved, buried, and stepped on, but it is there, and can be reached under the right circumstances. This includes all known terrorists and evil dictators. The right circumstances for reaching that goodness do not include bombings and assassination attempts.

2 – I cannot in good conscience say the Pledge of Allegiance. My patriotism is expressed through informed voting and paying my taxes; but my allegiance is to a kingdom not of this world. I pledge to no other. Even if I could pledge my allegiance to this country, I could not say *that* pledge because I attempt to only say true things and it includes the patent and obvious falsehoods that we are "One nation under God" and that there is "Liberty and justice for all." This I have not observed to be true.

3 – I cannot swear an oath in court, not on the Bible or any other book. I take that book very seriously and that book contains the instruction to not swear oaths because it implies that you have two standards of truth. That book says to let your "yes" be "yes" and your "no" be "no", and leave it at that.

4 – I believe that *all* war is incompatible with the teachings of Jesus. He said that we were to love our enemies, and I think that this meant at the very least that we should not kill them. Our present war is immoral, as has been every other war; and yes, I include World War II and the American Revolution in that list.

5 – I do not believe in the death penalty. We may indeed need to keep some citizens safely locked up for life. But I would not put any human to death as a consequence of crime. And that includes

Timothy McVeigh or Ted Bundy. It's the "Love your enemies" thing again.

6 – I respect my fellow voter's rights to disagree with me; to fund and support a military. But I think that military recruiting, like other sinful behavior, should be limited to consenting adults. It should be illegal to aim military recruiting at secondary school students.

7 – I do not believe in living beyond my means. This is also in the teachings of Jesus on the subject of simplicity. I try and limit my debt to the house and an occasional short-term car loan. I am not a very simple Quaker; many do much better than I do in this spiritual discipline. But if everyone in the US shopped even as simply as I do, the economy would crash, big and bad.

8 – I try to send as much of my money as possible outside of the US economy. I think we should be poorer and the poor nations should be richer. I do this by supporting organizations that reduce poverty. I do not pay much attention to whether or not the people helped, or their governments, agree with US foreign policy. The cool subversive benefit of this is that the government lets me forego taxes on this money, which means less money for the military and other projects of which I do not approve.

9 – I am not actually keen on national borders in general. I am not worried about illegal immigration from Mexico. Fine folks, by and large. Figure out how to tax them. I would gleefully support a national sales tax that paid for universal health care and schools. I think the national anthem sounds great in Spanish.

10 – I think that informed, non-violent, conscience driven dissent is extremely patriotic. I also think that it is sexy.

So there you go, guys. I'm sure you know my numbers. Feel free to check in regularly. Visit our little meeting if you like, you will be welcome.

Noisy Quakers

Be still and know that I am God.

—Psalm 46:10

It was a very noisy Quaker meeting.

For some of us, this is unusual. Quakers are known for having a
big taste for quiet. We practice a listening spirituality. Whatever
else we do, the core of our worship is supposed to be listening to
the present Christ, and if we are given a message for the community we are supposed to speak it. Because we have been around
for 350 years with no centralized church government, the practice of this has become extremely divergent. African Friends sing,
loudly and long, often dance, and then listen to the present Christ
discerned by the designated preacher. Some American meetings
also follow this practice. At the other extreme, you will find British meetings that will actually boast about how many decades
it has been since anyone spoke in meeting – they have elevated
the listening process, and appear to have forgotten the purpose
of the listening. There is an urban American meeting that in the
mid-1800s would go out on Sunday morning and put straw over
the cobblestones of the street so as to muffle the hoof beats of
passing horses. Some of us like quiet just that much.

The majority of Quaker meetings and churches include some
quantity of sitting still, being quiet, and listening. It is not always
easy. It is counter-cultural. It makes many people uncomfortable.
It's not rock and roll, but we like it.

The meeting I usually attend is a Quaker hybrid. We sing a little.
We pray out loud a bit. Then we settle down and shut up. Someone usually receives a message to speak, often several someones.
The messages are usually right on target. We like the peace that
we get between the messages. Most of the people in the room are
new Quakers; they are acquiring a taste for the silence.

One morning, two strangers walked in. A man and a little boy.
The son looked around. He looked panic stricken. He turned to
his dad and said loudly. "Oh no! Not church! Don't want church!"
The boy was looked to be on the autism spectrum. I greeted the

father and he said to me, "This may not work; we may not be able to stay." I said, "Please try, you are welcome here. Your son is welcome here."

Our room is pretty small. We sit facing each other in concentric semi-circles. There isn't really any place to hide. The father took his son and sat on what constitutes the backbench. The boy was not happy. He did not want to stay. The father tried several tricks to get him to settle. The boy vocalized, every few seconds, for the next hour.

We sang. The boy declared "No sad songs!"

We prayed. The boy said "No. No. No. No church!"

We settled into silence. The boy moaned, clucked, muttered, and talked.

"Don't wanna be quiet!" he called out.

After a few minutes, some other vocal ministry arose. It was sweet. It was true. It was just what Jesus would have said. It didn't directly address the situation; it addressed the needs of the meeting. The boy said "Good one!" and proceeded to yip.

After a few more minutes, a scripture passage was raised. The boy crowed.

I experienced what some Quakers call "gathering." It is a deepening of the silence. A kind of mystical feeling of the bottom dropping out of the meeting. A transcendence; a visceral experience of the presence of God. It was a gathered non-silence.

The time passed swiftly.

The meeting rose. Friends greeted the father and the boy. The father attempted to apologize. No one was having any of that. We knew that we had experienced a first rate Quaker meeting. The purpose of meeting is not to escape from the world to a place quiet enough to listen, but to learn to listen well enough that we can listen anywhere, under any conditions. It had been a good and rewarding morning's practicum. We were grateful. There was not a single kvetcher, not a single grumbler, not then, not later.

One of those present was a new attender, a new Christian, a new Quaker. She was a transgender woman. She had lots of tattoos. She was checking us out, watchful. She had been burned by church people. She walked up to me after meeting and said,

"Well, hmm. I guess you really mean it. I guess everyone really is welcome, wow. Walking the talk, hmm."

God told the psalmist, "Be still and know that I am God." Quakers like that verse. Many think the stillness referred to means silence. It does not. The Hebrew verb means to relax, let go, stop trying so hard, release. In order to see God, you have to stop striving, stop relying on your own strength. You have to give up your notions of how things should be. You have to let go of preferences and pet peeves. You have to open yourself up to the uncomfortable.

Then God shows up.

Selling Fear, Greed, and Falsehood

I live in a nice old-school kind of neighborhood. The housing is mixed, the mature trees are breaking up the sidewalks, front porches often have furniture, people walking by will usually greet you, and – the mosquitoes being not too bad – nothing is screened in. This I like.

Being that kind of neighborhood, we have people going door to door. The occasional uniformed cookie salesperson still pulls a Flexible Flyer up the sidewalk – I suspect that the devil himself might be selling thin mints – they are that tempting. We get religious people, usually the Witnesses or the Mormons – I try to be polite. Oregon has a political climate that makes it easy to get things on ballots, so we get petitioners, some of them fervent volunteers and some paid by the signature. I won't sign when they are doing it for the bucks. And we get regular salespeople of several varieties. Except for the cookie imps, I refuse sales at my front door; I prefer to decide when and when I am going to shop.

Then up walked this young man. He found me in a pretty good mood, and he was a pretty boy. College vacation job, no doubt. So I was a little more tolerant than usual.

"Hi! Could I please ask you a question?"

(Points for not calling me ma'am – points for saying please.)

"Oh, sure, ask away, but I may not answer."

"Do you rent or own this home?"

"Well, that's a mighty personal question to ask a stranger."

Oh, I'm sorry. I'm Dan and I'm with Blah Blah Security Systems."

"Nice, to meet you Dan. I'm Peggy. Selling security then?"

"Oh, no, I'm not selling anything today. I am the point man for our company, and today I am just out gathering marketing research. But we are concerned with security."

Then he launched into a spiel about the dangers of living in "crime soaked" Salem, Oregon. It was pretty funny. I smiled a lot, but didn't quite laugh. See the top paragraph about front porch living – until last year when the dog died, I never had a key to my own house. I mostly don't lock it when I am away and cannot conceive of locking it while I am home and awake. We lock the doors at night, but my kids know which windows never get locked. Eventually, I interrupted Dan.

"Son, for the sake of honesty, I need to tell you that you are actually wasting your time here on this porch."

"Aren't you concerned about security?"

"Never felt safer anywhere, anytime."

I didn't bother to tell him about my recent trip to a war zone, or the fact that I pack my sense of safety with me, so that I almost never feel less safe either. He tried to restart the line.

"Peggy, a lot of your neighbors are worried about their security."

Okay – then I laughed.

"Son, you aren't going to sell me a security system."

"Ah, but see here's the thing! I am not trying to sell you a security system today. We are just trying to make a presence in the neighborhood. We would like to pay *you* to put our sign in your window for your neighbors to see. Then, when our sales people come around, folks will have seen the name, and will feel like if you trust our company with your safety, then maybe they should too. And the thieves will think you have the system, so it will deter them as well. Cool, huh?"

"So you think false advertising is cool? Really?"

"Nothing false about it!"

"I am not afraid of crime, but you want me to pretend that I am so that my neighbors' sense of concern will rise, and they will think that I have installed this system, even though I haven't, and I am going to try to fake out the thieves, and you want me to do this for money, and you don't call that false?"

Danny boy was starting to look a wee bit confused. For the third time, I tried the simple truth.

"Truly, Dan, you are actually talking to the wrong woman. I can't say it any plainer than that. Have a nice day, son."

I walked in the house.

"Don't you even want to know how much we will pay you?!?!" Dan shouted after me.

"No, I don't; it makes no difference."

Dan walked away. Poor Dan, he had his pitch down so nicely. I wonder how transparent they were at sales-boy school. Did they tell him that they were selling on the two pillars of fear and greed? I wonder if they had numbers for how many people are motivated by these things. He certainly was presuming that I was. He was confused when it did not work.

Motivation – that which moves you – that which underlies your actions – this is a good thing to be acquainted with. If you know what moves you, and even better, if you can influence or choose what moves you, you will have the power to resist those who would move you in their own interests.

But to look at your own motivations, you have to be willing to look at your own dark side. Young Dan had no idea that the middle-aged lady before him would be much more moved by power and control than by fear and greed. But even if he had, it would not have done him much good, because I know those things about myself. I have taken them off auto-pilot and cruise control. I have surrendered them to a higher power. That's my security system. If they get the better of me, it is not without plenty of warning, plenty of chances to turn another way. I am not likely to confuse them with better motivations like compassion and loyalty, as I would have in the past. I am not perfectly secure from the darkness, but I am not an easy target. I'll bet my soul has a sign in the window.

I walked around my neighborhood last evening. I could not find a single house with the security company's sign in its window. I am proud to live in this neighborhood. I feel kind of sorry for Dan, but we all have our lessons to learn.

Call Me Irresponsible

I was in a rural town in Southern Oregon doing domestic violence prevention work. Traveling preacher. Traveling feminist. Public Quaker. And the guy in the back was yelling at me.

We were having a series of educational meetings: warning signs of abusive personality, universal rights of women, how to get a restraining order. That sort of thing. At the time, the county we were in had the highest rate of domestic violence in the state.

The first evening a man came in and stood in the back. He was pretty sketchy looking. Not a big fan of the bath. Not a big fan of clean clothing. Apparently not a big fan of me and my material, either, because every time I said anything, he shouted at me. If I said "X," he yelled "Not X!" If I said "Y," he shouted, "Y is a lie!" and added a few cuss words. I could have had him removed. One of the local leaders asked me if I wanted them to shut him up or throw him out, and I said "No, leave him be. For once I am not preaching to the choir – this guy needs to be here."

So I just kept going. The next morning, the guy came back, but this time he took a seat and confined his comments to loud grumbling. He came back every session. Sunday morning, he came and sat in the front row. He had clearly washed his face – just his face, and maybe put on a clean shirt. I preached on the high opinion that God has of humanity; how we are loved, and how this love is extended to all, even the perpetrators of bad acts. Part way through my message, at the reading of some scripture passages about how God feels about us, this fellow suddenly caught my attention. He was shaking, silently; it looked as though he was having an epileptic fit. Then there was noise – sobbing – and it was clear that the man was having some unaccustomed emotions. This time, the elders did take him out, and I am told that he confessed to a long bad life and especially to a lot of spousal abuse. The elders paid a visit to his home and provided assistance to the woman who lived there. The last time I saw the man, a couple of years after that morning, he was sitting on the floor of the meetinghouse, playing with the babies, clean, sober, and transformed.

This week they called Barack Obama irresponsible. This, for saying that he would be willing to talk to our nation's enemies. Not compromise with our enemies, not make concessions to our enemies, just communicate with them. In his words to "to look them in the eyes and say what needs to be said."

"How foolish, how inexperienced! They will use you as a tool for propaganda!" say the more experienced.

Well, as for me, if this is inexperience, then we need more people with less experience. Because the "inside-the-beltway" position is a position of fear, not of courage: fear of being used, fear of looking bad, and fear of failure. In their thinking you do not go in and talk to the enemy until your agents and minions have already wired the deal. Then the leaders go in, pretend to hold talks, and look like heroes. They give the example of Nixon and the Chinese, where Kissinger brokered the deal in advance.

I say we need more heroes, not more people who want to look like heroes. Moral courage takes risks. It does the thing that is unexpected.

Many of the people who criticize Obama's position claim, quite publicly, to be followers of Jesus. This confuses me. Jesus said:

> Others have told you, "Love your neighbor and hate your enemy." But I tell you: Love your enemies and pray for those who hurt you. (Matthew 5:43-44)

I am certain that "love your enemies" includes talking to them. It certainly precludes trying to kill them. It does not necessarily mean letting them have their way, but I think it does mean letting them have their say, and trust that the truth will be apparent.

I do not want to live in a theocracy. I do not expect politicians to run the country according to my religious opinions. I do not wish to legally impose my moral standards on others. But I do wish people would stop proclaiming loyalty to the teachings of Jesus when they are really living out the philosophies that He specifically denounced. It would be more honest. It would be clearer.

If they really want a faith-based position for foreign policy, I have one to suggest. It is the words of George Fox, one of the founders of Quakerism. He had this advice for his followers traveling about the globe:

> Let all nations hear the sound by word or writing. Spare no place, spare no tongue or pen, but be obedient to the Lord God; go through the work, be valiant for the truth upon the earth; and tread and trample down what is contrary. Ye have the power, do not abuse it... Keep down and low; and take heed of false joys that will change... This is the word of the Lord God to you all, and a charge to you all in the presence of the living God; be patterns, be examples in all countries, places, islands, nations wherever you come; that your carriage and life may preach among all sorts of people, and to them; then you will come to walk cheerfully over the world, answering that of God in everyone; whereby in them you may be a blessing, and make the witness of God in them to bless you. (G. Fox 1656)

To summarize Fox:

Proclaim the truth you know.
Use every method of communication possible.
Trample deceit. (Not trample deceived persons!)
Do not abuse your power.
Stay humble.
Live what you believe.
Presume that "the other" has God in them, as you do.

Heresy, you say? That of God in everyone? That of God in Vlad Putin? That of God in Osama Bin Laden?

I give you the Gospel of John, first chapter, ninth verse

> That was the true Light, which lights up every person that comes into the world.

John was not naïve about evil. He lived with the Romans; they killed all his fellow apostles before they got him. He lived through some of the most appalling persecutions, genocides, and atrocities that human kind has ever committed. And he believed that every human had innate goodness somewhere in them.

It is possible to speak truth, even to evil. But you have to speak.

This column was written in the summer of 2007. Barack Obama was barely a candidate. He had already earned my support. Sadly, he never talked to Bin Laden, He simply had him killed. That job is tough on a person's ideals.

Point – Counter – Point

When I was a kid, all sorts of people sat at lunch counters: men, women, working people, old ladies in fancy hats and gloves, children with enough coinage to get a handmade soda. These days, restaurants with counters are rare, and it's hard to get anything more than pie at the counter. Mostly men sit there, often old men. Solo women take a booth. So sitting at the counter has become a kind of micro-subversion.

Recently, I had a great Off-the-Grid motorcycle ride – a no agenda, no contact with home, free weekend. One of the things that made it great was that every meal I took in public, I took at a lunch counter. I don't always want to rub elbows with randomly selected humans, but sometimes I get in the mood.

On my first leg out, I stopped for a mid-morning gasoline, pie, and coffee break. The up-front gal aimed me at the booth. I re-aimed.

"Can I sit at the counter?"

"I have plenty of booths, honey, right over here."

"Thanks, I'd like to sit at the counter – these fellows won't mind, I hardly ever throw food."

Two middle age guys looked up at me. I put my helmet down on the counter. One guy grinned.

"Well! I bet you aren't riding a Goldwing"

Here we go... a standard conversation. I presume this happens to other people – you know, when your normal way of being provokes predictable comments from the hoi polloi. I have a stable of them. The one where I subvert little girls. The one where people confuse me with the Amish. And the one where motorcycle dudes feel the need to comment on me and my bike. These convos are so familiar that it is like *Name That Tune!* Two notes in, and I know where we are going with this. I have learned to play with these chats, seeing how the outcome changes if I change my lines. With dudes and bikes I sometimes succumb to the temptation of a wee bit ó the snark. Snark is one of my besetting sins.

"No, I am not riding a Goldwing, and honestly, I wouldn't ride one if you gave it to me for free." (Oops, snark!)

"Well, then – I don't like you!" He laughed and turned to the next guy, who got up and paid for his pie.

"Well, sir. I am completely okay with your dislike and the side order of judgement. – Mind if I eat pie?" (Probably snark.) The waitress arrived and chuckled as she poured my coffee.

"Aw, I was just kiddin' – I ride a Goldwing."

"I had guessed that."

I let the silence sit while I got my triple berry heated up. Then I decided to try to turn this chat toward the friendlier.

"I ride a Kawasaki Vulcan 750."

"Well, that a nice bike, a good size for... you." (A female person)

(Swallow snark) "Thanks – I've been riding this bike for 20 years; we are well suited for each other."

"Actually, the Goldwing is so big, it's only fit for the freeway – it's not like you can ride it downtown here just for pie. It doesn't actually get out much. Where are you headed?"

"I'm not sure."

He looked perplexed. I explained the off the grid trip, in which I go where the wind blows me, sans electronics, and even I don't always know where I will end up. The waitress was back, trying to refill full cups.

"Wow, that sounds like fun. My reckless buddy asked me to ride with him to Reno once, but Jeez, that's too far..."

We bonded by comparing our worst weather days. His was a rainy day exploring Mount Saint Helen's after it blew; mine was on Mancos Pass in Colorado.

"You used to live in Colorado?"

"Nope, I was on my way to Texas and back."

He stared, blankly, checking his mental map.

"So you pretty much don't have any immediate family, do ya?"

"Oh, not at all, I am married and have grown kids and a grand-child – I am a regular matriarch."

Now he was looking a little confused. "Does your hubby ride?"

"I am married to a beautiful woman named Alivia." The waitress was no longer pretending to pour coffee; she was just standing there watching this exchange.

"Well, okay, fine, does your.... does *she* ride?"

"Yep, but that doesn't change my need for the occasional solo ride – she understands."

Now his tone has changed, he is speaking softer; it's gone from challenge to confessional.

"Honestly, I'm jealous. My wife would never tolerate me going off by myself or going farther than a day ride."

"That's tough; I'll bet your Goldwing is missing you. You know, I never have asked permission, but it is important to have a blessing. Sometimes you have to earn that blessing."

"When do you have to be home?"

"Monday morning – I have to be at work."

"What do you do?"

"I'm the vice principal of an alternative high school – On Sundays I am a Quaker minister... but they understand, too."

And then the traditional silence ensued.

A Perfect Morning in Newberg

I decided to make a pilgrimage to Newberg Friends Church, Oregon's oldest Quaker church. I love this 19th century room, and I love its 21st century people. I love the saints and angels that seem to hang around. I have been to beautiful weddings and even more beautiful memorials there. I have heard some great preaching there, and I have preached triumphantly from the pulpit. Never had a bad day in that room.

I was especially looking forward to hearing my friend Gregg Koskela preach. He is a great preacher, and his voice is a balm to my soul. I love to hear him pray; I love to hear him preach. I envy his three girls who got to hear him read bedtime stories.

But Alas! It was missionary Sunday. World Gospel Mission people leaving Kenya for Uganda. No Gregg preaching, sigh. But hey, Africa! – I can dig everything about that. So I was happy as they preached about Abram leaving Ur. They wanted people to know that they weren't leaving Kenya because of problems or disappointments, but because God was calling them out. They talked about the sadness and the fear. It was good.

And then it happened: the propane pilot in my toes lit, and flames started curling about my ankles. And as the fire rose, I knew I would get to speak during open worship! Yippee and Yikes!

You see, Jesus had me on a bit of a leash at Freedom Friends Church. Pastor, facilitate, pray, pray much, clean toilets, pray, occasional small messages, but no fire, no Quaking. It had been seven years of no fire – and I love fire. Occasionally I was given fire in other places – but none at home, which didn't seem fair. But Jesus knows His own business.

So there I was, lit again, in worship. Oh, how good it felt! It doesn't always show, or come through my voice, mind you, and it seems to have no correlation to how the message is received. Sometimes I am called to speak without the feeling. But, oh, how I love it when it comes. It is sweet, undeniable confirmation to me. Ding! God's blue plate special, pick up! How I love to sling that hash!

What came was a simple, brief message, also on the topic of Leaving:

"My name is Peggy Senger, and this is what I know about leaving. And I know this EXPERIENTIALLY. If it is God that calls you out from your people, then it is LOVE that calls you. Love is indestructible. It is not contained by time, nor defined by place. It is not contained by doctrine or denomination. It is not even bounded by death. If any leaving is caused by love, then the leaving itself is an illusion. You can't actually be gone from those who love you or from those you love. Because the connection is made out of Love, and because Love is God – that connection is unseverable. We have been present to each other. We are present to each other. We will always be present to each other – Forever."

Then a young man on the other side of the room rose and read this scripture.

> But You my servant, whom I have chosen, whom I have taken from the ends of the earth, I have called you, and I have not rejected you, even though you are exiled. Fear not, for I AM with you, do not look around and be dismayed, for I AM your God. I will strengthen you in your difficulties, yes I will help you. I will hold you up with my right

hand of righteousness and justice. The people who are angry at you will be confused. Those who strive against you will come up with nothing. You will look for those who want to argue with you and you will not be able to find any. For I the Lord hold your right hand. Fear not, I will help. (Isaiah 41:8-13)

Sweet, sweet, sweet.

After worship, Gregg and I chatted. He said "Here's the thing I want to say about your message. See, I feel that we, the people in this room, should have said that to *you*." He was feeling the unnaturalness of Freedom Friends not being in official fellowship with Newberg Friends, because FFC affirms God's Gay children. My friend is a real Christian that way. He is capable, and willing, to love and be in relationship with people he doesn't understand, or even disagrees with.

So very kind.

But Gregg, you do send me that message. When I walk in and see your face as you recognize me, and I see that you can't help but smile at the sight of me. The God in me winks at the God in you. And then God plays with us all, and crafts a beautiful, perfect little worship piece using every crayon in the box, and we all know, *know*, that love is real and indestructible.

Amen. It is enough.

A Tale of Two Gatherings

It was the best of times...

Okay, there is no "B Side" to it; it *was* the best of times.

My invitation and intention was to preach at the 2012 Illinois Yearly Meeting of Friends. They meet in white clapboard, 1875, meeting house just outside McNabb, Illinois. Mid-state – surrounded by corn fields and the footprints of my ancestors.

What a lovely group they were. One remarkable thing was the lack of complaining. It was 100 degrees in June – I heard no complaints. I heard no complaints about the food. (Okay – the food was great.) I heard no complaints about the porta-potties, or from the dishwashers when the pump went out. I heard no complaints about any part of the program. I heard not a complaint in five days! A committee for every function, all run without votes, or hierarchy, or Robert's Rules. Parents and kids, teens and elders, so sweet and kind.

I was one of three speakers. Three nights, three speakers, no co-ordination between them. The Spirit kindly tailored the evening messages together like Armani's dreams – shirt to vest to coat, perfectly. The core of the message that I was given for the first night was this: *We cannot afford to dismiss or disdain any of our cousins; biological, theological or political. And no matter how weird we think they are, we are more like them and they like us, than any of us want to admit.* It was good preaching, and like all good preaching, dangerous – especially to the preacher.

Many of the Friends camped on the grounds. Peggy does not camp. So I slept in the nearby town of Henry, Illinois. Henry is a river town; when the ghost of Mark Twain gets tired of the tourists in Hannibal, I am sure that he floats over to Henry to get a little rest in peace. Henry is a town that Ray Bradbury would place on some alien world – the picture perfect mid-western town with absolutely no visible means of support. I probably shouldn't say it here, but when I end up having to be in the witness protection program, I am going to ask them to place me in Henry. Perhaps that is a significant proportion of the present inhabitants – it would explain a few things.

My home for the duration, the Henry Harbor Inn, turned out to be the weekend site of the Miss Riverbottom Festival, hosted by the Henry Yacht Club. The Festival is a gathering of all the local boating clubs on the Illinois River – I didn't see a boat bigger than ten yards long. They rolled in a couple of days early for site preparation. There were many committees necessary to pull the thing off – food, registration, program, hygiene, sales etc. Having filled the Inn to capacity, many people camped. I was the only person with a room who was not associated with the Festival. I was marked immediately for being slightly overdressed (as I also was at McNabb.) Each morning I hobnobbed a bit with the organizers. Each evening I sat outside with them for a bit. There was no point sitting in my room, because the music was rattling the doors and windows. There was a Beer Garden ten feet outside my bedroom door. So I put on my boots and wranglers and joined them. I was still overdressed. The stage was across from the Beer garden. The music was varied. There was country rap, country disco, rockabilly, country metal and regular country.

There were lots of teens and little ones. I never saw anyone carded, but I didn't see any underage drinking, either. All the kids had their parents and their parents' friends drinking and dancing all around them. It was pretty dang wholesome. The beer choices were Bud, Miller and Old style, all in plastic cups. All the fancy people were drinking Miller.

One of my favorite conversations was with the gal bringing the beer.

"DON'T SUPPOSE YOU HAVE ANYTHING IN A BOTTLE?" I shouted.

"GLASS BOTTLES ARE NOT A GOOD IDEA OUT HERE. BUT, HEY, YOU'RE THE PREACHER LADY, AREN'T YOU? IT'S PROBABLY OKAY," she screamed. "DO YOU WANT DOMESTIC OR FOREIGN?"

"DOMESTIC MEANS?..." – "BUD OR MILLER."

"YOU HAVE A DOS EQUIS?" – "SORRY."

"CORONA?" – "NOPE."

"HEINEKIN?" – "RIGHT OUT, I'M AFRAID."

"THEN WHAT'S FOREIGN?" – "WE HAVE BLUE MOON."

"ISN'T THAT MADE IN COLORADO?" – "YEP, LIKE I SAID, FOREIGN."

"I'LL TAKE ONE."

"BRING THE BOTTLE INSIDE WHEN YOU'RE DONE, OKAY, SWEETIE?"

"FUR SURE."

The highlight of the Miss Riverbottom Festival is the Miss Riverbottom Contest. Each club puts up a contestant who sings and dances. The winning club gets to host next year. The contestants are all STRAIGHT, White, Male, Drunk and in DRAG.

Meanwhile, over at McNabb, there was also dancing. Old-school style. The caller (a gracious, tolerant non-Friend) lined them up for a dance into "ladies" and "gents." I noticed that at least one of the "ladies" was a young man in a bonnet and that at least one of the "gents" was wearing a hoop skirt. After they lined up, the caller said "Okay, I see that not everyone is in the right line – but it doesn't matter if you are male or female, it only matters that you know if you want to be called a "lady" or a "gent." He rolled right with it. They danced with joy and abandon.

The weirdness quotient in each place was delightfully high. It was all fun. The sober, collaborative pacifists were at least as out of sync with the times as the drunken yachtsmen. I traveled between the two groups each day, slipping between alternative universes that were so far and yet so near unto each other.

I checked out of the Henry Inn on the last morning of their Gathering, before the decision on the Queen of the Festival. One of the organizers saw my suitcases and said, "Aw, you're not leaving yet, are you, preacher?" I allowed as to how it was needful. "You're not gonna leave us without a blessing, are you?" So I stopped, and the committee he was clerking took off their rhinestone-studded pink straw cowboy hats, and I prayed over them.

"Lord, we thank you for this good time." (The people said *Amen*)

"We thank you that all has been safe so far." (*Amen!*)

"I ask you to watch over this gathering, and put your angels in charge of the children and the drunks and do not let them fall into the river. *(AMEN!)* And Lord, tonight, let everyone get along and play nice. *(AMEN!)* And let everyone look at their spouses with love in their eyes, and let their eyes not wander anywhere else. *(AMEN!)* And Lord, we are not sure that you get involved in such matters, but if it be Your will, let the best Miss Riverbottom win!" *(AMEN!!!)*

I never heard anyone at the Riverbottom complain, either.

Waiting Worship

Waiting at the airport. I was early; I had planned that. Then I became earlier, as my expected person was delayed – once, twice, and then three times. I ended up with eight hours of wait time.

I was able to see the blessing in it pretty quickly, since it was 102 degrees outside and the airport had refrigerated air. I had the ability to purchase a good meal and a good book, and I like the airport. It is a great place to people watch. Every type of person on every type of business passes through. The extremely elderly and newborn babes are assisted on their way. Business, commercial and personal, is pursued with determination. The entire repertoire of human drama gets replayed every hour or so, re-cast with each arriving plane.

As I can be a bit of an empath, I have a distinct seating preference. I stay away from the screening and departure area if I have a choice. People there are sad, either leaving or being left. They are anxious and in a hurry; they are frustrated, and sometimes angry at all the security nonsense. I prefer waiting in the arrivals lounge. The anxiety there is the good kind. It builds and builds as people wait, watching the clock and the corridor, until it bursts in an explosion of joy when they see the much-anticipated one.

"Mommy!!!" screamed the three-year-old who escaped dad, got neatly around the guard and into his mother's arms, and everybody, including the security guard, smiled.

Grandmas, babies, soldiers home from war. Nothing stronger than the wave of relief coming off the weary young mother traveling with three under-fives when she sees her parents waiting to help – "Made it, made it, worth it already!" The dramas are the same regardless of ethnicity or class. It's all pretty intoxicating.

I spent a lot of time watching one young man. Twentyish, cool in a 70s sort of way; self-possessed, long curly hair, a neat beard, dark shades. He's wearing baggy jeans, but a clean shirt – probably his best shirt. It has buttons.

He paces, checking the time on his cell phone, checking the arrivals board way too often. He is wise enough to have discovered an important life secret: always bring flowers to the airport. The flowers are purple daisies – dyed – poor man's flowers, which makes him more endearing.

He holds the flowers like a straight man holds flowers: blooms down, drooping, casual, light grip, like he's carrying a bat up to the plate. He doesn't care about the stupid flowers. He cares a lot about the girl.

I wait with him, wondering what she will look like. Wondering if she loves him as much as he loves her. Hoping she hasn't missed her connection. Would she have preferred the one red rose? Hope, belief, doubt, swirling around him like a cyclone.

The wait is getting to him. He presses one hand on his heart and blows out a deep, shuddering, stress-filled breath. He adjusts himself – hold on, tiger. Then his phone rings and ends his agony. She is on the ground and can't walk the length of the concourse without calling him. He grins, and charges the gate just like the three-year-old.

She's pretty – very pretty – and she runs to meet him. Hugs, hugs, rocking hugs, and he kisses her on the forehead. Then he remembers the flowers. Of course she likes them.

Waiting is so holy. Anticipation is so holy. Joy is so holy.

We Quakers say that we practice "waiting worship." We sit, silent, waiting, expecting the present Christ to arrive. Our meetings are sacred arrivals lounges, or they should be. I wonder how often we experience the level and quality of anticipation and joy that you see at the airport.

Maybe we should bring flowers.

The Porridge of the Quakers

I awoke at the Okapi Hotel in Kigali, Rwanda on the morning after a particularly difficult bus day. I was having second thoughts. I was traveling solo on public transport from Bujumbura Burundi, through Rwanda and on to the Democratic Republic of the Congo. The problem was that the previous day was supposed to have been the easy day. The day ahead was the one predicted to be challenging. When your friends are all genocide survivors, you learn to take seriously their view of what is problematic. Sometimes you have to be more concerned than they are, because they tend to think that anything that doesn't involve hand grenades is pretty low key. But if they tell you to worry, you should not ignore this. My friends describe an actual shoot-out as "activity" and genocide as a "situation." The previous day had not risen anywhere near the level of activity, and yet I was whipped, emotionally and physically. A night's sleep in a middle-class African hotel had not restored me. I was not sure that I should proceed. I had no comrade input. But the reasons for taking the next bus were fairly compelling. I was expected to teach the following day. The students waiting for me were working with victims in an active war zone. They had no training in trauma theory or resolution. They had way too much experience with trauma. If I bailed, no one else was coming anytime soon. I was carrying tools they needed and I had no way to send the tools without bringing my person.

I did what Quakers do at such times. I got quiet. I centered down. I prepared to listen to the present Christ. And I received from the present Christ what I often receive – calm, peaceful silence. A sense of the Presence, to be sure, but no direction, no reassurance, no warning. In my experience the Divine does not usually repeat Itself. If I have my marching orders, I have them. I can act on them or not; the Presence does not leave me, but once I am clear, the directions are not usually repeated.

On that morning, I really wanted more. As I left my time of worship and reflection I prayed, quite sincerely "Look, I know You are here, but I am exhausted and afraid, and I need some clear, obvious indication that I am on the right path and that it is safe and good for me to proceed – or else a clear stop sign. You have about an hour – Earth time."

I went down to breakfast. African hotel breakfast is very nice. It comes with your room, and it is buffet style. The coffee is always excellent. There is always fruit and bread. The fruit – how do I tell you? If you have eaten a perfect, home grown tomato in August, or sweet corn picked and cooked in the same hour, and compare those to a January grocery store tomato or canned corn, that is the qualitative difference between what you know of as a yellow sweet banana or a pineapple and what comes with an African breakfast. Central Africans were taught bread making by the French – 'nuff said there.

At the typical hotel breakfast buffet, there is also always a hot dish option. It is usually some form of stew, frequently green cooking bananas and spinach-type greens swimming in viscous orange palm oil. I never really acquired the taste for the breakfast stew, but the other parts were so ambrosia that I didn't care.

On that morning I was almost alone in the dining room. An attentive young man in a white coat was overseeing the room. He greeted me and poured my coffee. I chose bread and pineapple. The hot dish was covered.

Mostly to make conversation I asked "And what is the hot breakfast this morning?"

The young man turned away and grimaced.

"Oh, Madame, the hot breakfast this morning, she is terrible!"

Now, I was curious, what could be more terrible than spinach banana stew?

"Really? What do we have this morning?"

"Madame, please, believe me. Can I get you some eggs? Chef would be very happy to make you an omelet."

Now I just had to know.

"Truly, I must know, what is it?"

He reached for the warming tray lid. Arm extended to its extreme, he turned his head and shoulders away and made a face of repulsion.

I was expecting toxic biohazard casserole.

"Madame, I am so sorry, it is the porridge of the Quakers."

He uncovered a perfectly beautiful dish of Quaker Oats.

"But Monsieur, I, myself, am a Quaker!"

"What? Madame, you, a Quaker? But this is wonderful! We have made this porridge for you! I will get a bigger dish!"

And he ran and got a giant serving dish and served me up the largest bowl of Oats that I have ever attempted to eat.

I tried to share my oats with Jesus, but he was not taking up His share. He was at the table with me, however. And He was with me on the bus going forward.

Backwards and in High Heels

Many young women take a gap year. Some travel. Fewer travel solo. Almost none decide to ride solo around the globe on a motorcycle.

It was the early 1980's. Elspeth Beard was a 24 year old architecture student, living in London, when she decided to take her 1974 R60/6 Flat Twin BMW out for a spin around the planet. She went Westerly.

North America was good to her. She landed in New York, rode up into Canada, cruised down to Mexico, and then back to Los Angeles, where she shipped the bike to Australia. She worked in a Sydney architectural firm to replenish her funds, then built herself a set of aluminum paniers and took out across the Outback. In Queensland, she cartwheeled the bike on a dirt road. Heavily concussed, she spent two weeks in hospital and then put on the same 'bone dome' helmet and took off again. At Perth, on the west coast, she put the bike on a ship for Singapore. When she arrived there, her passport, visas, documents, and valuables were stolen. Six bureaucratic weeks later, she rode across the Thai/Malay peninsula. As she was heading back to catch another boat, this time to India, a dog ran under her tires and she crashed into a tree in the garden of a poor Thai family. They kept her, nursed her back to health, and fed her dog soup.

She repaired her own engine. She took the cylinder off, straightened the bent studs as best she could, and packed the cylinder base with enough gaskets and goo to get compression back. Then she shipped the bike to Madras and rode to Calcutta, and on to Kathmandu. There, nearly two years into her adventure, she rendezvoused with her parents, who had flown out to check on their daughter. She was skinny, as she had contracted both hepatitis and dysentery. She would not consider going home with them. She did do a foot-trek into the Himalayas for a side-trip. She came down and out through India, and stalled at the Pakistani border. She forged herself a document, which surprised her by working. She entered Iran with seven days left on her visa to get into Turkey, making it with just hours to spare, despite being so weak from the Hep that she almost couldn't stand. There she rested a bit, down to 90 pounds from her starting 143. Stronger, she crossed into Greece. The ride across Europe was anti-climactic. She made it home to London, three years older, many pounds lighter, and with a fresh 48,000 miles on her odometer.

She went back to school and became a successful architect and a mother. She still rides.

Where God Talks to Girls

I enjoy helping weddings happen.

That day, everything was going well. The guests were steadily arriving at the family home. The bridal party was all accounted for and dressed in their finery. The flower-covered wooden arch was ready. I was out among the guests, greeting people and watching for that moment when it would be time to gather the groom, cue the musicians, and start the proceedings.

A small girl tweaked my radar. She was examining the wedding cake at very close range, clearly dealing with the temptation to put just one finger into the icing. She was leaning up on the table. I engaged her in conversation and reminded her of the funny videos where people knock over the cake table at a wedding. She wisely eased back a bit.

She was about eight. Long brown hair and very blue eyes, magnified by thick glasses. A dress imprinted with Disney princesses. It was clear that she was all into the wedding thing. We talked about how soon the wedding would start, where the bride was "hiding," and when the cake would be cut. We looked over the guests together.

"I wonder which one is the preacher?"

"Ah, that would be me."

She looked up at me, mouth open. She pushed her glasses up her nose.

"But you're a girl!"

"Yep" I said, not correcting the girl/woman thing.

"I've never seen a girl preacher!"

"Look all you want, baby. Sometimes, God asks girls to be preachers."

"Not at MY church."

"What church do you go to?"

She named a large, conservative denomination.

"Ah, well there are lots of churches, and some of them, like mine, think everybody can preach. I am a Quaker."

"A Quaker" she said, like it tasted funny but not all bad in her mouth.

We talked a little more about God, and what God might ask you to do, and then it was time to start the wedding.

Later, over cake, I asked her what she thought of the wedding, and how it looked with a girl preacher.

"It was nice, you did a good job, you talk real loud, and the cake is good. Do you really have a church or do you just do weddings?"

"I really have a church. Nice folks. Probably a bit different than your church. Someday, you should come visit."

She looked up at me, pushed her glasses up her nose again, and pursed her lips.

"I think I would like that – a church where God talks to girls."

Speaking Truth to Power

When I was a young adolescent, Wednesday night Bible study was mandatory. A volunteer churchman was teaching the mixed class of adults and teens on a muggy summer night. He was going on about the creation story in Genesis with a special emphasis on the place of man and woman in the story. He was trying to make the point that, because man was made first, this clearly put him in charge. I spoke up and said something that indicated that I didn't think this was the only possible exegesis. This brought the undivided attention of teacherman who said;

"Really, Miss Peggy; and why, then, do you think that God made man first?"

"I dunno; if at first you don't succeed, try, try again?"

I don't remember his response, although I think there was minor sputtering involved. I do remember that my mother stifled a laugh, and shot me a look. I expected that look to involve disapproval. I was surprised to see amusement, and maybe a little bit of pride in my mother's eyes. At the time she said nothing. Later she spoke to me, in private, and her words were about refraining from the temptation to humiliate and mock people in public.

You see, my father was a strong, good man – a natural born leader. But he did not rule my mother. She had a sense of self, rooted in God's love for her, and it could not be shaken, oppressed, or ruled. She was my father's – any man's – true equal. At her breast I got not only physical antibodies, but also spiritual and emotional antibodies. I grew up resistant to oppression. I learned to listen, but I let no one do my thinking for me. I found my voice early. I practiced using it until it became strong and even occasionally disciplined.

I learned my Bible, and I learned it well, but I also learned that the purpose of religious education is not the indoctrination of beliefs, but the inoculation of invincibility.

A couple of decades later I found myself sitting in the anteroom of a guitar studio. I was eavesdropping on my thirteen-year old daughter and her wise, gentle, and gifted guitar teacher. Mr. Walt had student recitals twice a year. Emily liked her guitar and she loved Mr. Walt, but she hated recitals. At the age of eight she just went along with them; by ten she was resisting but could be bribed. At early adolescence she found her voice. She told me that she wasn't going to play in this year's recital, and none of my tricks worked.

I liked the recitals. I liked seeing my beautiful child shine. I sat there hoping that Walt would talk her into it one more time. He asked, he cajoled, he tried minor guilt and gentle manipulation. Emily held her ground.

Then my thinking took a radical shift – I felt my own, now deceased, mother's presence in the room, and she was rooting for Emily. I realized that my daughter was holding to her sense of self in the face of the temptation to please someone she respected, and wanted to please, but with whom she disagreed. I changed my allegiance.

Emily continued to play her guitar, but she never played in another recital. The inoculation took; like her mother and grandmother before her, she was and is invincible – any time she wishes to be.

Getting Your Glinda On

So you seem to have a problem. It appeared to come out of no-where. Poof! All fire and green smoke. You didn't see it coming, and you didn't ask for it. Any causal relationship you have with this problem is strictly accidental. But it's getting real personal – threatening, actually. It's not only going after you, but your lit-tle dog, too. Other people are running for cover and hiding be-hind their lollipops. You've tried running before, and that hasn't seemed to do anything but put you in ever weird and increasingly weirder circumstances. And at the moment, you wouldn't know where to run, anyway – life has gotten just that weird. What's a good kid from down home supposed to do?

Listen to the fluffy lady behind you. Sure, she seems as weird as the problem, but she does seem to know what to do. It's time to get your Glinda on.

Glinda is an attitude. Glinda isn't useful in every situation, but she comes in handy more often than you'd think. There is some deep situational wisdom here. She has that light laugh. She is queen of the eye roll. She *owns* the dismissive wave. You know her lines: "You have no power here! Be gone before someone drops a house on you!" And to the girl: "Hang on to those shoes – they must be very powerful if she wants them so badly!" She is the archon for being relaxed in the face of a threatening situation. Here are her secrets:

1 – Know where you are. Know the ground upon which you stand. The great Ancient Warrior Sun Tzu talked a great deal about grounds. He knew it was always unwise to take the fight to some-one else's turf. The transport alone will bankrupt you! The locals are likely to be hostile. Your resources will be limited to what you can carry, and your supply lines will always be in danger. Better to be patient, and if the threat is real, make them fight in your yard, on your terms. Think this doesn't sound very Christian? The Apostle Paul said that after you were armed to the teeth with things like truth, and peace, and integrity, all you had to do was stand still. You will not be moved. What ground are you on? Is it stable? Do you have deep enough resources? Are the inhabi-tants your friends? If so, then take a deep breath and smile when

trouble shows up. It is not likely to have much depth or staying power. (Sign that you are not on your own ground – flying monkeys! Time to roll!)

2 – Know that the showy and bilious are often more afraid than you are. Don't be impressed by the noises and smokes. They are just that – noises and smokes. Those that threaten others are always looking up for that falling house. And boy, do those houses fall! Might be a good idea to step back a bit.

3 – And then there are those sparkly shoes! Wow, red glitter becomes you! You didn't even know you had them, did you? It may take you a while to figure it out, but you have some personal power going on. Someone equipped you with everything you were going to need in this land. (Spoiler Alert!) You can rescue yourself, any time you want to. All you have to do is remember who you are, where you came from, and what you were created to be, and then believe and act on that. You don't need no wizards or balloons. The Kingdom of Heaven is your rightful home, and you can live in it anytime you want to. You can live by its rules, and you can reap its benefits.

Yeah, sure, some days you are going to have to leave your safe zone and take it to the threat. You will have to work in places that don't acknowledge your rules. You will work with people who don't know who they are and what they were created to be. There will be a few monkeys to swat. But you get to wear your shoes. Your personal power is portable. If you lose it, it is because you surrendered it – they can't take it from you.

So take heart, little one. Most days, you can laugh at the bluster. Tell it to go away, and it will. You have plenty of time to walk your road and figure things out. You are being watched. Help will come when you need it. Your friends may be goofy, but they are faithful. Home is here, home is now; all you have to do is own it.

What Women Deserve

Young, poor, and pregnant is pretty scary. This was ancient times, and there were no in-home-pregnancy tests. You had to go see somebody. I didn't have my own doctor, or any insurance, so that left me to the free clinics and to people who had agendas. I found my way to Planned Parenthood. I was nervous. They were kind. They were respectful. They gave me a test – I was pregnant. I was also days away from starting graduate school, and I was waiting tables full time at a pizza joint to pay for school. It was about the worst possible timing. I was not happy. The doctor (nurse practitioners were unheard of in those days) could see my unhappiness. He sat with me for a few minutes. He listened to me. He made no judgments or suggestions. When my words and tears had run out, he asked me if I wanted to know about my options. I told him that my option was to be a mother, because aborting a healthy fetus did not fit into my faith, values, or ethics. He smiled and he said, "I think you will make a fine mother," and he told me where to get free pre-natal care, and about a program for free food for pregnant women, and where the free counselors worked. I was very grateful for his listening, concern, and advice. It helped.

Five years later, I had another unplanned pregnancy. Ironically, I was getting ready to put the previous baby into kindergarten and re-start my education. There were still no at-home tests. I was still pretty poor. I was between health insurance plans. This time, due to hours and transportation issues, I went to a "Crisis Pregnancy Center" near my home. There was no doctor; instead, nice Christian ladies staffed the center. They were happy to help me. They gave me a test. I was pregnant. I wasn't very happy this time, either. The lady asked if my pregnancy was planned. I said no. She got really nervous. She started spilling statistics. She made some presumptions. I thanked her and tried to leave. She got more nervous. She tried to set up a video. I declined her offer, thanked her again, and got up to go. She actually blocked my way to the door and said, "I'm not supposed to let you leave without showing you "Silent Scream." I escaped. She yelled after me, "Please don't kill your baby!" I didn't, of course, and I also never got near those people again, or the churches that supported them.

Eventually, I did restart my education, earn a master's degree in Counseling Psychology at an evangelical Christian seminary, and raised two daughters. In my 25 years as a pastor, counselor, and now educator, I have walked many women through many difficult decisions, including unplanned pregnancies, serious birth defects, and grief over pregnancies lost and ended. I have learned that the decision about whether, and when, to become a mother is never black and white. It is not one that women make frivolously.

This I believe: every woman deserves a quiet, calm, unanxious, unbiased listener. Every woman deserves to know all her choices, and every woman deserves to make her own choice free of coercion from any direction. She deserves to have her decision respected. She deserves to have her basic needs met, and this includes safe housing, adequate nutrition, and affordable health care, including contraception. We can afford this for every mother and every child. For me, this is a faith-based position.

Planned Parenthood was there for me when I needed them. They did a good job. They listened to me, and they respected my faith-based values better than the Christians did. I have sent my daughters to them. I hope they will be there for my grand-daughters.

Terrorism

What is terrorism? It is the attempt to punish or control a group through fear, by attacking a representative sample of that group.

Seven people were murdered in California in 2014 because a mentally ill young man was homicidally angry at young women who would not have sex with him.

> College is the time when everyone experiences those things such as sex and fun and pleasure. Within those years, I've had to rot in loneliness. It's not fair. You girls have never been attracted to me. I don't know why you girls aren't attracted to me, but I will punish you all for it.

Connecticut teen Maren Sanchez was choked, pushed down the stairs, and then stabbed to death by a fellow classmate because she declined to go to the prom with him.

Guns, knives, bare hands – it doesn't matter. Saying "no" is, and always has been, a dangerous act for women and girls. In every time and in every place and in every culture. It is dangerous.

The media has decried these events. Everyone decries these events. But they name the perpetrators as "extremely disturbed individuals." They are, but that is not all that they are. They are also terrorists. They are absolutely no different from the Boston Bombers, or from any other terrorists.

The clear intention of the terrorists here is to punish women who say "no." The intentional effect is to make all women just a little bit afraid to say "no." It has worked since the dawn of time. It is not rare. In 2005, 1,181 women were murdered by their partners (source: cdc.gov). Those were partners who lived together. The added toll of women dating, women going about their business or to work or to school or just walking the streets, are not counted as part of this reign of terror. Sixty-four percent of mass shooting victims are women and children. (Huffington Post 2015) Their killers are angry men.

These attacks are treated as if they are aberrations. The one-off lunacies of deviant individuals. It might be said that woman killers are not an organized group. (Excuse me, Taliban? – Malala Yusafzai?) But when an idea is this pervasive, you don't have to organize. The terrorist acts out of the collective consciousness. The individual is troubled because our culture is troubled. An emotionally disturbed individual picks up the emotionally disturbed content of the society.

Terrorists are discernibly different from those who kill for reasons that are not reality based – the psychotically mentally ill. These young women were killed for saying no, or being representative for those who said no. A real act happened. A fundamental human right was expressed – the right to say no. They were killed for expressing their basic human rights.

They are different from those who kill for their own sadistic pleasure. Yes, those women died because they were women, and seen
as consumable commodities, but not for actual actions that they
took.

I choose to believe that most men never think about raping or
killing a woman for being an intentional actor in her own life. And
I believe that, of the small subset who think about it, an even
smaller subset act upon it. I do not blame the majority for the
acts of the minority. But we are all culpable, and men especially,
for refusing to see it for what it is, an attack upon womankind.
Then we are culpable for not doing much about it.

The first step in changing the basic human culture of possession
and punishment is to name things correctly, and treat these acts
precisely as we would a terrorist attack by Al Qaeda or the KKK or
any other terrorist group. These are Hate Crimes.

Along with this, we need to name the victims for what they are.
They are martyrs. A monument should be made. If the writing
was tiny, like the Vietnam memorial, the Great Wall of China
ought to be about the right size.

But a better next step needs to be for every parent, every teacher,
every adult to tell every girl that she is completely within her
rights to say no to anyone at any time for pretty much anything.
She is also within her right to say yes to whom she will for whatever she wills. She will need to be educated about what respon-
sibilities come with her actions. The field upon which she acts
should increase incrementally throughout childhood, but her
right to act cannot simply be assumed; it must be affirmed, as-
serted, and protected – vigilantly. And, sadly, she must be made
aware that she is going to meet those who do not affirm her right
and will try to punish her for making her own choices. And that
they may try to kill her.

Death by Perfection

They tell us that the last word the pastor said was, "Why?" Seems like a good question when your wife has just emptied a shotgun into your back.

We may never really know what happened to the Winklers of Selmer, Tennessee, but what is being described as incomprehensible seems understandable to me. The pastor's wife killed the pastor. I think I can describe why this, or something near to this, could happen in many parsonages in America.

I have two caveats. First, no matter what happened, nothing – I mean NOTHING – justifies murder or abuse. Second, there is some missing information in this case, and once lawyers became involved, the details got edited.

I have spent 20 years in the counseling profession. I have been invited into the secrets of numerous "Christian marriages," many of them lived out in parsonages. I believe that there are thousands of people – pastors, elders, deacons, and their spouses – whose private gut reaction to the news of this crime was "There but for the grace of God go I."

From the reports of Mary Winkler's words after her arrest, I can see a perfect storm for murder brewing in that house and that community. Inside the home: he was verbally cruel, physically a bully, and sexually coercive. She was secretive, and foolishly fell for a Nigerian money scam to the tune of 17 grand. Outside the home: they were perfect. He was strong and she kept sweet.

Here is the recipe for a Christian matrimonial murder:

Start with a church culture that says that pastors and their families have to be, if not perfect, then at least better than everyone else. In these cultures, the pastor's family is seen as the proof of the Gospel. If they live a blessed, Biblical life, then God, the Bible and the church are proved true. If not – then they are hypocrites, and all their teachings are lies. This is way too much pressure. Nobody can live up to it, but a lot of people try, and ironically, what that trying requires is the ability to lie and to fake. Fake happy when you're not. Fake nice when you feel crabby. Pretend concern when you are really too tired to care. You cannot admit normal human mistakes. You cannot admit lapses in judgment, because if you do it reflects badly on God.

This kind of falsehood has a backlash. When you hold ugly in, it just gets uglier. When it comes out – and it will come out, usually towards the people you love the most – it can be truly nasty.

Now, add to this a theology that says that you *especially* cannot admit or fix a mistake if that mistake was a marriage or an ordination. You can't divorce your spouse simply because they are consistently mean to you. You can't admit that you were totally unprepared for marriage. You can't admit that, while the choice of the ministry sounded like a good idea at the time, you now have discovered that you are not cut out for it. Marriage and ministry are not choices, they are sacraments, and holy callings. You can't change your mind or admit a mistake about these things without being disobedient to God. Double all of this if your theology say that sanctification – removing the sin nature – is possible and you have claimed that for yourself.

Stir in a church culture that tells women in particular that they cannot stand up for themselves in the day-to-day business of life. The theologies and cultures of perfection, almost always have different standards for men and women. Women must be pure, and they must be subordinate.

If you live in a culture like this, and under a theology like this, a marriage of constant belittling, criticism, and bickering can be soul-killing. People always look for the big, bad secrets like adultery, sexual abuse, or physical abuse when murderous rage occurs. But consistent verbal meanness can be just as toxic, or more so. If you cannot talk about it or get help for it, the pattern persists and gets worse. And if the toxic couple also has to pretend that their partners are saints when they are in public, the dissonance and the private rage can reach volcanic proportions.

Now, take this situation and add in just a little of one or more of these common human frailties: a little brain chemistry issue, a bit of postpartum depression, a childhood abuse issue, a little familial mental illness, a minor league addiction, consumer debt problems.

Add in only one thing more – a loaded shotgun in the hall closet – and disaster lurks at your door. I would be willing to bet that the Winklers never saw this coming. Their family and friends sure didn't.

Let's learn something from this, okay? God is all about choices – any theology that makes you feel trapped is not from God. And God's reputation isn't really going to live or die on your perfection. Lighten up on your clergy and their family. Set a new church culture that tells the pastor that she or he may model how to get help for problems, not pretend to live without them. Let's start telling our young people that they can make mistakes, admit them, and fix them. Let's tell all our children that they have the power and the right to stand up for themselves, but that standing up doesn't mean being violent. The proof of the Gospel is less about how good your cleric is and more about how good we can be to each other in our humanness. Let's try harder.

Gorilla Wars

Some days you just get all your cards trumped. Some days I like it.

I was leaving the Democratic Republic of the Congo in the spring of 2007. Traveling by people's bus. I had been teaching for a couple of days for an ex-student of mine who was trying to set up a trauma-healing center in Goma. I was on my way back. I thought I was being brave.

Then a good-looking young blonde woman got on the bus. Her name was Ellen Brown, and she worked for the Wildlife Conservation Society studying and protecting mountain gorillas in the Virunga National Forest of the Congo. She was traveling to Kigali to pick up a visitor.

A little compare and contrast is needed for readers. In Central Africa, there are areas designated as national forests. In Countries like Burundi, which is 97% deforested, they may be the only forests. But they are nothing like an American National Forest. There are no picnic or camping areas, few walking trails. The rangers carry AK-47s and use them on a regular basis. This is because various rebel groups have discovered that national forests make great hiding places. People live in villages in the national forests; they never moved them out. Those folks are in regular peril in the Congo.

Still hiding out in the Virunga National Forest, North and West of Goma, was the remnants of the Interahamwe, the fellows who instigated and perpetrated the Rwandan Genocide of 1994. Also nearby was the private army of General Nkunda, who claimed to be protecting the local Tutsis, who were hated by the Interahamwe. The Congolese government army was ineffectively attempting to rout out both groups. Add into the mix the Mayi-Mayi, a local militia who believe that magic water mixed with human ashes and applied to the face will protect you from bullets. They hire on as private security for the villagers.

Caught in the middle of all of this were a few families of the last mountain gorillas left on the planet. The Interahamwe had taken to shooting them for target practice. They did not even eat them, which by Congolese standards is a huge waste and insult.

Ellen told me that there were about 400 gorillas left in the region; many of them live on the Rwandan side of the border. Rwandan Gorillas have a better deal. We traveled that day through the town of Ruhengeri, Rwanda. It is surreal. There you are, bouncing along on bad back roads – washouts, views of consistent intense poverty, active volcanoes – and then you round a bend and the road is suddenly silky pavement, and there are streetlights, and a planted boulevard, and coffee shops, and white people sitting in the coffee shops. Ellen informed me that the town is entirely fueled by Gorilla tourism. The tourists, mostly Europeans, are flown in directly to the town and never see the rest of the region. They are taken out into the forest to see the Gorillas for one hour a day. Each Gorilla family has their own ranger who calls in by satellite telephone to the tour guide who brings the tourists out for the visit. I was told that the Gorillas know tourist hour, like the Queen knows teatime. They expect it, understand the rules of it, sometimes enjoy it, and get impatient if it goes on too long. I asked Ellen if this was good for the Gorillas. She said that if keeping them alive was good, then it was good for them. The Rwandan Gorilla population has risen by 10% in the last ten years. The government is very interested in keeping them alive and thriving.

The Congolese Gorillas do not have such a good deal. There are the bullets flying by. Rough on teatime, that. Ellen told me with great sadness and disgust about finding a Gorilla matriarch shot in the head and dumped in a latrine. The Congolese Gorillas have their rangers, too. But they are also dodging bullets. They are tasked with arresting people chopping trees to make charcoal. The twenty million people in the Great Lakes region of Africa cook every meal over charcoal fires. Burundi is mostly deforested. Rwanda has made cutting trees illegal. So sneaking across the border into the Congo to cut and burn trees is a going concern. Good enough business that people are willing to try to evade four gun-happy armies to try to get the wood.

I asked Ellen if she was afraid to be living in, and driving around, Virunga. She claimed she was not.

I pray that Ellen and those rangers and all those Gorillas stay out of harm's way.

Modesty

I was preaching the Gospel in a Friends Church. It was the 1990's, and I was still in my thirties. I loved preaching the Gospel. It was a beautiful spring morning, the house was full, the meeting felt gathered, the message I had brought came out smoothly. I was grateful for having been used. It was a good day.

After worship an older lady took me aside.

"I really appreciated your message, Peggy. I really appreciate your ministry in general. But may I tell you something?"

"Of course"

"I only tell you this because I know you are a mature Christian and I know you can hear my heart in this." (I have now learned that this is always your warning to escape.)

"Okay."

"I know that you care about presenting God's Truth. I know that you would not want anything to hinder your ministry. I know you would be open to ridding your ministry of any distractions."

"Well, I guess I would be. Are you aware of such a distraction?"

"Yes, honey. It's how you present yourself – it's how you look."

"Really – I had no idea." I gazed down at myself. I was wearing sensible pumps, hose, and a business suit. It was robin's egg blue, but it was exactly the style of suit that any lawyer would wear in court, and that I did in fact wear as a professional counselor.

"I think you may not be aware of what a distraction you are to the men sitting in the pews. Men have trouble with their thought-lives sometimes, and we women have to help them. It's our job to not put a 'stumbling block' in front of them."

"I'm a little confused."

"Well, let me speak plainly, then. I think your ministry would be greatly enhanced if you would dress a little more modestly and less fashionably, gain a few pounds, and stop coloring your hair – maybe put it up. I think the men could receive your fine preaching much better if you changed the package a bit."

I stood there in stunned silence. I think I may have actually thanked her for her input. I may have promised to take it under consideration. It wasn't the first time I had heard this theory, but it was certainly the most personal and blunt exposition I had encountered.

I was sure it was just a fluke, a left field thing. So I took it to my spiritual director – a very wise Quaker woman and minister. She disagreed about adding poundage, an obvious health issue, but acknowledged that we are to be thoughtful in how we present ourselves. She didn't argue too hard against the point. She thought there was a core of truth in it. She did encourage me to "rise above" the critical and, to her thinking, possibly jealous presentation. Her nuanced, gentle, and gracious response only modified the basic premise that it was my job to at least consider that my physical appearance might be a problem for someone else's thought life, and that I might want to do something about it. I was flummoxed.

As I sat with the thing, and prayed about the thing, it didn't get any better.

The first realization I came to was the obvious and screaming inequality of it. Never, in my decades in the church, had I ever heard a male minister criticized for simply looking too good. Male preachers obviously did better when they were physically attractive. My sense of justice objected. I just don't like double standards.

But this observation did not seem to address the issue thoroughly. Something else still bothered me. I didn't figure it out until a couple of years later, while taking some training in addictions recovery.

The problem was co-dependency.

Co-dependency is the flipside of addiction. They feed and fuel each other.

Co-dependency is defined like this: somebody has a problem with their desire mechanism. But they can't or won't admit it. So someone else close to them, who doesn't have the primary problem, starts changing their own behavior in order to make the problem or the consequences of the problem go away.

Say I like to get drunk. It causes me problems. But I don't see them as problems, or I won't do anything about them. You live with me. You see the problems clearly. But you can't or won't make me take responsibility for them. So you search out my hidden booze and pour it down the sink. I buy more booze. You call my boss and make excuses when I am late, because my problem embarrasses you and threatens our livelihood. You yell at me a lot. But I do not change; I say that your nagging ways drive me to drink. And so it gets worse.

This is the real problem with co-dependency: it does not work. It is completely ineffective. In fact, it perpetuates the very behavior it chooses to address. This is what happens when the person with the power to change a behavior – the person doing the behavior – does not take responsibility for it. The person who is putting all the effort into the problem actually has no power to change the problem.

They will go crazy trying.

The answer is for the person with the problem to deal with the problem, and for everyone else to let them have their consequences. Let them feel the discomfort until they want to do something about it. "Let go and let God." This works.

So what is this so-called thought-life problem? It is purported that men's sexual desire mechanism is so strong and unmanageable that they can't engage in normal activities with women around without it sabotaging them. If women cover themselves in an attempt to help men with their thought-life problem– willingly as in some churches, or unwillingly if you have the Taliban around – all it does is allow men to be lazy about self-regulation. And it won't work. Because as we all know that if you cover shoulders, arms become sexy. If you cover knees, ankles become sexy. Sexy is in the brain of the beholder, and that is where the change needs to take place.

Maybe.

Because, actually, there is nothing wrong with sexy. All God's creatures have it. Sexy only becomes a problem when it gets in the way of other things that God also made, like your ability to listen. Like your ability to respect. Like your commitment to equality.

When sexy becomes so big in your brain that it crowds out those things, then what you have is a problem with idolatry.

And nobody can fix that but you.

The Madonna of Santa Fe

Walking down a small back street in Santa Fe, the sidewalk was minimal; the adobe wall on my right hand was solid. My left hand could have touched any passing car. It was a one-lane sidewalk.

I heard the slow, rumbling approach behind me. Then I heard the young men in the car. They were speaking Spanish, but their intent required no interpretation. They leaned out the open windows. I took a deep breath, blew it out, and ignored them. They matched my pace, rolling along directly behind me, providing color commentary.

Then I noticed an old man walking toward me. He looked at me, he took in the boys. He could see what they could not – I was visibly pregnant – and it just popped his top.

He jumped off the curb in front of the car. He stood there screaming at the boys – in Spanish, of course. He waved his arms wildly in my direction. The only word I caught, multiple times, was "Madonna." I turned. The boys got the message. The old man continued to yell and pound his fist on their hood. The chastised boys put it in reverse, backing away from the avenger.

I slipped around the corner, unnoticed.

And that, was in fact, the problem. Nobody on that street had seen ME. The ones in the car saw the biological usefulness of my backside. The one in front of me saw the biological usefulness of my womb. All had opinions about my status as a woman. Their opinions were in severe conflict.

None of them saw the strong young woman who was neither flattered nor frightened by the unasked-for attention. No one saw the young woman who wanted no sexual attention, no protection, no vengeance. What I thought or felt mattered not at all to them.

But hear me now.

I am not my biology.

I enjoy all the things that my body can do. But I am not my body.

I treasure my body, giving it respect without worship. It is my friend and my servant. But it is temporary and I am not.

My sex, my gender, my orientation are temporary.

I am created in the image of God, and I cannot be defined by temporary things.

When my blood and sinews, hormones and neurotransmitters, are all rot, I will remain.

Some of what walked that street will remain.

But those blind men on that street that day would not recognize me.

Because they never saw me.

The Widows of Gitega

Gitega is Burundi's second largest city. It's a little wild up there. One of the suburbs had their new precinct captain assassinated on his third day in office while I was there. Some say the rebels did it; others say that it was his predecessor. They put up a replacement, and he lasted one day before being killed. They couldn't find anyone else willing to take the office – big surprise!

I was speaking at a conference called, "Let's Unite to Stop the Violence Against Widows!" The Burundian group I was working for was sponsoring this event at a Catholic retreat house. There were thirty women invited, all widows, young to old, one pregnant and six with nursing babies.

In Burundi, the widow is very close to the bottom of the power ladder. The only people lower are street children. Widows often have no functional protection, legal or physical. You can steal from the widow, or rape the widow, with impunity. Because the widow cannot afford bribes, she rarely has recourse to law. Because she is impoverished, and they would have to support her, her own family does not want her back, and if she speaks to a man who is married she is suspected of planning to steal a husband, so her married friends turn against her, too. Often her biggest problems come from her former in-laws, who want the house or land back, and may be willing to push the children of their dead son or brother into the street to get it.

So I was there from far off planet America to speak to the condition of these women. I was asked to talk to them about women's rights! I felt irrelevant.

They came in their best – wrapped in color – one yardage for a skirt and another around the shoulders. I was told that most of them had borrowed the clothes. Some of them even had shoes – plastic slippers of the type we would call flip flops. For them, this was the best three-day vacation of their lives; the austere Catholic hostel was the Ritz; the food, the best they had eaten in a long time. This was the first intervention – just to pull them up out of grinding poverty for a few days.

The second intervention was that they were invited to a conference. In Burundi, only important people go to conferences, and only the rich attend any kind of schooling in adulthood. They told all their neighbors and relatives that they were attending this event, and it raised their prestige. The gift of a notebook and a pen is significant: only seven of the thirty read or write, but just owning paper and a pen makes you special. Their stay was paid for, and they were given a small transportation allowance. When they were given this stipend at the end of the second day, they held an impromptu dance. I don't believe that a single one of them used the allowance for a bus ride home. They walked home, however far that was, with their babies on their backs; the stipend bought food or paid the small but impossible school fees for one of their other children. And some of those children would have a notebook and a pen.

The babies nursed, and the babies cried. The babies made puddles on the floor like puppies. Sometimes the mothers mopped up the puddle with the baby's blanket and then wrapped the baby back up in it – sometimes they didn't bother. The day was hot and dry; it took about thirty minutes for a baby puddle to evaporate. Most of the babies looked healthy. They were happy because their mothers were happy. They did not yet know that they had been born into the lowest position in one of the least developed countries in the world. I was looking at the bottom of the world totem pole. I was sad. They laughed.

We opened the sessions. My translator, Felicitè, started with an exercise that we would call an icebreaker. She had each of them stand and say their own name, and then repeat the name of each previous woman, going around in a circle. That was clearly a thing they had never done before. They were shy, hiding in their shawls, putting their hands over their mouths, whispering. This did not go unchallenged. "Stand up, speak loudly!" she encouraged them. One by one they stood, and spoke their own names out loud, and other women listened and tried to remember. They said "I am ME," and then they affirmed that, "You are YOU" and "WE are US." Suddenly the activity took on real power.

Then I was on. They were clearly fascinated with me, but a little skeptical. They are a storytelling people so I told them the story of my grandmother and how she became widowed by the influenza epidemic in 1918. How she managed to raise her three boys on her own in the great depression. I told them that a hundred years ago in the US, the plight of the widow was not much better than their own, but that things had improved as social reforms were made, and women started to vote, and fought for their rights. Then I outlined for them the universal rights of women as designated by the Beijing Women's Accord. I told them that this was what all women of the world hope for. They were amazed to find out that their legal rights in Burundi are better than women's rights in some countries. They can own property, they can vote, they can worship as they see fit, and they can change their religion if they please. Their rights may not be respected or enforced, but at least they exist, and can be fought for. They found out that a rich Saudi woman might be less free in some ways than a poor Burundian. But we all know that they would change places if they could.

When I told them they have a right to the physical integrity of their own bodies, they look confused. I clarified.

"You have the right not to be raped or beaten." A hand was raised.

"Not raped or beaten by soldiers?" the woman asked.

"Not beaten or raped by anyone!" I said.

"But husbands...?"

"Not even husbands."

There was a second of silence, and then they laughed, loud and long – this was the funniest thing they had heard in a long time. Most of these women would be glad to have a husband – even one who raped and beat.

Over the course of the next two days we ate together, and talked together, and played with the babies. On our third morning, we were displaced by a group of Burundi government ministers who wanted to use our room on short notice. We were women, so of course we were displaced. We were sent to another part of the grounds. It was a little more than two miles away. I had a car and a driver, but it was a nice cool morning and I decided to walk with the women. So in my high heels, I led the parade of colorful women up the badly rutted dirt road. The arriving ministers sped by us in their SUVs, covering us with their dust. The new room was actually nicer than the old one; it belonged to the archbishop. The babies peed on the archbishop's floor, too. But lunch was served two miles back at the first place. So after a morning of teaching, with an afternoon to go, I measured my strength and took the car to lunch, while the women walked. This did not feel very good to me, but I knew without a doubt that they were stronger than I. Even the ones who had AIDS or malaria could out-walk me with loads on their heads and babies on their backs. I felt wimpy.

We were supposed to get our room back for the afternoon, but the ministers were slow to leave. We sat and watched them depart. One very important guy's off-brand Asian SUV wouldn't start. We sat around and watched as the men tried to push-start it, and jump-start it, and didn't have much luck. I explained to the women that this brand is known to suck, and that this minister should have held out for a Toyota like the other ministers. The women laughed. I am pretty sure that the minister understood my English as well as the translation. He was not enjoying being laughed at by widows, but since they were beneath his notice, he could not notice. He was also not sure who the white woman was, so he ignored us. God has such a funny way of balancing the books some days.

I decided that the ministers' slowness should not rob these women of their teaching time, so we gathered in the shade of a tree. I was taking questions, and we were discussing how to talk to your children about difficult things; things like death, AIDS, rape, war, ethnicity, and poverty. My translator got a little nervous with my answer to a question about how to tell your children that soldiers had killed their father. The soldiers of the ministers, with their automatic rifles, were still only a few feet away from us. She asked me to go to the next question. I protested that we were only telling the simple truth about everyday reality. She pointed out that in Burundi the simple truth could get a person killed. We changed the subject. I was angry and afraid.

The last of the big men left and we claimed our room. It was time to say goodbye, and the women decided to dance. They started to sing – rhythmic, harmonious, and with joy. They took the floor. Their arms sailed, their feet kept the beat. Every part of their bodies moved, as they weaved in and around each other, singing. They pulled me off my chair and I joined them. The whoops and hollers at the sight of me dancing with them raised the roof. We danced for an hour. Everyone was soaked in sweat; the smell was tremendous, but we were happy.

I thought I had nothing to teach these women. I thought that my world was too far from theirs to cross the barriers. I thought that I would find them broken by their condition.

I thought wrong.

Witnesses

There are some things I was taught as a child to understand literally that I no longer understand that way. I do not think Noah got polar bears onto a boat. I do not think that all this magnificent Creation around us was made in just seven, 24-hour days. But some things – some very important things – I *do* still understand that way.

I do believe that He was resurrected. Bodily, on the third day. I will always believe this. For many reasons- but foundationally, fundamentally, deal-breakingly, because I will not betray the women.

All the Gospels say that Magdalene and a few other women were the first witnesses. Mark, the first writer, says that they were not believed. Matthew leaves that little shame out. John inserts Peter, and most likely himself, into the story; he does not mention incredulity.

Luke tries to make amends. Luke is interesting. Tradition says he was a physician in Antioch. Tradition says that Antioch is where Mary, His mother, fled. Luke has stories, like the birth story, that are women's stories. Luke says this: "Their words seemed like non-sense (idle tales) and they believed them not." They were not legal witnesses – no woman was. What a betrayal that must have seemed! – Or maybe they were just used to it. The eleven must have felt embarrassed a short time later. I hope they apologized.

Well, I guess some of them did. Mark put it into the story. Matthew and John seemed to want to forget – it would have been so easy to forget, to erase. But Luke was not letting them get away with it. He put the radical, ground-shaking witnesses in the story, and he documented the shame of their brothers. If you were cleaning up a myth to make people look good, you would take that bit out. The fact that Luke leaves it in, rings true. It is making amends, which always comes out of a place of truth.

Others could have erased it later. But no one did. Not the first tellers of the story, or the first writers, or the successive copiers. The Nicene Council - Patriarchs all – chose to believe the women, and document their witness and leave in the shame. For two millennia, no Pope or Patriarch, no potentate or preacher, no man has been able to wipe those women out of the story. No one has had the nerve. Until lately. It has become fashionable to doubt miracles. But to do so, you must discredit the reporters of the miraculous.

I will not discredit the voice of Magdalene, nor her spiritual mothers and sisters. I will not stand with the unbelieving brothers, the skeptics. I will not turn them into metaphor, or allegory, or hagiography. I will not let my modernist sensibilities blackball their words in shadow – less than other words, even the words of the Master. I won't make them smaller. Their part has been shrunk enough already. I won't discount them; they are already a bargain.

I know what it is like to not be believed when telling the Gospel Truth. I also know what it is like to create metaphor, and allegory, and hagiography. I have told tales and sold nonsense. I, a story teller, know the difference.

These women told the most important truth ever told. And if their witness is discounted in my presence, I will not be silent.

Because I believe them. Quite literally.

Ascending Acoma

St. Esteban del Rey Church crowns the top of Acoma Pueblo, New Mexico. My younger daughter and I were visiting my elder daughter and her husband. It was Sunday, but there was not much interest in the group in finding the Quaker meeting that I knew was in town. The month was October, clear and crisp. I suggested we take a drive out to Acoma Pueblo, an hour's drive outside of Albuquerque. I had not been there in decades, but I knew the drive was beautiful, and I could enjoy my daughters' company and give them a history lesson at the same time.

We ended up on the walking tour through the village, which is perched on a small Mesa that rises 367 vertical feet out of the desert. They call it Sky City. Our tour guide was Dale Sandoz. We were lucky to get Dale. She is a matriarch of the Eagle Clan of the Acoma people. She is small and round, "Like the cedar trees that grow at the base of the Mesa – strong, dry-country growth." She splashed water on the ground from her canteen as a gift to Mother Earth, to secure a safe tour. The Acoma are matriarchal: all property passes from the mother to the youngest daughter, "Because we expect that she will outlive us all." A couple of long, tall Texas cowboys in our group discovered that you do not walk in front of an Acoma matriarch without being rebuked – "But you ladies can walk wherever you like." Acoma governors are all men. "Women have more important things to do – so we nominate them, and if they do good – we keep them, if not, we don't." The village has been continually inhabited since at least 1150. The houses are two or three stories high, and none have electricity or water. They are made of limestone blocks (the traditional material), or adobe, or cinderblock – Dale regrets these innovations – "But there are no zoning laws up here, and you can't tell a youngest daughter what to do with her house."

We started our tour in the church. It is huge – at least three stories up from the plaster and dirt floor to the massive ponderosa pine beams that were carried many miles from Mount Taylor in 1629. "Because they were holy, they never once touched the ground between here and there. The men took turns carrying them, and rested them on platforms at night." The Spaniards gave them a bell as a peace offering – and a peace offering was dearly needed because of the massacre of 1598. Thirteen Spanish soldiers tried to steal grain and were killed by the Acoma. One of them was a relative of the governor, Juan de Oñate, and he retaliated with a brutal assault on the pueblo that saw the women taken as slaves and the men killed, or left alive but with their right foot cut off. Children were pulled screaming out of hiding in the kiva; their throats were slashed, and they were dragged through the village behind horses. The atrocity shocked even the Conquistadors, and Onate was eventually prosecuted. The Acoma were "given" a church. I'm not sure what "given" means when you spend a lifetime of the people – 40 years – building it yourself. The Acoma chose Saint Stephen for their patron. When they heard the story of the man who prayed as he was being stoned to death, "Lord, do not count this sin against them," they recognized him as their own. Dale says that they freely accepted the religion of their oppressors because they recognized the truth in it beyond the actions of its adherents. This woman is so *not* oppressed! She says that "99% of Acoma are Catholic and 100% practice the ancient religion – because they are so similar." At the altar are four pillars carved from those ancient ponderosas, carved as twisted, entwined beams of white and red "for the two religions that are practiced here." Symbols of the people are painted on the walls of the church alongside paintings of saints and a prominent picture of purgatory. There are only a few pews up front to accommodate the elders – the rest of the space is left free for dancing. A small window is aligned to admit a ray of sunlight to fall directly on the Santo only on the winter solstice. It is a most integrated place.

We walked out through the burial yard and through the village. I bought a small pot. I was deeply moved, but it took days for the full truth to sink in. The Acoma built that church twenty years before Quaker George Fox stood and preached for the first time. The Acoma had found Christ in the church of their murderers. They found a faith that spoke to their condition. They found "That of God" in the ugly other. They found a model for forgiveness in the worst of situations. We consider these to be Quaker testimonies. George would have had no truck with the Spanish Church; but he would have understood the Acoma.

One of those near the stoning of St. Stephan was the Apostle Paul – spiritually preserved, perhaps, by the prayer of his victim. Paul's image is also on the Acoma altar.

I wonder if the prayers of the Acoma have saved Oñate.

Don We Now Our Gay Apparel

Girl Arrested

Dressed in a complete boy's suit from top to toe, a rather pretty 17-year-old north side girl was arrested yesterday by Deputy Sheriff Roddy, and soon thereafter was taken to the county farm, where she will be held until the county court can take proper action concerning her case, which it is expected will result in a sentence to the State Reform School for girls at Morrison.

This is the same girl who six weeks ago, after being missed from home for a week, was found doing man's work for the Fitts Manufacturing company. At that time she had secured a horse and buggy and driven eight miles in the country to the home of a family she knew; there she appropriated a serge suit belonging to the young man of the family, and after bobbing off her luxuriant head of hair, came to town and secured an up-to-date boys' haircut. She then hunted a job and got it. Upon being discovered, she was returned home.

Last Friday, after having been given $85 dollars by her mother to pay bills (which she did not pay) and after "borrowing" $20 more from the home, making a total of $105, she donned the suit she first wore and went down town and bought a complete set of boy's attire, including toilet articles, candy, gum, pocket knife with "loud" pictures on the handle, and watch and fob, secured a room on Union avenue, and was probably hunting a remunerative job. Roddy hove across her path and took her into custody.

This girl belongs to a good family, has a good and prosperous home, but she just wants to be a boy.

The Pueblo, Colorado *Chieftain*, October 24, 1917
(author uncredited)

I Used To Be an Ally

I used to be a straight ally. My personal views about equal rights for gays started to form when I was in college in the late 1970's; I publicly started to express those views in the early 90's. I put a rainbow sticker on my car in 1998, when Matthew Shepherd was killed – I figured if you could get killed for being gay in this country, better they should be confused and get a straight preacher than an actual gay person. In 2004, I co-founded an inclusive Quaker Church and resigned my ministerial status with The Northwest Yearly Meeting of Friends to do it. That grieved me greatly. I lost some friends and the esteem of many over that – but I gained the esteem of others. I started writing publicly about it in 2006, when I started a blog. I spent a lot of time listening to people like gay Quaker activist Petersen Toscano. I showed up with my body at the State Capitol whenever Tara Wilkins and the Community of Welcoming Congregations asked for it. I thought I got it. I even thought that I got the fact that being a straight ally was a lot easier than being gay.

I did not get it.

In 2007, my straight marriage of 30 years blew up and I was single for the first time as an adult. I took inventory of my mind and soul in a whole new way. I realized that I had never really understood why it was not possible to love someone regardless of what body they came in – it actually didn't make deep sense to me. Peterson said, "Peggy, we have a word for that – it's called Bisexual." That made sense, and I realized that I didn't choose that, either. It was simply true for me. In time, I courted and married my best friend, Alivia Biko, a lesbian. And I thought I got it.

I did not get it.

I estranged some with the decision to marry Alivia. I gave a lot of smug people an "I told you so" that wasn't true, but I just put up with it. I thought I was paying my dues.

I was not.

It has now been years of happy with Alivia. I mostly travel in circles that are happy with and for us. I don't sit under the preaching of fundamentalists these days. Liv has medical issues, and her doctors and the local hospital treat us with great respect. Both of us can be out at work – our bosses came to the wedding. We get seated at restaurants. We travel without fear. I traveled to Africa and my Quaker host there, when told, smiled, shrugged his shoulders, and said "Congratulations." I started to wonder if it was too late to get in on that oppression thing.

I signed a protest letter asking for equal rights for LGBTQ students at George Fox University with no ramifications whatsoever. I was happy to see this conversation starting at my Quaker Alma Mater. I knew it would be a long one. I knew it would get messy. I thought I was ready for that.

I was not.

I was happy to show up at a Forum on Human Sexuality held at Fox. I knew it was going to be messy and hard, but Good Lord, there was Nathan Meckley, the pastor of the Metropolitan Community Church sitting up there like a regular expert, gonna get his say, on *that* campus. Amazing. It appeared that they could not get even one of their own seminary professors to take up the conservative Biblical position – because they had to send across town to the Baptist seminary for Professor Gerry Breshears. The Panel was rounded out by Oregon Court of Appeals Justice Darleen Ortega, a Quaker, and Erica Tan, clinical Psychologist and adjunct faculty at Fox. Just having this discussion was real progress, and quick progress.

Unfortunately, I started to get queasy from the get-go.

Phil Smith, from the school, started off suggesting that we all come to the table with the idea that we might be wrong, and that if we came with that idea we would get a better result. And it sounded sorta good, but part of me started crawling.

See, when I came to the table as an ally, what I had to put on that table was my beliefs, some of them heartfelt and precious, but still my beliefs. For some people, like my Evangelical Quaker pastor friends, they might be putting their jobs on the table if they decided they had been wrong. However, like a lot of the faculty at Fox, they could change those beliefs and keep quiet about them to keep those jobs. Now, though, I was being asked for a whole different thing. If I came to the table with the "I might be wrong" attitude, I would have to put my love on the table. If I am wrong about my love for Alivia being designed and blessed by God – then what? Another divorce? A sexless marriage? Are any of the straight people in the room, allies or not, willing to put those things on the table?

Of course not. That would be wrong. Because the default setting is that their love is good – only *my* love, *my* marriage, is hanging in the balance. It is not an equal equation, Phil. It is asking of me, something you would never ask of yourself.

Then the Baptist got his say. He started with one of those beautiful evangelical confessions and apologies, and I think he meant it. I think he believed it. "Sorry for all the hurt, the bad words," he said. He copped to homophobia, personally and corporately. He said they had all been wrong about the choice thing – they knew now that it was not true. He said that "The only law of Jesus was to Love your neighbor, and this is what the church should be doing."

I let the shields down and thought, well, maybe this *is* progress.

Letting the shields down was a mistake.

Because he immediately launched into a whole new round of dismissive, painful, condemning language and judgments. According to him, His virgin-initiated straight marriage was chaste, everything else was something less. *Everything.* This was supposed to make us feel better. The word he used for my most holy, delightful, God-centered moments with Liv was *porneia.* But he didn't want us to take that as special condemnation, because so was straight guys using porn, and people who get divorces, and people who have sex before marriage. It's all *porneia.*

Everything except what he does – that is Holy.

But he didn't want to be seen as judgmental. Those weren't his words and ideas after all, they belonged to Jesus. Jesus is the only one who comes to the table without having to take the "I might be wrong" pledge. And because he was only bringing Jesus's words, Prof. B didn't actually have to put anything on that table. He really thought he was doing grace and being fair.

I would rather have the Westboro Baptists. Horrible, but honest. They are better than the guy who does "Nice, nice, nice, I really love you, you are my friend, I just want to have you over for dinner.", and then he sticks you with the shiv between the ribs.

Because my heart is between my ribs. What he was calling porneia is the absolute best thing that has ever happened to me. Our sexuality is an indivisible piece of that. Our love, every bit of it, is dedicated to Christ. I talk to Jesus every day and He never talks to me like this.

I wanted to puke. When I was an ally, I would have wanted to puke from disgust. This is different – I wanted to puke from pain. Torture puke is far worse than disgusted puke.

Without thinking, I started curling up in a ball. Protecting my vital organs. I was sitting with my friend Stan Thornburg, who noticed this, and draped his coat over me, thinking I was cold. I was not cold – I was cowering. This guy had me in full retreat. He had sucker-punched me. He landed it.

The rest of the evening was various parts of taking a breath, a cool cup of water (Nathan and Darleen), and being asked to swallow more poison. For the most part, it was lauded as a real good evening by most folks. I suppose it was.

I could now write the smarmy evangelical apology I owe for all the insensitive things I have said and done as an ally. The times I have thought that my gay friends were being a wee bit too impatient, or too sensitive, or too thin skinned, or for the fact that they might not be looking at the big picture or the long run. Ow. Puke.

But I now know that the time is past for justice. My heart is not too sensitive; my skin is not too thin. The picture is no bigger than my bedroom. The run is no longer than the today I have with my love.

The people who have been putting up, for years, *for their whole lives*, with hate, and then fake-grace wrapped crap, are not troublemakers. They are saints.

Losing Your Voice

I was sitting in the front seat of a Land Cruiser just outside Gitega. I was working as a peacemaker and a teacher, and I was in trouble – deep trouble.

We had been delayed outside of town and it was about to be dark, the kind of dark we rarely get here in the US. No streetlights, no house lights, no lights anywhere for miles – that kind of dark. There was a civil war going on. The roadblocks went up at dusk. Both sides put up roadblocks. Both sides attempted to control movement, and both side resupplied by banditry. Niyonzima was on his home turf and fortunately knew the road blindfolded. We were flying towards town like angels towards the Throne of Glory. We rounded a corner to see a truck stopped in the middle of the road. This is not unusual: if you break down, you just park it in the road and leave it there for a few days till the parts come. We flew around its right side. We never saw the thin cord lying across the road – the only indication of a roadblock. What we heard was the tat, tat, tat of automatic rifle fire – probably over our heads, but maybe at our backs. My friend stopped and we were surrounded by a patrol that was probably government soldiers but might have been rebels. We could not tell. They cannot always tell. It didn't matter, because they were hostile, drunk, and pointing AK-47s at us. There was no problem with being drunk on duty in either army. The Burundian government sometimes paid their troops in beer. My host spoke quietly and calmly through his window to the captain of the patrol. I smiled and tried to look relaxed. I had just enough Kirundi words to hear the others say "woman," "truck and woman," "white person." Their smiles were not comforting. They were gauging the benefits of pillage against the potential costs. What they really wanted to know was who would come looking for us if we disappeared. My friend was talking about our organization. He later told me that the captain asked about the logo on our truck. He told them about our mission. He said that we were "Making straight hearts made crooked by war." He told the captain that I had come to teach this process. The captain exclaimed "But our hearts are very crooked – we need this!" and chided him for being out past curfew and told him to get the Mzungu into town before something bad happened.

My friend pled our case and talked us out of a very dangerous situation. His voice and our truth were our only weapons, our only protection, that night.

At least he had his voice, and could speak our truth.

Dan Hunt of Ontario, Canada, lost his voice in 2006. When James Loney, a Christian Peacemaker in Baghdad, was kidnapped in November, he was in double jeopardy. He was a westerner suspected of collusion with the occupying force, and he was a gay man. While the families of the other hostages spoke out in the media, reminding the world of their plight, James' partner, Dan, went into hiding. While the other families could seek broad help, support, and prayers, Dan had to be quiet, out of fear that James's orientation would become known to his captors in a land where one of the few things that most people agreed on is that the penalty for being gay is death.

When you lose your voice out of fear for your life, or the life of someone you love, you have been robbed of a sacred, God given right. Of all creatures on this planet, we humans are given the gift of voice – the ability to tell our own story, to share what we know, to share ourselves with each other.

We must fairly say that James took the first risk; open-eyed and clear-headed, he walked – not into simple danger – but compound danger, to be a peaceful presence in the midst of chaos. I call this courage. The kidnappers put his life in yet more immediate jeopardy. But if the kidnappers asked Norman Kember about his life, he could talk truthfully about his dear wife at home. James would have to lie and say he was single, or face a worse death than he already faced. It was religious fundamentalism that robbed him, and Dan at home, of the freedom to speak truthfully about their lives.

I define religious fundamentalism as the assertion of absolute truth and the completeness of one's own beliefs and practices to the intentional exclusion of the possibility of truth in the beliefs and practices of others. And whether it is Christian, Jewish, Islamic, or whatever kind of fundamentalism, it is a scourge and a plague on humanity. When it is mixed with the power of governance, you get false theocracy. When it is mixed with weapons, you get death. You get the Puritans and witch trials, the Taliban blowing up Buddhas, the bulldozing of Hebron, the Janjaweed riding in on horseback in Darfur. It is the progenitor of inquisition, crusade, pogrom, and jihad.

Our founding fathers had some real genius. They protected the human voice. They protected religion while separating church and state. I am a Quaker, a once persecuted religious minority. I have benefited greatly from their wisdom. One of my Quaker foremothers was legally hung in Boston, pre Bill of Rights. Part of my religious practice is that I am not willing to kill, not for anything – that is just the simple teaching of Jesus. But there are things I would die for, and the separation of church and state is one of those things, and the free voice of people like Dan and James is another.

On that dark African night three years ago, my friend's truthful, gentle, persistent, fearless voice saved my life. I pray that we never spare tongue, nor pen, nor anything else in the protecting and publishing of every human voice.

A League of Extraordinary Gentlemen

I struggle with hymns sometimes. You know what I mean; all I had to do was see the title after the worship leader called out the number, and a groan came up within me. "Not that old clichéd rag! – oh, spare me." Haunted hymns. Hymns I could only hear in voices that I no longer wanted to listen to. Voices that brought back so many of the fundamentalist memories that I had worked hard at putting outside the garden gate. Bloody hymns – lambs bleeding and dying at every turn. I had long ago given up the slaughterhouse metaphors as not relevant to my life.

But I was the speaker at this Christian retreat, and walking out of the room, while it would have been tolerated, would have caused concern among the brethren. And they were brethren. I was the only woman within shouting distance.

> Blessed assurance, Jesus is mine! ...
> This is my story – This is my song
> Praising my Savior – all the day long.

George Beverly Shea, Billy Graham's worship leader always pronounced it stow-ree, and drawled it out nice and slow – it rhymed with glow-ree. I can't hear that song without hearing George. I tried to drag myself back from the stadium of thousands to the small circle of men. I looked at the present leader, Jonmarc. He didn't look like George and he didn't sound like George. He was younger and lankier, and he sported a motorcycle jacket, soul patch, and some hipster eyewear. Boy did he have a story. A story that involved pretty severe, unwanted alienation from the people who loved him and whom he loved. Some serious flying monkeys on his back. A story that involved a stint in the summer camp for the criminally inclined that some people call prison. And when this man was in prison, did the church of his childhood visit him as commanded by scripture? No, it was these men who came, every week, outcasts visiting the outcast. His story is a story about Jesus, whom Jonmarc just couldn't quit.

> Oh, How I love Jesus ... the sweetest name on Earth
> It tells me what my Father hath
> in store for me every day

> And tho' I tread a darksome path,
> Yields sunshine all the way.
> Oh how I love Jesus, because He first loved me.

That pulled me from the present back to a hot summer camp meeting under the trees. Mosquitoes whining at the screens and nasal-voiced old women singing their love for their master. Those old women infected me with a virus of faith, and I caught their vision for preaching. But they didn't prepare me for the fact that they were sending me out into a world where many people would simply deny the fact that a female could have a genuine call to preach the Gospel. I have sat more times than I wish to count with people who looked me in the eyes and said that I did not exist – that there was no such thing as a God-ordained female minister. The choices were, was I delusional or a liar? A very weird and discouraging situation. But not one of those folks ever told me that I could not be a Christian – that there was no such thing as a female Christian. The men sitting around me had lived through that level of denial. They were all gay men. And they were all Christians, but they had been told for most of their lives that those two things were mutually exclusive. They had had their foundational reality rejected, again and again.

So I came and told them that each and every one of them was here on planet Earth on assignment from God, and that they needed all of themselves to stay on task. They needed to be integrated to do it. That their gender, their orientation, their history, or the opinions of the world had no power to stop them. They chose to believe me, because their very own spirits shouted that it was true. Music to their ears.

> Oh Lord, my God, when I in awesome wonder,
> consider all the worlds Thy hands have made ...
> Then sings my soul...
> How great thou art!

There are lots of kinds of worlds beyond and beside planets and galaxies. There are the infinite worlds that each human child co-creates with God, by treading a path from the Eternal Heart into a womb and a body and a time and a place and through a life and eventually back to God. We come into the world all but spiritually deaf and blind. With only echoes of glory stored in our souls. We walk through our childhoods, needing to be told who we are and what our purpose is. We need acceptance, encouragement, and nurture. We need example and model. We need the company of saints. We need comrades. We need a band of brothers.

But some of us get abuse and torment. Some of us get fed a steady diet of lies about who we are and our place. Some of us learn to hide rather than to shine. Against all odds, some of us believe anyway. Some of us keep looking. Some of us refuse to quit and die. Some of us keep seeking until we are found.

This is a persistent human story that causes awe among the watching angelic cohort who have never existed a moment without a direct connection to God, who have never been denied, never marginalized, never oppressed, never abused, never living a moment without knowing who they are and what they are supposed to do. We amaze them!

I looked around me and I saw 20 men – old and young, rich and poor, educated and not, white and blue collars, with challenges, with disabilities, with histories.

I saw heroes, survivors of trials, defeaters of lies, defenders of truth. Men with the superpowers of forgiveness, resilience, persistence, repentance, and recovery. Men who are taking up their tasks with courage and faith, determined to judge themselves only by the simple question of whether they were obedient to their assignment today. Applying grace to their failures. Determined to do as well or better tomorrow. Learning to judge others – not at all.

And when, after the singing, after the scripture, after a lovely Quaker silence, after all the ancient, beautiful, bloody, broken words, they came around with the bread and the wine. Then the brother spoke to each brother, called each by name and said, "Child of God, this is the body and blood of Christ – *never* forget how much you are loved!" Then they came and said, "Sister Peggy, child of God, this is the body and blood of Christ, *never* forget how much you are loved."

Once again I took Christ and Christ took me, in the presence of heroes and saints. I won't forget. I heard the voices of angels singing "Holy, Holy, Holy," and saints singing:

> Brethren we have met to worship
> and adore the Lord our God.
> Will you pray with all your power
> while I try and preach the Word.
> All is vain unless the Spirit
> of the Holy One comes down.
> Brethren pray
> and Holy Manna will be scattered all around.

Holy Manna indeed. Thank you, brothers.

Star-Bellied Sneeches and Modern-Day Cossacks

The Halls of Democracy are sometimes filled with hostility.

The Capitol Building of the State of Oregon is a short distance from my house. I had received a phone call from a clergyperson I associate with, and she was trying to turn out bodies for a series of evening hearings at the Capitol. The legislature was considering two bills, one to limit discrimination against gays, lesbians, and trans-gendered people, and one to set up a way for the same people to legally protect their relationships in a manner akin, but not equal to, the institution of marriage. I could go, so I did.

My problem was that I was two weeks' home from a Central African war zone. I still had a pretty bad case of the social/emotional/ spiritual bends. It takes me about a month to re-adjust from the effects of genocide to the comforts and concerns of American life. I cannot do counseling during this time. I do not teach or preach, as it tends to turn into a rant. I just cannot immediately work up compassion for normal American problems after being emotionally present to people living in actual hell. I get over it. I reset all the dials. But it takes a while.

So that night, as I walked into the Capitol, I was not – shall we say – real enthusiastic. But I remembered that I normally felt quite strongly about this issue, and I figured I could be bodily present, if not spiritually present.

The first thing I noticed as I entered was that everybody was labeled. It was Dr. Seuss and the star-bellied Sneeches. Everybody was wearing stickers to designate their side. There were folks in the doorway discerning what party you belonged to and handing you your sticker. I don't really like stickers on my person. I was picked out by the Basic Rights Oregon person and offered my progressive sticker. I was not real sure how I was spotted, but I declined out of sheer rebelliousness. The young man then took another look at me and spotted my grandmother's cross, which I often wear around my neck. He actually took a step back, and said "Oh, sorry." That was my first clue.

The next thing I noticed was that the building was overflowing with people. I had trouble finding any of my friends. There was the main hearing room, and then many overflow rooms with closed circuit TV; and because those were all full, the lobbies were filled with chairs and people and additional TV sets. And security. Lots of security. The security people looked nervous. Second clue.

By observing stickers, I noticed that all the gay families were huddled together in the hearing rooms. The lobbies were full of their opponents.

The next thing I noticed was that the people opposing the bills all looked like each other. Really – they did. Round, be-scarved, middle-aged women who looked like nesting dolls, and droves of tall, good-looking, clear skinned, brown haired, blue-eyed men. A smattering of pretty blonde girls.

I found my clergy friend. "Who are these people?" I asked.

"They are all from one church here in Salem. It's a Slavic fundamentalist church. They can turn out 300 bodies any time the pastor calls for it. Thanks for coming, Peggy."

"Where are your folks?"

"They are all together in the hearing rooms; nobody feels comfortable mingling."

Well then, that gave me my mission for the night. Mingle with the Slavic Christians and see what was what. I don't like fear-based segregation. I do not often find that it is based in reality. I like to challenge it and look for the good in the other side. That's my default setting.

There was a seat open in front of one of the TVs right in the middle of a knot of young men. I took the seat. The energy was really quite amazing; I could feel it in the air. Primal, like big sexual energy, only about anger, not sex. Anger pheromones. I watched as people testified before the legislators – three for, then three against. The rule for the evening, both in the hearing room and in the lobby, was no vocal demonstrations. But the young men around me were having a hard time containing it. Quietly cheering the people who predicted the fall of civilization if a couple of lesbians made a civil union, and jeering, hissing, and spitting invectives at anyone who disagreed with that analysis. There were many dozens of testimonies that night. I got weary, but the young Slavic men did not. They seemed to gain steam from each chance to hate, which did not dissipate with the speakers who they supported. They had a one-sided reaction that ratcheted up with each round.

I was touched in some way by all the testimony. I was pretty put off by the fear-mongering, but when someone stood up and spoke eloquently on behalf of their alternative family, it warmed me, gave me hope and trust that love would eventually win out. One young woman did an especially good job, and I just couldn't help but say a quiet "Amen, preach it sister." The young men on either side of me, sat bolt upright and looked at me.

"Hi, my name's Peggy, I'm with the other side – I just didn't get my sticker." I put out my hand to the young man on my left.

He did not take it.

The next speaker was a clergyman from some progressive protestant denomination. He wore a Roman-style collar. He spoke of

God's love for all people. This really heated up my area. Much gasping and hissing. They really didn't like the pro-gay clergy guy.

The young man on my right sat with his fists and probably a few other body parts clenched. "Using God's name to defend an abomination! God should strike him dead," he hissed. I had the distinct impression that if God didn't do it, this young man would volunteer to be God's agent.

I suddenly remembered why I cared about this issue. These fine Christian folk, if they knew everything I believed and everything I preached, everything I live, and if given a free rein, would likely stone me dead without a second thought.

Think that couldn't happen in America? Quaker preacher Mary Dyer was hung in Boston Commons by fine Plymouth-Rock, Thanksgiving-Day, Christian folk. The framers of our constitution knew that well, and attempted to prevent it from happening in the new union. But they knew it was a real problem that needed to be addressed.

I remember something Garrison Keillor said about the Puritans, his forbearers. He said, "They came to America to practice religious persecution at a level not actually allowed under British law." He was right. The Puritans, of course, thought they were fleeing religious persecution and protecting their faith by hanging Quakers. The Slavic Christians gathered around me also fled religious persecution, and believe that they are protecting their faith.

There was one other person sitting in that group who stood out even more than I. An orthodox, possibly Hasidic, Jew – side curls, hat, fringe – the whole thing. We don't see a lot of that in Salem. From his sticker, I could see that he was in harmony with the Slavic Christians. When I got the chance, I moved and sat by him.

"Hello, Friend, so you agree with these folks?" I said

"I do, they are on God's side of this issue." He said, stiff, not looking at me.

"Don't they remind you of anyone?"

"I do not know what you mean."

"Like, I don't know, Cossacks, maybe?"

"You do not know what you are talking about."

"Probably not, no, I'm sure I don't. But are you really sure that if they managed to put down the gays like they wish to, that they wouldn't come next for, oh, say the Jews?"

Then he looked at me.

"Just a thought." I said, and I moved on.

What Chance Did I Stand Against Kismet?

– Example sentence, Oxford English Dictionary

Jason Kowolik was huge. Six-foot something, tattooed, and beefy – the US Army was glad to have him. But Jay's intelligence was too great to be a grunt, and his temperament was too kind to be a killer. So he worked as a translator for Army Intelligence during Desert Storm. Over time, he married two women and fathered two sons; he loved them all but could not make the relationships last. He earned a degree in criminal justice and worked as a cop, but hated it. He got sober the first time with AA, and treasured being a sponsor. He worked security at the State Mental Hospital and became a CNA, then a mental health technician.

That would have been enough for one life.

But the soul that enlivened Jay was not to be contained within that life. Jay came out, and married Scott. Being a gay man was new territory. Being an addict was old territory, but Jay conquered it again, this time with NA. Jay added some sobriety-based ink to help remember the battles lost and won.

That was still not enough.

A wanderlust of human experience called Jay further out. "Gay man" was just not fitting, so Jay Kowolik became Jaye Kyzmet, legally and physically a woman. How Jaye spelled her name changed on a regular basis, but it was a derivation of the Arabic word for Fate. When Jaye first walked into Freedom Friends, she was wearing a wig and a dress and a whole lot of colorful ink. Jaye could not be contained by the conventions of feminine beauty either, though, and she soon lost the wig to display a full bald dome of words and colors and flowers and symbols. Jaye stood out.

The ink was an attempt to anchor and commit her to her deepest ideals. She was wearing her code. It was also evidence of an exploration of pain. Jaye liked the needles. Being repetitively punctured was a meditative state. With the ink, Jaye could go deep into that place without risk of death.

She walked into the Quaker Church on the Island of Misfit Toys after a powerful conversion experience worthy of Fox or Wesley. Deep into a graveyard shift on the locked ward for the criminally insane, Jaye unlocked the door that opened her soul to God. She was reading Scripture, which was new territory for her, when she was overcome by a vision of Light and Love. She knew in that moment that this presence was Christ. The Presence affirmed everything she had been, was, and would be. The Presence told her to keep reading and to find community.

Jaye started looking for community. She also became a serious student of the Bible, memorizing large chunks of it whole – taking it all seriously. Biblical ink blossomed on her skin. Jaye's theological tendencies were, at first, on the edge of Fundamental. Jaye thought she had docked on the shores of certainty. Finding a Christian community of the Fundamental persuasion that would embrace a six-foot, bald, whole body-tattooed, transgender woman was tough, though. Impossible in Salem, Oregon. So she had to become tolerant enough to accept a group of Progressive Quakers who accepted her. Our meetings were enriched by her grasp of Scripture and her gift for the insightful question. Words of George Fox and lyrics by Alivia Biko found their place on her skin.

Jaye became a grandmother, learned to crochet a baby blanket, and attended a women's theological conference. She became active in the trans community. But Jaye suffered for the lack of a deep personal relationship, and she continued to struggle with the temptation to alter her chemistry. Her friendships started to embrace some people whose community was a rather famous Hispanic gang. We worried when gang symbols appeared on her legs.

Then she wandered off. Up into the Hills above Scotts Mills, and into a relationship that did not help with sobriety. We didn't see much of her. When we did, it was apparent that she had decided that weed was okay. The relationship was not okay, and one night, on an impulse fueled by jealousy, Jaye committed a crime. A small property crime, one that might have produced an arrest, but probably not any serious time. But Jaye had spent a lot of her life watching people who were locked up. It was a territory she was not willing to explore. She wasn't even willing to talk about it.

So she got a hotel room, paid for a couple of days, and put the "do not disturb" sign on the door. She laid out a Bible, a candle, a rosary, and a tiny Buddha to cover all her bases, and she used that old transport called drugs to propel herself into what she hoped would be the arms of that Loving Presence.

We hope she found home. Because this world could not contain her.

Bolt Cutters

Alivia and I were on a pilgrimage to the mecca of non-conformity: Berkeley, California. We were on a quest. We were expecting. Pregnant with that of God. Gestating a miracle, and looking for a stable where we could bring it forth.

We were carrying within our hearts a new creature named Freedom Friends Church – the culmination of everything we believed that God had been teaching us to this point in our lives. A place where Christ the present teacher could be passionately worshipped and radically obeyed. A place where the precious truths of Quakerism could be explained and lived out in a new millennium. A place of intentional inclusivity, where God's marginalized children of all stripes would be welcomed and given a place of service.

However, the sad truth of Quakerism at the turn of the 21st century is that we are polarized and fragmented. Our larger groups and organizations tend to be Christ-centered and non-inclusive (a thing we find to be contradictory), or inclusive and theologically muddy, (a thing we find to be lacking in unction and power). We needed another option. It seemed unlikely that our home, Northwest Yearly Meeting, was going to be able to give us such an option, or claim us as their own if we created it. So we were in Berkeley, investigating a possible option there.

It was a 'tender and broken meeting,' as the Quakers of old would say. We listened to a Quaker leader describe Friends' work around the world: hospitals in Kenya, oppressed but vibrant faith in Cuba, and heartbreaking tales of Palestine. She gave us the unforgettable picture of an old Palestinian man and his wife, separated for thirty-five years by an Israeli fence, meeting daily to entwine their fingers through the chain link, whispering of faithful love kept apart by institutional violence.

We listened to the leader of our hoped-for option describe how she had once considered her own ministry unacceptable, because she was a divorced woman, and how God had surprised her by calling and empowering her to serve in spite of this. She described her joy at being found acceptable.

Again and again through the day we heard the call for workers – help was needed. The fields were white. There was no heart there that did not feel the tug

I sat on the back bench and watched two brilliant, gifted friends – our hosts for the weekend. Two women, committed to the Light and to each other. One whose gentle heart was broken by the reality of an evil that would put up a fence, careless of the separation of love; the other – deeply gifted with insight, knowledge, and the ability to empower others – who had been begging God for a clear commission to the work. I watched my friends' hearts respond to the call. I watched the spiritual struggle, and the surrender. I saw my friend stand and ask if her service would be accepted. And then I saw the Christ-centered Quaker fence go up. "Policy," we were told, did not permit the service of Christ's gay and lesbian servants.

I slipped away and into a bit of a vision. I saw the work of Christ on one side of an endless fence, desperately in need of help; and on the other side, a Christ-called worker, fingers entwined through the fence, straining to be of use. I knew in that moment that it was my people who had erected this fence. Well-meaning, Jesus-loving, but fear-based people. I saw that I had been searching for a group of fence-builders to join. And then I saw Jesus, the lover of my soul, on both sides of the fence, and the Jesus nearest me handed me a pair of bolt cutters.

Theology for a Warming World

> There is a principle which is pure placed within the human mind, which in different places and ages hath had different names; it is, however, pure and proceeds from God. It is deep and inward, confined to no forms of religion, nor excluded from any, where the hearts stands in perfect sincerity. In whomsoever it takes roots and grows, of what nation whatsoever, they become brethren.
>
> —John Woolman (1720-1772) *On Keeping of Slaves*

If you take theology out to its edges, people call you a heretic and often try to burn you at some stake. If you live that edgewise theology, sincerely and consistently, proving its practicality and worth, you will annoy even your best friends. Quaker John Woolman did all of that.

He is, quite arguably, the best thing ever to come from New Jersey. As a young man, working as a scribe, he refused to copy wills that transferred ownership of human beings. He was so scrupulously truthful that young Friends made a sport of trying to catch him in the smallest inaccuracy. He did not wear clothing colored with dye or use objects made of precious metals, because they were produced with slave labor.

He traveled, making personal visits to slave-keeping Quakers, sitting at their fine tables, refusing to eat off of the good china, and paying the slaves for their service to him. He spoke with the tender sincerity of an 18th century Fred Rogers. He was actually gentler than Jesus. He also had the bold tenacity of an Old Testament prophet, walking in where he wasn't really wanted. One can only imagine the dread of the masters and the delight of the slaves when Woolman was in the neighborhood.

During the French and Indian War, he went out to meet with as many native people as he could – "That I might feel and understand their life and the Spirit they live in, if haply I might receive some instruction from them." He strove to "Attend to pure universal righteousness so as to give no offense to the gentile, who does not profess Christianity, whether they be blacks of Africa or native inhabitants of this continent."

He died at 52, in England (he had traveled in steerage), just after convincing the Quakers there to adopt a formal anti-slavery stance. It took American Quakers longer to come to the same conclusion. Possibly because they no longer had John Woolman to prod their consciences and pick at the scabs of their rationalizations.

Asking for Direction

Vancouver, Washington is not big enough to get lost in. This was during my itinerant days, and I was on my way to preach the morning message at a small Quaker church in a town that people often think is in Canada but is actually just across the Columbia River from Portland, Oregon.

Alivia Biko, my right hand, ministry partner, and musical director, was not able to be with me that morning. I had grown accustomed to the luxury of Alivia, and one of the luxuries was that I almost never had to drive on preaching mornings. This was a good thing, since I tend to go into a sort of unction fog an hour or two before the appointed time – and an unction fog is not conducive to driving. Knowing that I would be thus handicapped, I allowed myself extra time, took the non-smart cell phone, plenty of coffee, and made sure that I had a church directory for our group of Quakers. I thought I had things covered. I often forget Whose job that is.

I was enjoying some liturgical music by U2 as I went north. BB King was singing "When Love Comes to Town" with Bono and the boys as I crossed the Columbia River. This is one of the greatest testimony songs in Christendom, I often have to open up the moon roof, or "blessing window," as we call it, and raise a hand in affirmation when they get to this part:

> I was there when they crucified my Lord.
> I held the scabbard when the soldier drew his sword.
> I threw the dice when they pierced his side.
> But I've seen love conquer the great divide.

> (When Love Comes to Town – Bono)

I may have seen Love conquer all, but I completely spaced my exit. When I realized it, I just took the next right and wound my way on down into old Vancouver, trusting my sense of direction, which usually serves me pretty well. Except on preaching mornings.

I was all turned around and I knew it. Nothing looked familiar. I pulled over and consulted my directory. That was when I discovered my real problem. The church was only six months old.

I knew this because I had preached at their kick-off Sunday the previous November. This meant that they weren't in the directory I was carrying. They weren't in the local phone directory, either. I could not remember the name of the street they were on. I had 30 minutes to find them.

I prayed a bit and drove off in a direction I could no longer identify, and then I saw my salvation: a cab company. My definition of a town is a municipality big enough to have a cab company. A city has multiple cab companies, Uber if their fancy. In towns, the cabbies let you sit up front with them; in fact, they are sort of insulted if you sit in the back. I once had a cab driver in my home town of Salem ask me if I thought my name was Trump – sittin' in the back like that. I gave the excuse of having been raised in Chicago, and moved up front. Portland is a city these days – you sit in the back. But they still don't lock the front door, and there aren't usually bars or glass between you and the cabbie. I wasn't sure if Vancouver was a town or a city, but I was glad to see that they had cabbies – because cabbies know everything.

I pulled into their yard and walked up to the dispatch building. A big guy in a loud shirt waved me on into the back room.

"What am I doing for you this morning, darlin'?" He said.

"I'm lost," said I.

"*No you aren't.*" He said this with surprising vehemence.

"Well, I don't know where I'm going."

"Yes you do. You're goin' to church. Which one?"

"I'm preaching at New Life Friends, in just a few minutes."

"Hmm...What's it look like?"

"Ummm, it's a little funky old place between a New Age bookstore and an espresso booth."

Note: in the Pacific Northwest, coffee addiction and New Age proclivities are pandemic. We sometimes have three coffee shops per intersection. The description I gave might as well have been "It's on a corner, next to a street."

"Ah, I know your place." He said confidently, and he gave me directions.

I was less than a mile away.

Out of the chain smoking mouths of cab dispatchers – once again – God's very own truth. There is no such thing as lost. Knowing where you are going and knowing how you are going to get there are two different things. The knowledge doesn't have to be completely in your head. The reality is that I, and you, and the whole world, live in the palm of the hand of God, and we couldn't walk off it if we tried. When we step off, God's other hand is there to catch us like a Mr. Magoo cartoon. When we feel confused, we can always stop and ask for help, and help is out there.

Dispatch man walked me out to my car, and after I thanked him, he said this:

"Now, when you go in there this morning, – you're gonna be full of juice, you hear me? I'm tellin' you, you're gonna Ace 'em. Just go Ace 'em Baby, okay?"

So I did.

Little Words – Big Deal

I was seated front row center for the first week of seminary – Beginning Greek class. I was all jacked up for this class because, though I do not have any great giftedness for languages, I do have an interest. I was one of those geeky little kids who tried to learn Elvish after my first reading of Tolkien. I had self-taught myself a little Latin. I went to a college where they made you read Sophocles in the original. Now, many years later with a much rustier brain, I was going back into Greek to read the New Testament. I knew that Jesus himself probably did not speak Greek to the disciples – most likely Aramaic, possibly Hebrew at times – but I was about to get a lot closer to his words than the King's English would ever allow. I was excited.

I noticed that many of my fellow students seemed equally stirred up. We were in the First Chapter of the Gospel of John.

> In the beginning was the Word, and the Word was with God, and the Word was God... and the Word became flesh and dwelt among us.

This is some of the most beautiful poetry ever written, and some of the simplest Greek in the New Testament. This is why our brilliant teacher had taken us there on the first day. She knew that she could get us through it and that we would feel like translators right off the mark. She wisely also let us bump right into the frustrations of translation. The bigger words were easy. The verbs she gave to us on that day, but she let us struggle a bit with the little words, the prepositions, "in," "with," and "among." She explained to us that many of the words had multiple meanings and that the translator had to use wisdom, discernment, and context to decide which word to supply to the text.

This is when some of my fellow students started to get nervous. They also were there to get closer to the words of Jesus, but some were hoping to ease their frustration with the multiple English translations and find out what the "correct" answer was. They were searching for certainty, and the professor kept bogging them down in discernment. They were discovering quickly that the little words could change the meaning in a big way. "The Word became flesh and dwelt *among* us" can also be translated

"The Word became flesh and dwelt *in* us." In fact, "in" is a more common translation of the Greek than "among" is. The students saw the theological conundrum of the choice almost immediately. They asked the teacher for the right answer. She told them why most translators chose "among" over "in", but allowed as how "in" was also a correct choice. Some of my fellow students started to breathe funny. They did not like the idea of two correct choices. They had not come to find a deeper level of mushy, they wanted solid. She gave them context and translator's choice. Smoke started to come out of some of their ears. Some of them had spinners for eyes. Some of them started making plans right then and there to transfer to the Baptist seminary across town. I watched them for a minute with amusement – fundamentalists often amuse me. But then I got lost in the theological possibilities.

Prepositions of place count. Whether God is near you, or in you, matters – a lot. Since babyhood, I had been told that Jesus was *near* me, knocking on the door of my heart, wanting to come in. John the Evangelist seemed to be implying in a big way, in many places, that God and Christ were already *in* me, and had been since I came into the world and possibly before. That Jesus had planted the seed of Himself in me, in everyone, and was sitting there waiting for the right conditions to germinate.

This started a bout of thinking that continues in me to this day. You have to be in a kinda strong and grounded place to work on this puzzle. You have to be pretty comfy with paradox. The Apostle Paul talked about riddles wrapped in enigmas viewed in murky mirrors – yeah, that kind of clear.

Here is the problem. The Kingdom of Heaven is in me. It was in me in some form before I recognized it, and with my intention, called it to quickness. But it is also all around me; I can see it and observe it in my garden and in the stars. And is it also among us – in community with all its frustrations and foibles. I couldn't get more than a heartbeat away from the kingdom if I tried, it is that close.

And yet, Jesus said that He stands at the door and knocks, waiting, beyond some kind of barrier. The door is a metaphor for some kind of barrier. My fundamentalist childhood said that the barrier was my sin, that I was depraved. Fallen. That evil was inside me and that Goodness had to ask to come in. That has never set right with me.

I like all kinds of stories. In the theological metaphor that is "Buffy the Vampire Slayer," The Apostle Joss* sets things up where Vampires (evil) cannot walk into the home (heart) uninvited. Humans carry their glory and sin and possibility of redemption with them wherever they go. Goodness (God) is already in the house – it came in with you – and evil has to beg entry. For a professed non-believer, Joss is fairly Gnostic. Joss could be burned at the stake in certain inquisitions.

Me, too. I am a Quaker.

When I face a theological conundrum, I try to hold it as precious and deny none of it. I live with it until I wrestle a blessing out of it. But when I have to make a functional decision, my experience of God trumps dogma and exegesis. This I know and declare to be true: when I first called out to Christ as a knowing adult, and sought His presence, He answered not from a place external to me, but from inside my soul. I work for the Kingdom; I fight the Lamb's War with the presumption that Christ is ahead of me working *in* everyone. All I have to do is find where He is working and assist.

I have met evil, but I have never experienced it as internal. It is always dissonant. Always wrong. Always against whom I was meant to be. Evil talks to me from outside. Christ talks to me from inside. I do have troubles sometimes with my listening, but I don't have a problem confusing the two.

This has made some startling differences in the way I walk my Christianity.

I cannot "bring anyone to Christ." He is already there. No one is "lost." He knows precisely where they are and what they need and He is on the job. I don't have to spend any prayer time, any worship time, inviting Him to come – we can just get on with it. I do not have to beg Him to hear my prayer. He cannot fail to hear it. I do not have to shout like my African brethren; He is not deaf nor far away. Do you know how much time and energy this saves?

So what can I do? I can preach the Good News. The Kingdom of Heaven is at hand. As close as your own palm print, actually. I can fan the burning embers of desire for faith into crackling little flames. I can tell people the truth about who they really are and what they were put here to do. I can participate in the laboratory of sanctification that is spiritual community. I can walk the roads of my vicinity looking in the ditches for the wounded and dying. And sometimes I can stand out on the porch with the vampires and back them off a bit so that the people in the house can enjoy their redemption and do their work in peace.

I have found that the paradoxes and conundrums become precious mysteries to explore when I have time, not problems that cause my hard drive to smoke.

It's a good deal.

Joss Whedon wrote and produced "Buffy the Vampire Slayer." It aired from 1997–2003. It is brilliant.

In Between

I was called in for a spiritual and psychological consult about an old woman who was dying in a care facility. Her child, an ex-client of mine, made the call. I had never met the mother.

The care facility was run by a religious organization. It was a place I would have allowed my mother to stay. Praying people all around. A full-time chaplain. Pleasant and peaceful surroundings.

But this mother was having a terrible time. She was deep into dementia, and had not been verbal with family or staff in weeks. She had not recognized anyone in months. She was extremely frail, not eating and only rarely taking sips of water. No one knew what was holding her to this life. Her living relations had visited and blessed her journey. No one knew of any unfinished business.

But she was not passing, and she was having intermittent bouts of terror. Screaming terrors. Trying to crawl through the wall terrors. All sorts of meds had been tried; none had worked. The child asked me to come and see if I had any ideas. The child asked me to come and pray. The family wanted someone cross-trained in mental health and spirituality. I was not at all confident that I could do anything that had not been done, but I knew I could come pray with the child. So I went.

I witnessed one bout of the screaming. Way beyond "sun-downers," and at the wrong time of day. Eyes wide open, looking into space. God-awful screams. The nerves of the child and the nursing staff were on edge. They had given her all the morphine that anyone's conscience would allow.

I talked with the child, and then sat by the mother. I held her hand – papery and cold in the hot room. We settled into prayer, and I prayed vocally for her. And then she turned her head and spoke to me.

"Who are you?"

"I'm Peggy."

"I don't know you, what are you doing here?"

"You are right – you don't know me. Your child called me. I am a counselor and a pastor. You seem to be having a lot of trouble.

"I'm in between – and I'm stuck. Have you ever been to In-be-tween?"

"No, I don't think so. Tell me about In-between."

"Oh, you'd know. It's awful. I can't come back and I am scared to death of going over."

"What are you scared of?"

"He's there. He's telling me to come to him."

"Who is he?"

"My husband."

Now, I knew about the husband. A lifetime abuser of women and children. A first-degree controller. An actual living nightmare when on earth – now several years gone. I had never met him, either, but I was glad of it.

"Is there anyone else there?" I asked.

"Yes, my parents, but they are farther away and quiet. But I can see them."

I turned to the child. Were the grandparents okay? "Yes, kind people, dead many, long years." The child hardly knew them, but loved them.

"Go to your parents", I said.

"I'm scared. I'm scared of stepping across. I don't think I can change my mind once I choose. My husband says I have to listen to him, that I need to obey him."

"Don't, okay? Tell him to go away. I'm pretty sure it is safe to cross. Call out for your mother and stretch out your hands and walk to her."

"I'm scared!"

"It's going to be okay."

"You come with me!"

"I'm pretty sure that I am not allowed to do that."

"See, you're scared too!"

"I'll hold your hand, and your child will hold your other hand. Okay?"

And we did.

She took a deep breath and shut her eyes, and never spoke again in this world. She didn't die for another 48 hours, but she didn't scream either. She rested peacefully and slipped away quietly.

To her parents, I presume.

Because the cord of Love is strong even when it is thin.

Turning Around

We were on a back road outside of Cave Junction, Oregon, having a day off on an extended preaching trip. My best friend and ministry partner, Alivia was driving the Unctionmobile. Our holy transport was an inferno-red PT Cruiser decked out with some Holy Ghost flames, a dashboard saint of Margaret Fell (the mother of Quakerism), a trinity-red #3 cue ball stick-shift knob and a license plate that reads UNKSHN, because Oregon would not give me seven letters. Unction is a perfectly good word that my Methodist-preacher grandfather used to use for any special blessing that came from God.

We were driving through the enclave of Takilma, a small spot on the Oregon-California border populated by anarchists, peaceniks, heavily armed aging hippies, and an assortment of folks who wouldn't stand out in that sort of a crowd. We had been discussing the nature of spiritual journeys, and had reached the consensus that it is always better to go forward rather than back, no matter what the circumstances. Naturally, at that point, we realized that we had missed our turn and were on a dead-end dirt road on the wrong side of town. We humbly turned around and headed back into Takilma.

Then we came upon a walking woman. She was beautifully attired in exotic cloth and dripping with dreadlocks. She extended her thumb. In Takilma, this passes for public transport, and – not wanting to appear un-local – we stopped and loaded her in. Her ganja perfume was quite striking. She thanked us for the lift and gave us directions to a farm down the road, which she said housed the local volunteer-staffed radio station: read pirate radio, as in Radio Free Takilma. This radio station served the community, calling out the volunteer fire brigade or the staff of the free clinic, or telling a mom without a phone that she needed to pick up a child at the Dome School. In between community services, any resident could run their own radio show; turns out we were transporting the mistress of Reggae. When we left her off, we exchanged a mutual blessing, and Liv and I proceeded on our way.

Immediately my stomach knotted – you know that feeling – the one you have when you have missed something really good, or when you have ignored a nudging of the Spirit. Alarmed, I turned towards Alivia, and it was clear I wasn't the only one disturbed. She said in a sad tone, "You know, we should have given her a CD." Alivia is a musician, gifted with a voice that God doesn't give out very often, and she had just that week released her first CD – and we had a box of them in the car.

"Turn around!" I said. "Take us back, and I'll try to find her! Rats! God put a real-live radio lady in the car, and we almost missed her!"

Alivia executed a beautiful, full speed U-turn, and back we went into Takilma for the third time. We found what we thought was the track into the ferny woods on which our lady had disappeared. In this part of the country, you want to be a little cautious about whose vegetable patch you enter unannounced. I walked onto the land, hoping I was in the right place. I met a man coming down the trail.

"Hello Friend – I'm looking for the radio lady."

"Hello yourself. She just signed on – back there in the trailer."

I walked up a narrow path in the brush until I saw a rusty old beaten-down trailer. I barged right in. Inside, it looked like a space shuttle. The radio lady didn't look surprised to see me; perhaps this lady was not surprised by much.

I got down on one knee and pleaded.

"I had to come back. You see, I'm a traveling Quaker preacher, and Alivia, whom you just met driving the Unctionmobile, has this week released her first album of truth music. We're here to preach and sing the Gospel tomorrow in Cave Junction. We should have given you a copy of the CD before we dropped you off. Could you, would you, please, oh please, give my best friend her very first radio air time?"

"Of course, I'd be glad to" said the Reggae princess.

She asked me to write down what song she should play, as well as the info on our gospel gig. I picked track 4, "Art of Life" – lovely song, very nature based – not too Jesus pushy- just right for Takilma, I thought. "Now, go get back in your car so you can hear it," she said, and dismissed me with a regal wave.

I thanked our radio patron, hugged her, laid every blessing I could think of on her, and ran for the car.

"Drive Livi, and get that radio on!" She did, and the mellow tones of our new friend came through the stereo speakers.

"Friends, this is Sister Mona Lisa, and as you know, this is usually an all-Reggae show, but today we have had a visitation."

She went on to talk about her lateness for her shift, the unusual pick-up by traveling Gospel ladies in a flamed out car, and my return and request.

"It is amazing to me how the Most High makes Herself known in our lives" she said, "I thought I was late, but God had something else in mind, and now I have the great honor to give Sister Alivia Biko her very first air time. Praise Be. Blessings on you, road sisters, you just keep on preaching the Good News – here is 'The Art of Life.'"

Then we heard Alivia's voice. But she was *not* singing "Art of Life," she was singing "Walk On," a song that is a refrain, interspersed with powerful bursts of Scripture. Alivia was on the air for sure, but God, not I, had called the tune! I whooped, I hollered, and then I noticed that Alivia was pretty quiet.

"What do you think? How do you feel?"

No answer.

"Liv, are you okay?"

No answer.

Hand waved in front of her face. No response. I gently put a hand on the wheel.

"Okay, were gonna slow this car down, okay? – That's it, lift your foot off the gas pedal, pull over just a little, that's right, stop real gentle – I think I'll drive for a bit."

I got out and opened Alivia's car door, got her out, supported her buckling knees, got her in on the other side, and off we were again. She recovered herself shortly, after the tears started to flow.

Friends, take it from me. In Christ, there is no such thing as lost; not physically, not spiritually. You may think you are on a detour, but don't count on it. The Most High will make Herself known. Participate, listen, be open, follow your leadings, grab the opportunities you are given with both hands. Turn back if you have to. All things are possible. Glory – nothing less – is around the next corner. Don't miss her!

Even if she's wearing dreadlocks and has her thumb out.

Hell's Freezing Over

The lunch table was full of insightful, visionary, powerful, spiritual women. We were talking about what it would take for our corner of the Body of Christ to embrace an application of our professed testimony of equality. Specifically, what it would take for the spiritual sea to change enough to make gender identity and sexual orientation non-obstacles to membership and ministry.

"What if we just opened that door and walked through it and let them watch? – Maybe they'd follow," I proposed.

"Yeah, when Hell freezes over!" said one of my sisters.

That phrase haunted me for a while after that. It rattled around in my heart like a marble in a glass milk bottle. Then the bottle broke, and it was spilt milk all over, but I had a jagged glass epiphany.

That is our job. That is precisely our job. We are supposed to be freezing Hell. Turning the thermostat of evil down till the devil is wearing thermal underwear.

Hell requires conflagration. Badness expends huge energy. Evil itches and requires lots of scratching, which leads to angry inflammation. But Hellfire can be quenched.

The best way to chill inequality is to not cooperate with it, not to ignore it. Racism is not by any means conquered in our world or our church. But in the last century, it has been moderated by courageous people refusing to accept that it is the norm. Racism lives, but legal Jim Crow is history. People, a few people at first, just refused to be segregated. Black people and white people. They just stopped cooperating. Police violence and inequitable incarceration need awareness and interventions. It starts when we stop cooperating with silence and cover-up.

This is how you have a chilling effect on evil.

We were created to be effective. Each one of us individually, and all of us together. Individually, we can douse and stomp on fires of evil that spark up around us. As a people of God we can be the cool soft rain that puts the forest fire to bed.

Hell loves a mob: especially a trauma-crazed mob, an unthinking, angry mob. Hell especially loves an armed mob; guns are nice, but machetes will do. But it is amazing what a few people, or even one person, can do to a mob. Hell was having a picnic in My Lai, Vietnam, when Hugh Thompson, Lawrence Colburn and Glenn Andreotta landed their helicopter between their comrades and their comrade's innocent prey. They stopped the carnage. The devil considered those guys to be party crashers. They were called traitors when they got home. Eventually, they were decorated as heroes.

What we don't know is how many similar atrocities, in that war and in the wars since then have been stopped short by one person saying, "Hey, that's not what we're here for," or "Don't even think about it." They don't get written up as heroes for preventing evil, but it happens all the time. The devil doesn't want you to know that he gets thwarted a thousand times for every time he succeeds in getting drunk on mayhem.

Do not think that it is only warriors who block disaster. I have seen a pig-tailed eight-year-old walk into a knot of bullies and take a scared six-year old by the hand and walk them out with a "Shame on you – I'm telling" look.

The truth is that evil is a sissy. Our spiritual adversary and all his minions are cowards of the first order. Hell can be frozen by the kindness of a child, the courage of a man, the voice of a boy, the persistence of an old woman. What we have to do is wake up, speak up, and step right in.

Jesus Fire Dancer

One of my church folk invited me to come down to the Riverfront Park in our town and watch her spin about her head small, flaming objects attached to chains. Not everyone knows a fire dancer, but I do. Some of her friends were dancing with sticks aflame at both ends, and the dancers were accompanied by a group of people banging on drums. All this was done after dark, of course, on this cool, early April Easter Vigil.

It was all very tribal, very pre-Christian, or maybe post-Christian. The dancers moved to the beat we all heard, but also to melodies heard only by their spiritual ears. The fires made great "whooshy" sounds as they whizzed about, describing circles in the dark air as if some wizard was teaching geometry to an unseen class. The circles got big, the circles got small; ellipses and figure eights appeared around the dancers' heads, feet and sometimes between their legs. The attitude of the dancers seemed serene, reflective, in control. Occasionally, flames from one dancer would interact with the flames of another. I saw flames lick at clothing and hair, but no one ignited themselves.

All in all, it was a great Holy Saturday activity. I am a Quaker, and one of our testimonies is that every day is a holy day and that all activities can be sacramental; but we are free to participate in all that leads us towards God, and the Easter Story certainly does that. I have long had a fascination with the Saturday piece of the story, called by some the "Harrowing of Hell." To harrow means to plow, or deeply disturb the earth; to disrupt the status quo.

It is clear that both the Apostles Peter and Paul believed that Christ was not inactive during the time between Friday afternoon and Sunday morning. In icons He is sometimes pictured as a preacher, speaking the truth to the souls in Sheol. Talk about a captive audience!

Sometimes he is pictured as a liberator bursting the gates of Hell open from the inside. Eastern Orthodox icons depict Hell as cold and empty with one or two chained demons and Jesus, resurrected, surrounded by former inmates. That's a great picture.

Hell exists; but the door is open and the exit sign is clearly marked. It is the church that has rebuilt the gates of Hell and found useful the scare tactic of inescapable torment.

While sitting in the dark and cold, contemplating Holy Saturday and watching neo-pagan fire dancers, I received a new image of Jesus: Fire Dancer. In my vision, He shows up in the dark and cold of Hell and converses with the adversary:

a: Welcome. Always knew you'd end up here.

JC: Thanks. I make it everywhere eventually, you know.

a: Really? I think your traveling days are over, bud. Like the flames?

JC: Actually, I do like the flames. Mind if I play a little?

He reaches down and picks up two handfuls of combustion and starts drawing circles in the air. A crowd appears. A drumbeat starts from somewhere deep. He steps lightly and playfully, showing His mastery, His serenity, His cool. The crowd starts dancing.

a: Cute tricks, been done before, but it's going to get old.

JC: Anybody ever done this?

The circle of flame above his head expands explosively, and He hurls it towards the gates. Those evil old doors crack and fly outward, and Jesus the fire dancer leads a parade out, up, and away.

Jesus Gives Green Stamps

I was at the Redemption Center. My arms cradled the stack of eight by eight-inch newsprint books, pages warped by the spit that had glued the seemingly infinite number of tiny, green paper squares onto them.

Mother had despaired of ever finding the time to empty the kitchen drawer of the logjam of paper scraps acquired as a mercantile bonus at the grocery, gas station, and department store. They were just slightly too valuable to toss, but rarely valuable enough to warrant the attention of my busy, creative mother. So she told me that if I did the pasting, I could benefit from the exchange. It took all of a Saturday afternoon, but in the end I had ten completed books of S and H Green Stamps. So it was with those vast riches that I entered the land of redemption.

At that time, any municipality worthy of the name had a Redemption Center where you could trade your books for goods. Honestly, I do not know how they covered the overhead. But in those magical places were rows and rows of shiny small home appliances, knick-knacks, sports equipment, baby supplies, and toys. Things that middle class mothers desired, but could not fit into their everyday budget. A store where you could buy without money. After an agonizing search, I left dragging a croquet set – fun for the whole family, and an act of altruism on my part.

But it must have been spring, near Easter, because I also remember sitting in church shortly thereafter trying to figure out what "Jesus, our Lord and Redeemer" had to do with Green Stamps. Life can be perplexing for children in religious families.

This memory wafted up recently while I was sitting in church singing, "I know that my redeemer lives," my favorite Easter hymn. I've been to seminary; I am perplexed at a much higher level than I was as a child. I know that Redeemer is a Hebrew word. It does not appear in what we call the New Testament. The word never comes out of the mouth of Jesus or off of the pen of Paul. The statement, "I know that my redeemer lives" comes instead from old father Job. The story of Job is considered to be one of the oldest stories in written human history. It is a story, not just about suffering, but about response to suffering – Job's response and the crummy responses of his "Who needs friends like these?" friends. Job's response is a stand of faith; faith in himself, in the God he is angry with, and in the scales of justice. He says, "I know that my redeemer lives and that I shall see Him." Job refuses to allow his friends to talk him out of his self-image of decency, and his belief in the decency of God, despite ample evidence to the contrary.

The only named example we have in scripture of a functioning redeemer is in the story of Ruth. The redeemer is the good man, Boaz. Naomi, a widow, and her daughter-in-law Ruth have, through no fault of their own, come upon very hard times. Boaz is a near kinsman with adequate resources, and thus by religious law has the right, responsibility, and privilege to set things right. He does so, and has been remembered forever for his goodness.

It is for such a redeemer that Job hopes and waits. Job knows that his hope is beyond human resources, and eventually God steps up.

I do not know who first made the connection and called Jesus Christ the redeemer. I have no argument with this. Christ, who by His birth became a near kinsman while keeping the resources of heaven, had and has the right, responsibility, and privilege of redeeming a world that has fallen upon hard times. He said his mission was to bring good news, bind and heal wounds, and set captives free.

But the teachings of Jesus Christ do make it clear that we are also to be redeemers. The Sermon on the Mount is all about using Heavenly resources to make things right in the world. We are to raise up and encourage the poor, to protect the small, weak, and hurting, to set captives free. We are to be a blessing to this Earth, not a curse – a force for justice. We understand that redemption comes through relationship, not through might.

We are near kinsmen to the poor of the world, the abused, the mentally ill, and the violent. We have the resources. We have the responsibility. We have the right. We have the example of the faith of Job, the actions of Boaz, the teachings of Christ. The world is our redemption center.

Geek Squad Jesus

I spent a portion of my childhood inside an organ. Our church organ was old, even during my childhood. It had fallen upon hard times, having been sold with the building by the Lutherans to a small, poor, band of Evangelical Methodists. It was as big as a small house, from the motor in the basement that filled its mighty bellows to the 16-foot pipes soaring above the sanctuary. My mother played it every Sunday. Trained on piano, she taught herself how to play the two keyboards and the extra keyboard of foot pedals. She had nearly perfect pitch, and this organ that hadn't had proper maintenance in decades must have driven her to distraction. This is how my father came to be the organ's repairman.

He claimed it started with a toaster. She wanted to throw it out. He told her it was perfectly good, it just needed a little work. He was kinda cheap. She handed it to him: "Fine, fix it." So he took it apart and figured out what was wrong and fixed it. He was proud. She was cautiously impressed. She said, "You think you can fix anything, don't you?" He allowed, as this might be close to the truth. She said, "Fine – fix my organ." And his career as a repairer of fine wooden tracker pipe organs began.

He climbed around inside that thing for years. And when there was occasionally something he wanted to reach in a space too small for an adult, he sent in one of us children. We learned obedience – touch this, not that. Put your feet here, not there. He was good with machines, and good with children. He was bold. And he knew that you couldn't fix the organ from the keyboard, you had to get inside it to do the job.

I cannot help the fact that he shaped my theological impressions. I wouldn't want to.

I do not think that the death of Christ had anything to do with punishment. Even Pilate knew that what was before him was a farce. So what *did* happen on that day outside Jerusalem almost 2000 years ago?

I think something broken got fixed. I see Jesus the Redeemer as Jesus the Repairman. Tech Support, if you will. See, there was this system called "Time and Space" and running on this system was a program called "Humanity." And it got all buggy. The code called "The Law" just wasn't working. So the System Designer had to crack it all open. Get inside, wipe some stuff, patch other stuff, write some whole new stuff.

It's a frustrating job, but somebody's got to do it. It helps if the somebody doing the fixing knows what they are doing. It also helps to have patience. Sometimes, people are just dumb; they do not interface well with the program, and you have to very patiently explain to them, again and again, how the thing is supposed to work. But if the code is all glitchy, you have to get your hands dirty. And you can't fix the code from the desktop.

So for me, the incarnation, life, teaching, death, and resurrection of Christ are all part of the same repair job. He got in, bringing with Him tools, skills, and a supremely solid connection to the Designer. He ran the program, personally. Diagnostics were completed. One of the buggiest parts of the program was death, so he ran that too. But death was not the end; resurrection – the reboot to end all reboots – was needed. And he emptied the recycle bin called Hell while He was at it. The Law was overwritten, the concept of clean and unclean wiped. Do you know what a time saver that was? Efficiency upgrade deluxe. Religious practice within the confines of tribal groups was made obsolete. Limitless grace was written in.

Then the lovely, fixed program had to be turned over to the users. So a help desk was established. Some people call it the Holy Spirit, some people call it the Present Christ, some people call it The Inner Light – there are lots of names for it. But it is there 24/7.

So we run the program. Seek the Kingdom. Pursue peace. Get serenity. Achieve enlightenment. War and hate are options under the free will part of the program; so are glory, sacrifice, and love. Calamity is just part of the set up. Calamity makes room for altruism and compassion. The whole thing works imperfectly, very imperfectly, but that is because of the human interface, not the program. The program works just fine. The human learning curve is steep, but that is also part of the design.

Everybody in the program has a task. Finding it and performing it is the work of being human.

I am a minister of the Gospel of Jesus Christ. I work for tech support. I run tutorials. I coach new users. I scan for viruses. I help people with their upgrades. I try to keep a very solid connection. Occasionally, I help people bust out of dead-end spots they get themselves into. It is a good gig. Frustrating at times, but very satisfying at others.

I come by it naturally. Dad would understand.

No More Scapegoat Jesus

Facing the righteous indignation of an eight-year-old is a terrible thing.

She stormed into the house, dramatically dropped her school bag, and slammed the door. My normally well-behaved and ebullient second-grade daughter turned on me with eyes full of rage. Nothing less than rage.

"What's the matter, hon?"

"She held us after the bell! All of us!"

"Who? Did what?"

"The teacher. Ian and John were talking, but she punished us all! She made us stay after. *She made us put our heads on our desks! I wasn't talking! I listen! She had no right to punish me!"*

I started a brief explanation of classroom management and why a teacher might try the admittedly lame tactic of using group pressure to control the few bad apples. Then I stopped. She was having none of it. She wasn't mad at the boys. She was furious with the misadministration of justice. I asked her if she wanted me to talk to the teacher. She wanted me to talk to the principal. She wanted me to get the teacher fired. She knew to her marrow that punishing the innocent for the sins of the guilty was injustice of cosmic proportions. She couldn't believe that they would let someone with such an obviously faulty moral compass teach children.

I knew right then that transmitting any semblance of Christianity to this child was going to be a challenge. Because sometime, someplace, some Sunday school teacher was going to explain the core of the Christian message as this: You, little girl, along with everyone else, are guilty. God needs to punish somebody, because that is just how it is, somebody has to be punished. It doesn't really matter that you get the right person, so the Good News is that somebody really good can step up and get punished in your place, and then you get off Scot-free.

I knew this kid would be buying none of that.

Unfortunately, I could not put the kid in stasis until I figured this one out. I started then to try to find different ways to talk about God, Jesus, and why death and resurrection are an important part of the story. It has taken me decades. The child is grown and gone. I am still working on it. I am not finished, but I have some handles.

The break for me started to come when I began to look seriously at the metaphors used for Christ. The most important one is this: "Behold, the Lamb that takes away the sins of the world." This phrase comes from the earliest explainers of the Christ story: the Apostles, those who knew Him, and those who sat at the feet of the first witnesses. They were all Jews. They were using a Jewish metaphor – the temple sacrifice, which must have been especially poignant for those who had witnessed the destruction of the temple in the year 70 AD, the end of the animal sacrifice system. Jesus, they explained, was God's Lamb. Which brings us right back to "He was punished for your sins." Unless you go back and look carefully at the instructions for the temple rituals.

I spent some time in the Pentateuch looking at the instructions. The sacrifices are all about community and restoring community. Bad behavior negatively effects community. Bad enough behavior breaks community. There is an element of justice and even, in the last resort, banishment from community. There is also a way to restore community. I discovered this when I found out the difference between the scapegoat and the lamb.

Nobody talked much about the scapegoat in the church I grew up in. But there it is in in the book. Once a year, the priest was to do a ritual, in which all the sins of all the people were symbolically placed upon the back of a goat, and the goat was pushed out the gates and into the wilderness, presumably to meet a bad fate. What happened to the goat didn't really matter. The punishment was being sent away from the community. The sins got sent away, not the people.

The lamb was a whole different deal. The lamb was clean, spotless, good, and the lamb was not punished, the lamb was consumed. The lamb was fit to be eaten; fit to be taken in. The lamb was giving your best stuff to the community to show that your intention was to be restored. It was about making amends, not escaping judgment. The lamb was taking responsibility. The lamb was investing in community.

Then the light bulb went on. I had been taught a scapegoat Jesus theology mislabeled as lamb theology. Jesus was the best God had, invested in us, not punished for us. Jesus was fit to be consumed, taken in: this was the message He himself taught at the last chance dinner. The Romans thought death was a punishment. But God is not just a bigger, badder Caesar. God understands that death is the universal human experience, and that joining us even in death is a connection of cosmic order. The ultimate community building experience.

But just wait one heretical minute! Did not Paul talk about "propitiation for our sins"? Yes, he did. I think Paul was spending way too much time hanging around with the Romans. I think it was starting to wear off on him.

So I don't believe in scapegoat Jesus anymore. I don't believe He was punished for my sins. I believe He taught me what to do about my sins: recognize them, send them away (i.e. stop), and then re-invest in community with my best stuff. Make my own amends wherever possible, and trust in the eternal resources that He made possible by joining my community to cover what I cannot. Come back, it works.

So what happened to the indignant little girl? She doesn't sit much under the teachers of orthodox Christendom. I think she absorbed the best ethics of Christianity and Quakerism and let the rest go. I am okay with that. But most tellingly, she is a teacher.

God Does Not Need Your Praise

The church pew was polished hardwood, so was the floor. I couldn't have been very old, because my patent-leather Mary Janes were swinging freely, well above the floor. We were all singing the Doxology; of course, at that age I didn't know it was called the Doxology, it was just the song that came after they passed the pretty wooden plate with the red velvet liner. I had been singing this song since I was about two, singing it by rote memory, syllable by syllable completely without understanding:

> Prays God Frum who mall bleh sings flow
> Prays Hih mall cree chairs hear bee low
> Prays hih ma buv yee hev in lee hose
> Prays Fa thur sun and hole ee Ghost
> Ah, MEN!

I had been singing this on call in my baby soprano to much applause. But as far as I was concerned, it might as well have been Latin, or Martian.

And then on that one Sunday, about age five, something in my brain clicked, and I realized the song was in English and that I understood the words.

> Praise God from whom all blessing flow!
> Praise Him all creatures here below!
> Praise Him above, ye heavenly hosts!
> Praise Father, Son, and Holy Ghost!
> Amen.

It was quite a little epiphany. And it was my first chance to actually do any praising, since it was my first understanding that any praising was going on. I dutifully reported to my mother that the song actually meant something.

But it started my little head a thinkin'. First, I had to work out my confusion about the Trinity. I had a notion about God the Father, and Jesus was a regular figure on the Sunday school flannelgraph board, but this Holy Ghost guy was confusing. Back then he was definitely billed as the Holy Ghost, not the Holy Spirit, and this caused great confusion for me with Casper the Friendly Ghost. This was made worse by visiting the church of my Pentecostal cousins, because every time the Holy Ghost showed up, all the grownups started yelling and running around, which was precisely what happened in the cartoon.

Life can be confusing for children in religious families.

Then, after a while, I started to wonder about the whole idea of praising God.

I had a great mother. She believed in praising children for their good behavior and accomplishments more than punishing them for their wrongs and failings. I knew my mother loved me, and that she enjoyed her children, but even as a kid I understood that there was an ulterior motive in the praise. She was manipulating our behavior, and mostly it worked. It was a good system.

So I mean, really, did God need to be flattered, to have his good behavior reinforced? To prevent Divine temper tantrums? Did He need to be told how good He was? And weren't we God's children, so shouldn't *He* be praising *us*? To let us know when our deeds were approvable? Church music telling God how good He was began to be a problem for me. (When I was a kid, God was definitely a "He.")

Things did not get better with the introduction of pop music into the church in the 60s and 70s. In a decade, we went from preachers who tried to convince kids to smash their records of "the devil's music" to preachers in white-guy afros trying to do Jesus pop/rock.

In most protestant churches, music wars resulted. In bigger churches, segregation of worship services by musical preference became common and continues to this day. Refugees from the Christian style wars started their own churches where they did not have to argue about it. They embraced the theory that cool, hip new music would bring people in the door and you could work on their belief systems later. This is still a popular theory. In many churches, the balance of the worship service changed from an egalitarian mix of music, prayer, and preaching, to lots of praise music with a medicinal capsule of doctrine slipped in at some point.

Most of this music was neither hip nor cool; it was third-rate treacle imitating the second-rate treacle of the popular genre. Melodramatic, sexually frustrated, mostly drug deprived teenagers, especially the girls, loved it because you could work yourself into a nice emotional state with a semi-orgasmic conversion experience at the end, all the while keeping it public and holy. And we were told that this was precisely what God wanted. That God just eats this stuff up. That Heaven is pretty much going to be an eternal praise service with a kick-butt band. Well, at least we could hope the band would be better.

I watched this and wondered what kind of God this was – some cosmic, insecure Hollywood starlet who needed a multitudinous posse of sycophants to prop up the divine ego? I had better self-esteem than that, and I was 13.

After taking a long break from the whole thing, I came back to my faith, and back to Christian music through my hillbilly roots. Bluegrass and southern harmony had a lot more meat, reality, and integrity than the vast majority of "Contemporary Christian Music."

But as I became more involved in organized religion, I had to deal with the praise issue on an adult level. There was no doubt that scripture praises God and recommends praise as an activity. King David did it, Jesus did it, and Paul did it. Two thousand years of Christian history has included the practice. I really couldn't just blow it off. But I could never come to grips with a God who needed our praise, or who was moved by it.

Then one day, while swinging my heels over the edge of another pew, I had another little epiphany. God doesn't need my praise. God isn't changed by my praise. I need to speak about the goodness of the world and the world's Creator because it detoxifies my soul. I hear constant messages about how this life stinks and how the world is going to hell in a hand basket and why I should be very afraid, and maybe despair, and none of it is true. I have to counter that poison with something. Gratitude and praise is that something.

When I sit in my Quaker meeting, we have no preacher and no band. We reach a nice balance. We sing a little, often positive affirmations of God's goodness – no shame, no guilt. We find the truest stuff that we can. Some of it is new, some of it is very old, some of it we have had to write. We try to avoid treacle. We detox ourselves and start to detox the space around us when we put the truth out there. We pray a little, and then we get real quiet and listen. No big Sunday emotional feast that leaves us hungry by mid-week. And no notion that God sits hungry, waiting for us to show up and offer a meal of flattery.

How I Became Invincible

I was on the kitchen counter, considering taking refuge on top of the refrigerator. My initial screams of terror had given way to rapid, shallow breathing. My eyes were dilated; my heart was pounding. My brain was sending out signals about imminent death. My adrenaline level was high enough that ripping through a wall to escape seemed sensible – anything to get away from the nauseating, skin-crawling horror before me. I was Jackie Kennedy crawling over the back of that Cadillac. Oh, God, save me!

The mouse on the kitchen floor was perhaps two inches long, if you included the tail. My seven-year-old daughter was standing nearby, laughing hysterically.

There were some parts of my brain that were fully aware of the stupidity of this whole scene. But those parts were totally trumped by my old brain. And my old brain was attempting to save me from a saber-toothed tiger.

Welcome to the world of phobias – fears that don't make sense. The problem here is that wires get crossed, and the feeling of danger and the actual level of danger are severely mismatched. It can get you laughed at by children, but it isn't funny if your alarm bells are going off.

The old brain is arguably useful if there is a real, imminent, life-threatening danger, and the best answer is running or hitting. For most of us, of course, this situation is rare to the point of non-existent. Yet so many of us still spend so much of our time afraid. And there are plenty of hucksters, and worse, who want you to feel afraid even when you don't need to, because the old brain makes you very obedient. They want to make you phobic of life.

Actually, most of the time, we need our fancy new brain with all its reasoning capacities and creative problem-solving abilities. When the old brain plays its trump card, you lose everything that makes you human. Reason, speech, altruism, relationships, and the ability to pray – they all get thrown off the back of the wagon like granny's pump organ on the Oregon Trail. So much baggage.

But there's nothing you can do about it. It's automatic, right?

Wrong!

I have discovered that my brain, even my old brain, is within my control. A brilliant guy* who trained me to listen to trauma survivors taught me this. Listening to detailed stories of rape, genocide, and torture is not fun. But I learned that I could be present to people in their horror without becoming horrified. I could be that resilient by choice, and by a very simple procedure.

All I need to do is take a deep breath, and soften and expand my abdominal muscles and pelvic floor muscles. It's harder work than it sounds, but if you can do this, you can take the pressure off the vagus nerve at the base of the spine. That nerve is what sends the signals that tell the brain to panic. This procedure is the exact opposite of the gasp and clinching that we do when frightened. Anything that I receive thus – softly – cannot, will not, and does not hurt me. I practiced this for a few years and got really good at it in counseling sessions. I became very resilient; my burnout risk plummeted.

Then I saw that smart guy again. He listened to my report and he said.

"Um, Peggy, you do know that you can do that all the time if you like, right?"

"What, just live soft? Like, all the time?"

"Uh, huh."

I tried it first on some times when my feeling of safety didn't match my real safety. It worked. It was work, but I could turn off my fear response if I wanted to. I did not have to face the ridicule of children, HA!

Then I waited for a chance to try it out in a setting of actual threat. I found I could quiet my old brain and keep all my capacities on-line. Present. Mindful. Dangerous instead of endangered.

Yea, though I walk through the Valley of the Shadow of Death, I shall not fear evil – Thou preparest a table for me in the midst of mine enemies. (Psalm 23)

You can't eat in a truly panicked state. To have the table set in the middle of a battle is an amazing picture of how things are supposed to be for us. Relax, take a load off, eat.

If I forget, and I do sometimes, I can still get freaked. But I don't have to; I can turn it off, if I want. If I don't take care of myself and sleep and eat and play, I lose some of my strength to do what I know I can do. But it is my choice.

I am resilient, with the option of invincibility. It is what I was created to be.

For we are more than conquerors, through Him who loved us. (Romans 8:37)

I have always known this theologically. I am a child of God. I am safe when things are quiet. I am in the palm of God's hand when things are nutty. I am safe if you don't agree with me, if you don't like me, or even if you are actually out to get me. I am safe if I am dead, because I am not my body and I live in God. I can choose to feel that foundational safety any time I choose.

For right now we are children of God, what we will yet become remains to be seen (I John 3:2)

With deep and abiding gratitude to God and Dr. J. Eric Gentry of Sarasota, Florida.

My Favorite Superpowers

I was walking down the street with my four-year-old daughter. Well, actually, I was walking; she was running ahead – full tilt. I wasn't worried about her, because she was a pretty well-trained child, and I knew I could rein her in with my voice. I was enjoying the sight of her moving like every baby racehorse ever born. As she approached the corner, I called out, "That's far enough, honey." She started her deceleration. Then she turned around, tiny hands on tiny hips and eyes of blue flame surrounded by a sunburst of yellow hair. She was clearly a little put out with me.

"Mommy, there is something I have to tell you."

"Okay, baby, what?"

"Someday, when I am running like that, I am just going to take off and start flying."

"Wow!"

"I thought you might be scared – so I am telling you."

"Thanks, hon, you're right, that might scare me."

"I'll be just fine, but if I am flying, I might not come back when you call."

"Thanks for the warning. You would come back eventually, wouldn't you?"

"Yes – I'll always come home for lunch."

"Great to know that – you gonna let me hold your hand to cross the street?"

"Yes."

Ask a preschooler if humans have, or can acquire, superpowers and you will often get an affirmative. I am told that this is true even where children don't have TV or movies.

What an amazingly old story. Hercules old, Moses old, Buddha old. Shaolin, Shaman old. It is also new. Jedi new, Marvel and DC new. I cannot think of a culture in which there is not a story line of mixed god/humans, or humans who attain a superhuman level of enlightenment and skills that go with it. The crux of the story is always what they do with the powers – save themselves, save the planet, or seduction and self-appropriation of the power to the destruction of themselves and others. Mr. Jung called these stories archetypal, meaning hardwired into the human mind. I think it is so universal that it must be true. God has put into us a truth so strong that every four-year-old believes it. And even after we crush the literal possibility out of the minds of our children, it is a truth so strong that it oozes out of our consciousness every time we tell a tale.

We are meant to be so much more than we are.

John the beloved disciple, John of Patmos, writing a letter:

> Beloved, we are even here and now God's children; it is not yet disclosed or made clear what we shall be, but we know that when He is manifested, we shall resemble and be like Him, for we shall see Him just as He really is. (1 John 3:2)

We have gotten immune to hearing "Everyone is a child of God", blah blah, metaphor, blah. John's ancient readers would not have heard it that way. They would have heard "Right now you are Hercules; what you are going to become can't even be described, but it will make him look like a sissy."

I have come to believe that this is true, that we are supposed to be superheroes. I have come to know this experientially. I am going to tell you about my top five favorite superpowers. You will probably dismiss this because it doesn't involve capes, and tights, and leaping tall buildings. You will say, "I don't want cheesy metaphorical powers, I want a light saber, I want bullets to bounce off my chest." But I say to you, the light saber is the metaphor. These powers are real, they are available, and if you surrender to the Divine, you will get your own set. And when you discipline yourself and learn their use, your life will be transformed.

Power #1:

I have become frequently impervious to insult and offense. This was the first power that I discovered and so named. I was shown that just because someone is offensive, it does not mean that I have to be offended. I can choose, and offense is so rarely a good choice. Offense is a huge waster of time and emotional energy. I have much better uses for my time.

Power #2:

I can forgive those who actually hurt me – the ones who do it accidentally, and the ones who do it intentionally. This power breaks chains of bondage. It crushes walls of isolation. It allows me to move through regions that otherwise I would have banished myself from. It erases enemies. It short-circuits revenge. It stops wars.

Power #3:

I have started to have what I call "Quixotic vision." Like the old Don from La Mancha, I have started to see people as God sees them. This is amazing. Some of the human trash of our society, the ones we warehouse, or worse, abandon to the streets, are beautiful and saintly. Some of the most physically beautiful, smart, and powerful, are actually wizened, shrunken and deformed in their souls. The scariest part of this power is looking in the mirror.

Power #4:

I can travel through time. Not kidding here. I am connected to a supernatural being that exists completely outside of time. Through that One, I can communicate and work in other places and times. So far, this is mostly through the work of prayer. I have prayed for my grandparents; I pray for my grandchildren who are not yet conceived. When I work with a person who was damaged as a child, I pray for the child they were, sending them strength and hope, to arrive at the day of their healing. I pray for my own death. I believe that the universe changes when I pray. Not always the way I want it to change, but it changes.

Power #5:

I am becoming hyper-resilient. One of my favorite story heroes is Buffy the Vampire Slayer. A cool thing about Buffy is that she takes her hits but she heals fast. A good night's sleep after the worst day fighting evil, and she is back at it again. Me too. If I take care of myself, sleep good, eat right, and escape to my fortress of solitude every so often, I do not run out of energy or hope. If I disconnect from my Divine power source through will or inattention, I fail. If I ignore the restorative spiritual disciplines, I might as well have a back pocket full of Kryptonite. I wilt. I whimper. I lose all my other powers. I screw up. I die.

So there you have it. I am "out" as a superhero. Deal.

But I leave you with another lesson from Buffy. At the series finale, Buffy and her friends defeat the ultimate evil by finding a way to break the Buffy-world rule that "Once to every generation there comes a slayer." They elevate every potential slayer to full force, all at once. They kick evil butt. They unlock this truth: we are *all* supposed to be superheroes. There are infinite powers. There are infinite skill sets. Evil doesn't stand a chance.

Let's go save the planet.

It's still okay to hold hands when you cross the street.

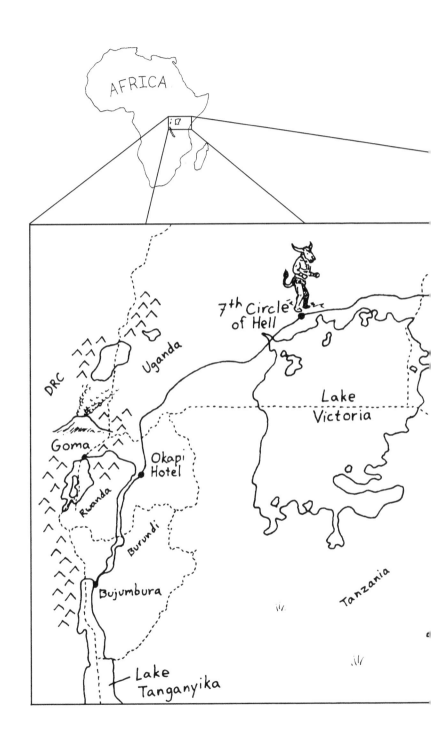

Last Homely House

Nairobi

Kenya

Mombasa

Pirates
Be Here

.

Africa

I am prepared to go anywhere, provided it be forward.

—David Livingstone

There is a large rock just south of Bujumbura. It marks the place where David Livingstone and Henry Stanley stayed for two nights in 1871 while ascertaining that Lake Tanganyika was not the source of the Nile.

David Livingstone was stark raving mad. Many of the great British explorers were. But he had a motive to his madness: he was an abolitionist. He hated slavery. He believed that economic development in Africa would end the slave trade at its source. He also subscribed to the theory that Christianizing Africa would help, although he spent much more time exploring and documenting botany than preaching. It is officially noted that he made one, and one only, convert to Christianity in 15 years. He knew that economic development needs trade routes. He also knew that roads in sub-Saharan Africa weren't happening any time soon, and that rivers make pretty good roads. So he started mapping the great river systems, hoping for navigable connections. His holy grail was the headwaters of the Nile.

He walked – as in, on foot – across the entire width of the African subcontinent. Then, having done that, he signed up to do it again from south to north. Demonstrably insane. His wife, Mary, missed him badly and came to Tanzania to visit him – she died within weeks of malaria. Livingstone himself seems to have been saved from malaria by his pioneering daily use of quinine. It did not save him from several other diseases, or dysentery, or parasites.

He was never lost, although Europe lost track of him for six years. Stanley was a journalist sent to find him or his grave. What he found was a broken and miserably ill man, who still wanted to go up the length of Tanganyika – so they did.

He refused to come home with Stanley. He died two years later in the care of Chief Chitambo, in present day Zambia. Two of his bearers carried his body a thousand miles to the coast, where it was shipped to England. Except for his heart, which they cut out and buried where he died. Losing your heart to Africa is a very real risk.

Freedom

My severe allergy to all things pre-dawn did not stop me. I had slipped silently out of bed and closed the doors to the children's rooms. It was chilly, so I wrapped up in a blanket and made myself a cup of coffee. I turned on the TV, twisting the volume knob down low. It was February 11, 1990, though it was ten hours further into the day in South Africa. I had gotten up, waking without an alarm, to watch the live coverage of a man at the pinnacle of human dignity. There was Nelson Mandela, walking out of prison after 27 years of unjust captivity. The African sun warmed me from ten thousand miles away. As he pumped his fist in the air, my heart pumped pure joy, and tears washed my face.

They had offered him his "freedom" five years earlier, on the condition that he renounce the revolution that had gotten him there. To their shock he turned them down. For the next five years they negotiated with him the conditions of his release until there were no conditions. They needed him to give them liberty from the shame of having held captive an innocent man. Their big mistake? They were under the impression that they had freedom to offer him, when the fact was that their apartheid, and their prison bars, had never taken this free human's birthright. They had nothing to bargain with, leaving them to beg.

His revolution had been built on the truth of equality, and so, in time would be won, whether he fought or not, whether he walked the earth at liberty or sat with the truth in a jail cell. It was the oppressors who were bound, held captive by their tiny ideologies, and so it was they who eventually pleaded with the free man to give them their liberty.

I just had to see it, with my own eyes, in real time; that kind of shining, stellar, stunning truth and beauty demand attendance.

I was reminded of that moment recently when I heard someone make the following remark. The context was a situation where the speaker was looking at the possibility of an uncomfortably mixed group. The comment was: "If (they) were here, I might lose the freedom to be myself."

Wow, what kind of tragically fragile freedom is that?

A freedom where external circumstances can cause an inability to access and express your core identity is no freedom at all. I wish this was a rare condition – but I think that it is rather common.

Jesus said that we would know the truth and that it was the truth that would make us free. Freedom is just this – a practical, working acquaintance with truth. If you know the truth about yourself, that you are an immortal being, created to exhibit glory, truth, honor, joy and love, then no one can take your freedom from you. No one can intimidate it out of you. No prison can confine your soul or its expression. No gun or bomb or threat thereof can kill your freedom.

We have fear-mongers at the highest levels of culture, politics, and religion, all telling us that our freedom is fragile and under attack. They attempt to bring us to that Orwellian place where we surrender all expressions of our liberty in the name of protecting liberty. They want us to isolate ourselves within walls of fear, and then to preemptively attack outside those walls.

What nonsense!

Your freedom, our freedom, is inviolable. It is built on the truth of equality and justice, and so will triumph, no matter who attacks. You can take it anywhere, in anyone's presence, without risk.

We say that there are those who have died for the cause of freedom. Actually, they have died nobly in the cause of physical and political liberty, which are *expressions* of freedom. They were willing to die because they knew that they *were* free, and could spend their lives as they saw fit. Unfortunately, the vast majority of battles have not been fought on such noble grounds.

I know individuals who, because they know they are free, have refused to fight and have chosen to sit in prison as an expression of their freedom. They are freedom fighters just the same.

The Apostle Paul told the folks at Galatia that, having attained freedom through the recognition of Christ's truth, they were to stand fast and to never again submit to the yoke of mental slavery. Interestingly, he did not tell them to fight for, or even to defend, their freedom – just to stand in it. Be free, and let the chips fall where they may. He did not warn them of people stealing or attacking their freedom, he told them not to pick up and put on themselves the yoke of slavery. He did not tell them to be afraid. And he most likely wrote from a hell-hole of a Roman prison.

If you don't feel free, the answer is inside you. Your freedom is a given. The truth of who you are, is a given. It is up to you to stand in it, express it, and get a working knowledge of it. If you express your freedom – and you should – there will certainly be consequences, and they won't always be pleasant. But the consequences, whatever they are, do not make you unfree.

One of my favorite footnotes to the story of Nelson Mandela is his birth name. Born the son of Thembu royalty, the name given to him by his prophetic father was Rolihlahla, which means "Troublemaker."

The free always are.

Supply Lines.

I was a missing link, and I didn't even know it yet.

It was late fall of 2001. I had just finished a multi-day training with J. Eric Gentry, one of the top trauma healers around. Post 9/11, disaster training was all the rage. I was just putting in my continuing education hours – or so I thought.

Dr. Gentry teaches like he's fattening geese for foie gras – rich and fast. I found it to be fascinating. I found it to be challenging. I loved the idea of being an agent of change in a really bad place and time. I thought I had the right stuff.

Then I went back to my rather mundane counseling practice in Salem, Oregon. Mostly middle class people, with manageable middle class disasters. I wondered if I would ever have the chance to use what I had learned about mass trauma. It wasn't really the sort of thing you ought to wish for.

A couple of months later I met a man. An African. I was editing an anthology of Quaker writings. This African Quaker had an essay that I needed to pick up. Fascinating fellow – David Niyonzima from Bujumbura, Burundi, Central Africa. He was studying mental health at a Quaker university. He was within a couple of months of finishing his degree. He had gotten a good education – if you were planning to be a psychotherapist in Portland, Oregon. But he was planning to go home, where a simmering war between the government and three rebel groups had killed 300,000 people in the last decade. He was about to become the only man with a master's degree in Counseling Psychology in a country of seven million trauma survivors. I asked him if he felt prepared to go do the work that was ahead of him. He gave me a look that signaled that he was trying to decide whether to be polite or honest. He chose honest.

"I am leaving with none of the right tools. I do not know what to do."

I asked him a few more questions. It was clear that one-on-one, paid, insight-focused therapy was not going to cut it in Burundi. Freud vs. Jung was not going to matter. Diagnostic codes for insurance companies were going to be useless. Feel good personality profiles would be culturally irrelevant. And the people who had sacrificed to get him this fancy degree were waiting for him to come home with the answers. He was a worried man.

Then I realized what my role was – I would volunteer to help with his supply line.

We spent a lot of time together in those last couple of months. I downloaded everything I had learned from Gentry to him and then I figured out how to get him some more. I started studying and making connections in order to pass it on. I have traveled twice to Burundi to teach teachers. David has taken what I gave him and multiplied it like loaves and fishes. He has made connections with many others in the field of traumatology. He has multiplied his supply lines. Tens of thousands of lives have been affected for the good.

I have learned the value of solid functional supply lines. No army of any merit can function without them. David and I are volunteers in an army of peacemakers, justice builders, and fear fighters. We are recruits to what Quakers call the Lamb's War. It is a good fight. It is a good army. We may look a bit rag-tag to some observers, but my supply line has never gone down. I have never run out of ammo or food. The medics always show up when I need them.

I am praying today for a young man that I know, who is not as well-supplied as I. He works for a different army – The United States Army. He is serving on an outpost in Afghanistan somewhere near the Pakistani border. He is doing his best. He is serving honorably. He has been told that he is fighting terrorism. He is about as far from civilization as you can get on this planet.

His army is an expensive one. We pay billions per week to support him. One of the things it gets him is a satellite link to his family. They can drive up to Fort Lewis every couple of weeks and get fifteen minutes of near real-time chat with him. One of the things the billions haven't gotten him is a winter coat. The other morning, his grandmother noticed that he was shivering. He reported that it was ten degrees Fahrenheit. He also reported that the Army had not gotten winter coats to his unit. He told her that he was recently reprimanded for wearing non-regulation gloves while on a dangerous convoy mission to re-supply food to the unit. His bare hands got the food. They did not get coats.

I am absolutely sure that someplace, the United States Army has a warehouse full of winter coats. That they cannot put one on this boy's back halfway through an Afghani mountain winter is shameful. This is not rocket science. It is not even satellite technology. It is basic army 101.

And it makes me very glad that I work for a very different army.

Grail Quest

My Friend was here for a few hours – well, he was here for a couple of days, but I got a few hours. I tend to take the airport run with David Niyonzima, because we can get in a meal and some good conversation. But this duty always comes with the insertion of his "Last Minute Tasks." These are always entertaining.

He usually has a shopping list, and counts on me for shopping expertise. There is almost always at least one impossible thing on the list. One year it was, "Peggy, we need to stop at a pharmacy and get a thousand tablets of Haldol." In Africa, if you had the money and they had the Haldol, this would work. No doctors need be involved. This does not work in Portland. He was mightily disappointed; African crazy people were depending on him. He does not like to let people down. He's reliable that way.

This time he had two requests.

The first was for a dear friend of his, a Catholic priest, who needed a communion cup for his church. "Silver. You know, they look like a soccer trophy with two handles. Bigger than a regular cup."

"Has the Vatican run out of silver, that they are not supplying their priests these days?"

"He is building his own little chapel at his retreat center, and he needs this thing. He is like a brother to me, and I want to give it to him as an honor. I have told him that I would look for one. I have a hundred dollars set aside for this, and I am told that such things can be easily found at Goodwill in America."

A grail quest. You don't get that every day. It is not that I do not believe that this man might not just have the purity of heart to pull off such a feat – he might. And it is not that I do not believe that this man might have a God who would get kicks from supplying such a request – he does. And if there was going to be a grail quest, I most certainly wanted to be there. But I felt that I needed to explain to him the odds. That Goodwill was a chancy thing, and that the quality was usually not that good, and that there was the time factor to make the plane.

"Ah, I see, you are saying that it is unlikely, difficult, and time consuming."

"Indeed – But I know of two such places between here and the airport, and if you want to try, I will take you."

"Thank you – you are always willing, my friend, but it is not the only thing I need."

"What else is on your list?"

"There is a little boy at Kamenge. He is about 2. His family is very poor. He loves me very much. He likes to sit on my lap on the elder's bench. I asked his mother if there was something he might need or want from America. She said he was airplane crazy, and wondered if a toy plane could be had. I wanted to look for that, also."

"That I think we can find. What do you want to do?"

"The child will not know if I bring something or not, only the mother. And I had such hopes for the cup... But I think I will bring the toy. I would rather please the child than the man."

So we looked at the toys. We found a nice shiny jetliner, but he would not have it because the engines looked like bombs to him and he was afraid the child would play war with it. Finally we found a little red Cessna, with a propeller. He smiled broadly and bought it.

In the car he held his prize.

"I am happy. The boy will be happy. I am content; let us head for the airport."

And I knew we had found the grail.

And I was happy.

The Temple of Safety

Bujumbura during the summer of 2003 was in trouble. Various rebel groups were camped in the hills around the capitol city. They had mortar rounds and rocket-propelled grenade launchers – and they were using them. The South African peacekeepers had helicopter gunships – and they were using them. The United Nations had pulled all their people out. The embassies were working with skeleton staffs of people without dependents. The US embassy folk had a safe zone and a corridor to the airport. They were not allowed to travel anywhere else. I was flying in to help a local NGO set up training centers for trauma healing. My local connections thought they could keep me safe, and promised to ship me out if they could not. I thought I was being very brave.

But right away things were not what I expected. I was stupid naïve. I had expected that once I was off of the international carriers in Nairobi and onto African air transport that it would be pretty much "Clutch Cargo Airways." I guess I was expecting propellers and maybe chickens – the sleek 737 for the Nairobi-Kigali-Bujumbura leg was unexpected. I also didn't expect the plane to be full – I mean, how many people would be flying into a war zone? I really didn't expect to see children on board. In the seats next to me were two Arab children, with their mother and baby sister behind us. I asked the older boy if he had any English – he did. Everyone else's children have more languages than most Americans. We had a nice conversation. They were on their way back to Buja from a visit to their grandparents in Dar Es Salaam. Dad was a businessman in Burundi, with a fine store, according to his son. Mother did not have as much English as her son, but he translated a question for me.

"How do you feel about taking your children to Bujumbura? – Does it feel safe to you?"

"It is a wonderful city, a good place to do business, a good place to raise a family." She said. She didn't seem in the least bit worried. I wondered if I had gotten the news all wrong.

I hadn't. But I spent three fairly safe months in Burundi. And I met a lot of children there, and most of them seemed happy.

Business was thriving in the midst of chaos. Kind of like the old west. Dodge might not be Mayberry, but the saloon business was treating Miss Kitty all right.

Apparently that mother had not listened to the fear-mongers.

I have been thinking a lot in the last few years about fear and fear-mongering. It seems that our culture is taking a real turn towards being a culture of fear. If you listen to any media outlet, you can quickly make a list of things that you are supposed to be afraid of, from dangerous bacteria that infest every corner of your house to the threat of various forms of global annihilation. Places that are supposed to be bastions of safety are now terribly dangerous. The hospital is the last place that a sick person should be. That clergyperson talking to your son is highly suspect. The evening news that was once delivered to us devoid of emotion is now served with heaping portions of concern, caution, fear, and outrage.

I do not think that this is a good trend.

Not that I am against practical safety. Airbags, Yeah! By all means, change those batteries in your smoke detector, and please, do wash your hands before you leave the restroom. But the constant diet of fear and the persistent selling of products and behaviors to assuage the fear seem to have gotten all out of proportion.

This is an old business. As old as virgins being tossed into volcanoes to appease the gods. And I think the comparison to idolatry is apt. To run the fear business you need a stick and a carrot – a supposedly noble or at least awesome deity, and fear of retribution. We have begun to worship at the Idol of Safety in earnest. The fear of retribution if we do not, is very real.

You know that something has become an idol when its name becomes a magic incantation that stops questions and debate and induces unnatural obedience. Remember Obi Wan Kenobi, and his Jedi mind tricks? "These are not the droids you are looking for." With the wave of his hand and hypnotic words, he lulled weak minds into a stupor. Now, in the United States, all you have to do is say, "This is for your safety, sir." and people nod their heads, take off their shoes and stand in line. They throw their personal possessions into sacrificial barrels, and avert their eyes as the Middle Eastern looking fellow behind them gets pulled out for extra screening.

The temples of Safety are everywhere. She has legions of acolytes. She drinks greater and greater portions of our national budget. And devotion to her is very exacting. You must be willing to give her your personal liberties. You will isolate into smaller and smaller groups, and in those groups you will think alike. You will not trust the other groups, whether they are across the street or across the world. Words will change. Isolation will become nesting. Courage will become foolhardiness. Mr. Orwell will be very busy.

Because faith in Safety focuses more on feeling safe than actually being safe, there will be the never-ending task of risk management. As long as one person in the room still feels unsafe, we will all change our behavior until that person feels better. But having lowered the threshold, it will be only a matter of time before the unease grows in someone – who will raise again the cry, "Unsafe!"

You got the smoke detector. Then you got the carbon monoxide detector. Then you got the radon detector...

You screened the little league coach for criminal behavior. Then you trained all the children to detect pedophiles. Then you made the rule that no child is ever to be alone with a single adult, ever...

It never ends.

For years after coming out of seminary with a degree in religion and counseling psychology, I tried to envision and make church a safe place to be, emotionally, spiritually, and physically. Eventually I found out that this was the trials of Sisyphus – futility itself – unless you kept out all the human beings. Then I decided that we were not created to be safe. We were created to be invincible.

Stormy Weather

Burundi is not always a place of easy sleep. When the old gods retire, they move to tropical climes. I knew this because those old Norse dudes Thor and Odin were duking it out directly over my tin-roofed house. The flashes of light not only illuminated the room, they illuminated the back of my brain through eyes squeezed shut and a pillow over my head. The thunder, which was occurring at ten-second intervals, was shaking the foundations of the house. The wind blew open the shutters three times, and my bed was soaked with rainwater. But as it was about 90 degrees Fahrenheit I didn't mind the water so much.

The call to prayer from our neighborhood mosque was due, but I think the singer had given up over the tempest – God was singing God's own call. "Sleepers Awake!" I will never again brag about the Midwestern thunderstorms of my youth. All those cards have been trumped.

Nothing about the place is mild. It is hard work to get up and live. The simple strangeness, and the energy it takes to adjust to it, tires you by 10 in the morning. The abundance is also exhausting. Five choirs at church that each sing twice, loudly and with exuberance. Drinking halls in the residential neighborhoods that dance all night. The Mosque a few blocks over with its loudspeaker. The food is strange and abundant. The driving deserves another essay.

But the most draining thing of all is the spiritual learning curve.

I got daily doses of the Disciplines that far exceeded the recommended minimums. Compassion and discernment with the four-year-old homeless street children. Forgiveness with the 47 cultural snafus that I created each day. Continual Attention was required to avert catastrophe. Adventure – Boy Howdy! My soul was on the rack – stretched to near breaking. Yet I learned.

The squandered resource of central Africa is human intelligence and initiative. There is not enough work to go around, and – due to poverty and lack of development – much of the work that is done is difficult, menial, and does not use the obvious prevalent intelligence of these people. They make jobs for each other right and left, but a lot of those jobs work at half-speed, and way below the level of competence. A secretary, who at home would be a busy office administrator, answers a phone maybe once an hour – and if she makes a few photocopies, it is a busy day. The rest of the time she spends waiting. Our driver works about two hours a day, and sits for six. We have a man just to open our gate. But even his job is more interesting than the soldiers of the new Burundian peace, who sit on the roadside every few hundred yards and stare into space for the whole day.

I spent many hours a day waiting: for the power to come back on, for the shared internet connection, then for the required minutes as I waited for an e-mail to be sent. I waited for Niyonzima as we drive and stop every few hundred yards to greet someone. I got better at relaxing while I waited, but I often found myself wondering if what I was doing was really the best use of me.

Then my eyes were opened to yet another level of my American spoiled child syndrome. I took for granted the fact that I would be near the top of my game most of the time – that all my work would be meaningful in some form. I don't like to do work unless that work is something that really takes me to do it. I like to be unique and to express it. I am just way too precious a commodity to be wasted.

I am a spoiled child of God. I am full of it.

So I decided to join my brothers and sisters, in their patience and graciousness and wisdom. I learned to sit quietly and contentedly and wait to see if there is some small thing that the Boss had for me to do today. And if all I did was stand at the ready, handmaiden to grace, then I would still count it to be a good day.

They that wait upon the Lord shall renew their strength.

Garbage

I was a long-term guest in an African household. My hosts' socially appointed role was to make sure that all my needs were met, and that I was adequately protected. My role as a guest was to be effusively grateful, and to bless the household spiritually and materially, as I could.

I was being a bad guest, and I knew it, but truly, I could not help it. My hostess, my sister in the Lord, my fellow mother, was unknowingly endangering her children, whom I now loved as if they were my own. If nothing else, the rules of the International Union of Mothers required that I speak up.

My friend ran a well-ordered household. It was hers to rule. Lower middle class though she was, she had a cook, a gardener, and a night watchman, as well as a couple of younger sisters from up country who worked for their school fees and board. I was housed in separate quarters, but inside her compound. I had my own young female helper. This was completely normal and pro-social behavior; to have the ability to employ people and to not do so in a country of vast underemployment is seen as selfish.

My friend had a lovely vegetable garden inside the compound walls. She also had a system for dealing with trash, as the city of Bujumbura did not have anything like trash collection services. The trash went out to the far corner of the compound, and the heap was burned and turned once a week. When well broken down, it was mixed with the droppings from the chickens and rabbits and spread over the vegetable garden. Nice and orderly. Except for one thing – the toxins.

Imports from China and Eastern Europe have made it to the edges of the Earth. There are the ubiquitous plastic grocery bags. The universal cheap plastic lawn chairs. Cell phones are cheap. Many things, including food, now come in colorful paper and plastic packaging. And battery powered toys, radios, and other devices are now common for the middle class. With absolutely no way to safely dispose of any of it.

It was when I saw the AA batteries, broken by fire, in the compost around the maize that I investigated a bit. I thought about it. I prayed. And then I took my sister aside privately to do my bad guest behavior. I praised her housekeeping skills. I praised her education and professional demeanor. I added as a very slight aside that as busy as she had been with the good work of God's Kingdom that she might not have had time to learn about the contents of batteries. I offered my information as a trifling aside. Heavy metals, toxic chemicals, damage to the soil, her plants, and the beautiful food that she grew and fed to her babies.

She laughed at me. Silly paranoid concerns. Irrational beliefs. Could I not see how pretty her corn and beans were? Had I not tasted the food? Was it not delicious? Could I not see how fat and healthy and smart her children were?

I praised effusively her cooking and her progeny. Then I very gently asked her if she would break one of those batteries open and let her youngest suck out the contents. She looked at me with horror. I suggested ever so gently that to break them open and put them around her beans meant that the contents went into the beans and into her child even if the beans tasted good.

I suggested that she separate her garbage into two groups, one pile for food waste, animal waste and plant waste; and another place for plastics, colored paper, and such. I suggested that only the food and animal waste go onto the garden. I suggested that the batteries be put into a storage container and just left alone – forever, if necessary.

She laughed at me again, a trifle wearied. She pointed out the obvious flaw in my thinking. The purifying fire of her little garbage heap. Did I not know that fire cleaned all things? I gently reported that I had been told that home fires are not hot enough to truly destroy all the bad things in plastic and batteries and such. She gently suggested that I put my hand in the fire and see if I thought it was hot enough.

I apologized profusely for my bad manners, obvious lack of knowledge about how things are done here, and let it be.

But the next week I noticed that there were two garbage heaps in our household.

Every other good mother of Bujumbura continues to burn her plastics and imported garbage. You smell it in the air every evening – purifying fires. And the babies mostly look fat and happy.

I continue my bad guest behavior by telling you this tale, I hope to be forgiven. But this is how we change the world, one woman talking to another, risking good manners for the truth, daring to listen and to change.

Generosity

I was on my way to church, and I had escaped my handlers. Three weeks in-country and confident of my directions, I had slipped out the gate of the compound before my driver had arrived to take me to worship. The gatekeeper shook his head at me as I left, but he did not have the power to stop me, and no language to caution me. I knew I would be ratted out within minutes, but I thought I could get quite a ways before I was caught. I was wearing my Sunday finery, and had put up my rainbow colored umbrella to protect me from the already hot sun. I had a little bag over my arm with just the basic necessities; my Kiswahili Bible, enough small change for a taxi, a little water, and a Japanese fan for survival during the three-hour service.

The day was fine. I greeted each passerby with a bright "Bonjour!" There was still a shooting war going on in Burundi, and the UN had pulled their people out, so there weren't any other women who looked like me walking about the town at liberty that day.

About half a kilometer from home, the van driven by my host caught up with me.

"Peggy, why are you walking? I was on my way for you!"

"It is a beautiful morning, my friend, and I know the way; I decided to stroll."

"Please, get in and let me drive you."

"Am I unsafe walking?"

"No, you are quite safe, I think."

"Then, please, allow me to enjoy myself."

"As you wish."

And then he went one street over and discreetly followed me downtown.

As I neared the city center, I picked up the usual entourage of street children. They seemed more curious than hostile, and I greeted them and proceeded.

I arrived at church feeling quite triumphant. I entered the back of the bamboo-sided sanctuary and noted that the Sunday school lesson was just finishing. I advanced quietly to the last empty pew and sat down, putting my bag next to my feet. I was at least forty pews from the door where I had entered. A baby, just walking, came up to me from the next bench forward. I leaned forward to pick her up and then sat back on the bench. It was in that moment that I noticed that my bag was missing. I stood, whirled, and saw no one behind me in the church. Not trusting my own eyes, I looked about. It was gone. The babe's mother asked me what I was looking for, and I told her. This started a genuine uproar. I was their invited guest and I had been robbed in the church. The men and boys ran into the street, the women searched all the nearby children. I tried to calm things down – but my hosts were truly shamed. I just felt stupid. It was later determined that a street child had crept into the church behind me and grabbed and evaporated in the manner that only a truly desperate urchin can do. I figured I had paid my tithe to the poor.

After church and the noon meal, there was much consternation back at the compound. The children in the family seemed especially angry, and made much talk about how those bad boys should be beaten. I was more uncomfortable by the hour. I asked the children to gather the household on the lawn. I went through my things and found a present for every member of the family. I found another copy of the gospel, and we had a reading on what Jesus said we should do when we are abused or taken advantage of. I gave out presents, and said that the lesson for the day was for me. I had been a victim of theft, and I needed to remind myself that, though people may steal your things, you cannot let them steal your spirit of generosity.

This was cheap and easy for me. A gesture, nothing more. But it was a lesson that I had learned from the many brave souls I have worked with as a trauma healer; people who have been victims of crimes as vicious and wicked as humankind can inflict – torture victims, victims of violent rape. I have noted who does well afterwards; in fact, many of these people thrive. The ones who thrive are the ones who practice the Spiritual Discipline of Generosity with a truly militant attitude. They refuse to lie down and die; they refuse to give up their hope, courage, or generosity. They take back their own sense of self. They find a way to turn their tragedy into a blessing for someone else. They may seek justice, but they do not seek revenge. Sometimes those who have had the most taken from them seem to find the most to give. They save themselves by walking this path.

They are planetary heroes.

We live in a world that loves revenge, a world drunk on anger. But those of us who claim to be followers of Jesus are supposed know a better way.

I wonder how the world would be different if in the fall of 2001, America had not only sought to apprehend a small group of terrorists, but had at the same time started a massive effort to make sure that every Muslim child on the planet had enough to eat for a season. What if we had responded with an outpouring of generosity, just to show ourselves that we could not be made afraid, could not be made miserly, not made smaller, by being hurt? What if we had taken the path of militant generosity?

I wonder.

A lot.

CSI Rwanda

I was on the bus to Kigali, Rwanda. I was on the big bus – the good bus. This meant that it was about the size, and maybe vintage, of a 1950s-era Greyhound. Sure, it had a few dents front and rear, and a lot of duct tape on the seats, and – most disconcertingly – decal appliqués of bullet holes on the sides (very gangsta), but it was clearly the good bus. I expected a quick trip. By the map, it was three hours.

Silly me.

We stopped to buy bananas. We stopped to buy peas. We stopped to buy goat on a stick. The border crossing ate up an hour. Okay, it was going to take five hours, no sweat, we're on African time. I was just fine with that. Then we were stopped and boarded by the Rwandan Police. Not once, but twice.

The first time was apparently for speeding. We had seemed to be within safe parameters to me, but apparently the Rwandan police had been cracking down on this after a bad week of bus plunges. I was a little surprised when the Police Chief boarded our bus and asked for witnesses against our driver. It was pretty clear that if we testified against our driver, he would be taken away and we would sit there by the side of the road. No witnesses for the prosecution, no sir. Finding none, he scolded us all quite soundly, and told us that he would let us go, and we could all die then. Our driver was released, gave us a thumbs up, and off we went.

Okay, so the trip was going to take six hours.

We were making good progress towards the capital. We were maybe a half an hour out when it happened. I had the front seat on the right side of the bus; I was directly behind the side mirror, and my window was wide open for air. We were on a very nice stretch of road, good tarmac, and it even had a raised curb, a bit like a sidewalk. The countryside was wooded on both sides. We were going along at a good clip. We passed a young man on a bicycle. I watched him disappear in the mirror. I looked away. I heard a hard "thunk" of a sound, and then very clearly, the sound of a bicycle crashing through trees. It is a distinctive sound. It went on, "crash, crash, ... crash." I sat up. I looked at the ticket-taker sitting next to me.

"That wasn't good." I said

"No" He leaned over me and looked out the window.

He had a few quick words with the driver and we slowed. Everybody looked out the window. More words – Kinyarwanda I wasn't getting. Clearly a discussion of, "Should we stop?" It was decided not. We proceeded.

A kilometer down the road, a smaller bus pulled up beside us. Its driver was shaking his fist at us; the passengers were leaning out the windows screaming at us. Our driver yelled back. No translation needed. The tension on our bus was rising. The next vehicle to come up behind us was a Rwandan Police pick-up. They pulled us over. Their captain boarded our bus with a very serious countenance. He asked questions and argued with our driver and our ticket taker. Then he announced that there had been an accident and that we were all returning to the scene. The bus turned. The captain left a lower officer and his AK-47 on our bus. He joined me on the front seat and propped the gun between us.

"Bonjour, Madam."

Good day? Not so much, sir, thank you.

Now a bit of an aside about Central African law. The law is Napoleonic. I am no great student of the law, but I was schooled a bit by my African friends before they let me loose in the countryside. The functional difference between our law and theirs is the presumption of innocence. They don't have that. A great weight is placed on the investigation, and on the testimony of the investigating officer; his determination of fact is fact, unless you can prove otherwise. And it is the investigating officer's job to determine responsibility and guilt or innocence on the scene. Traffic law is pretty matter of fact. If you hurt someone on the road, you are instantly liable for all of their injuries, and if you kill someone and it is determined that you are at fault, your life is forfeit for theirs, life in prison. I was praying for a young man on a bicycle.

We returned to the nearest hamlet. The accident victim was there. Living, *Jesu'ashimwe*, but bloodied. The bicycle was DOA.

Now it got interesting. All the bus passengers disembarked. All the villagers gathered around. The Police captain took chaotic testimony. I tried to figure my way out. I asked the lieutenant with the AK, if I could leave – it did not seem like I had a place in the argument. I knew that I could stick my white thumb out and get an instant ride with a UN, or UNICEF, or any other NGO vehicle.

"Oh NO! Madam! You are a witness; ALL witnesses must stay until the case is decided!" Yikes. Sequestered I was.

Now I knew why every passenger was so involved in the increasingly heated discussion. Their time was on the line, too.

Our driver's personal stake was big. The bus company was considered a rich target, and the supporters of the young man were arguing for guilt and a large settlement on the spot. Our driver was admitting no responsibility. The captain decided to see the actual crime scene. We were all re-boarded, along with the young man and his supporters and the wrecked bicycle. The bloody young fellow was given the best seat in the house, between the lieutenant and me. I gave him my water bottle. He didn't look like he had any major bones broken, but one of his feet was really bad. He seemed rattled. He smelled bad. He apologized when he got blood on me.

We retraced our travel at a snail's pace, heads out the windows trying to find the exact spot. "Here – where the trees are broken!" We stopped – everyone got off. A couple of passengers had taken on the role of counsel for the defense of the driver. Local residents were clearly the prosecution. We were accused of hitting the young man and knocking him off the road. We all examined the side of the road. We examined the side of the bus. Much argument and discussion, done at volume with gesticulation and shouts of approval and derision by the crowd. Our ticket-taker pointed out that there was this nice sidewalk. With an ad hoc translator, I was asked if I saw the boy on the road or up on the curb. I testified that I had in fact seen him on the curb. I could not say if we had hit him or not, but I was certain that we had not climbed the curb which was a good six inches high.

This curb was found to have lateral cuts in it at regular intervals for drainage. The cut just above the first broken tree had a very fresh dramatic scratch on it. Voila! The young man, startled by the bus, but not hit, had taken the curb cut wrong, precipitously decelerated and was ejected with his bike into the woods!

Professor Plum in the library with the candlestick!

The Police captain was convinced, but he still had townsfolk to placate. The bus company, while admitting no wrongdoing, decided on the spot to magnanimously transport the boy to Kigali, to the hospital, and give him an admittance fee. The locals were disappointed. Our driver was hugely relieved, and – with just another hour of talking and a stop at a police station – we arrived in Kigali eight hours after our departure.

All humans who are alive and awake and involved are called at times to be witnesses. Those of us who profess a life of faith are witnesses to truths that are not easily demonstrated, let alone proved. I have seen many religious arguments that have all the grace and serenity of African crime scene investigation. Perhaps we argue so gracelessly for similar reasons. We don't actually trust that truth will win out. We see the temporal and sometimes the eternal stakes as high and unchangeable. Win here and now or lose big.

Quakers have a testimony that is supposed to address this concern. It is called continuing revelation. It asserts that God will continue to work on our understanding of truth. It does not deny absolute truth, but honestly admits that we will not comprehend truth absolutely and that our understanding will change. It asks us to live the truth as best we know it, knowing that in the living, we will come to find that which is trustworthy. Traditions based most closely in the truth will survive the longest. It asserts underlying unchangeable principles, but infinitely changeable application. It requires more listening than argument. It requires trust in God and in each other. It presumes a loving and fair judge.

I like it better than roadside justice.

The Road to Goma

Breaking one of my cardinal rules for living in an alien environment, I was ignoring the advice of the local friend charged with my health and safety. Mzungu Ujinga – stupid white person!

I was getting ready to head out from Kigali to Goma. It is a long ride on the very best of days. Those days don't come around often. My friend was clear that I should be on the 10:30 bus, at the latest. It was the last bus that had a good chance of getting me to the border crossing before dark. I was going to have to negotiate that crossing without help, and in need of a visa. It might take time. No one wanted me to cross into the Congo after dark.

Before leaving, there was a task that I needed to perform. I had been charged with the duty of interviewing six secondary students at the George Fox Secondary School. They were orphans and at risk of losing their place at school for the inability to pay their fees. I was going to bring their stories back to a group in the US who had scholarships on their mind. It felt important.

My friend picked me up and wanted to purchase my bus ticket before seeing the students. He did not want to risk a sold-out bus and a late departure. We got to the bus office. He tried to buy me a ticket. Bad news. There was no 10:30 bus today, just a 9:30 and an 11:30. It was five minutes until nine. My friend stated his intention to buy me a ticket on the 9:30 bus. He was clear about this. He assured me that the students would wait. I knew my return trip would be even tighter, and on the weekend, when the odds of finding the students at school were not good. I asked him to buy me a ticket on the 11:30 bus. He told me he would not do this – he wanted me to get on the 9:30 bus right then and there. I asked him to pray with me for a moment. In those moments of silence, I felt a bond and a call to those young people that would not let me go. I could not abandon them. I thanked my friend for his care of me. I assured him that I understood the risk I was taking. I told him that I felt clearly led to go see the students. I asked him to buy me the 11:30 ticket. He politely asked me to buy it myself, as he wanted no responsibility for my choice. This is as clear as an African can be that you are being foolish beyond belief. I bought my own ticket for the 11:30. Then he took me to see the students.

It was a heartbreaking hour. I heard stories that will never leave me. We all wept. I had nothing to promise them except that I would tell their stories. Any possible help was many months away, and it might be too late for some of them. Walking away crushed my heart.

We arrived back at the bus station at 11:25. They were doing repairs on the bus. Duct tape was being applied to headlights. I snagged the seat in the center front, next to the driver. I am a famous puker, and looking forward and having air is a good idea. The bus was a Toyota ten-seater; they sold 17 tickets, plus luggage. It was good to be packed in tight, because there were no seat belts, as was evidenced by the spider shaped crack in the windscreen directly where my head would hit in a sudden deceleration. Seasoned African travelers like the center of the bus. The air is bad, but the person at the center often survives the crash cushioned by the bodies of their comrades. We left with a locally on-time departure of noon, straight up.

Kigali sits in a bowl, a city on many hills surrounded by mountains. Every road out of the city goes up. Every road is serpentine. Serpents would puke on those roads. Our bus driver was in a mood to make time, cutting curves and not stopping for vegetables or people. Until we were about half way up – then there was a large group of people by the roadside and on it. I do not know what caught his attention, but he slowed and called something to the passengers, and then stopped. Way too far into the roadway for my happiness. So we all got out. Our driver trotted up to the people, whom I could now see were distressed and pointing over the precipice. Driver looked over the edge and screamed. I don't like it when African men scream. It is never good.

It turns out that over the edge was the 9:30 bus. Our company's bus. Yes, that bus.

Some men had climbed down. There was not a soul to bring up alive. Even the center seat was a bad seat this day. Bodies would be eventually hauled up; the bus would be left. Phone calls were made to headquarters. People prayed. After a while, our driver decided that we needed to try to go on. We boarded our bus in a somber mood. He goosed it up the hill. He started swearing almost immediately. I looked at him. He pointed to the gauges. I watched as the engine heat gauge swung up and over the "H." He alerted the passengers to our situation. This bus was not going to make it to the Congo today. Many groans, tempered a bit by our status of being alive, and our awareness of how lucky we were. That status was challenged right off. He turned the bus, put it in neutral and switched off the engine. We coasted silent and swift as death itself down that mountain. We passed the bus plunge scene, and the roadside viewers looked at us with gaping mouths as we flew past. They must have thought our driver has gone insane with grief and was planning to take us to follow the lost bus. Our tires screeched at every turn. The smell of burning brake pads filled the cabin. The people of the bus were too shocked to pray. Finally, we reached the flats, crossed the river bridge, and coasted to a stop. People began thanking whatever God they worshipped.

I honestly cannot tell you why I did not find or borrow a phone and call my Kigali friend and bail. But I didn't. I bought cokes and sambusa with the people of my bus and we waited for the bus company to send us another bus. I am sure that we commandeered the 12:30 bus; it was only 1:00 after all. But soon, after an hour or so, we had another bus and a fresh driver. And again we ascended. It was about 2:30 PM.

As were starting the climb, I spoke in a loud voice and stated that I was going to lead the bus in prayer, apologizing for my English. I prayed loud and long. I prayed for the bus, I prayed for every part of the bus, I prayed for our new driver and for our old driver. I thanked God for our lives and I prayed for the souls of the departed. I prayed for our courage and for the road ahead of us. When I finished, a voice in the back said loudly, "In the name of Jesus – I agree with you!" It was the first English I had heard all day. I invited the man, named Daniel, to come and sit more forward so that we could talk. The people of the bus rearranged themselves for my entertainment. Daniel had lived in Boston for two years, and he told me the story of Mary Dyer. He was very pleased to see that female Quaker preachers were still risking their necks for the Lord. He had thought we had all been killed. Not quite, Daniel, not quite.

The next six hours were uneventful. I reached the border crossing a couple of hours after dark. The young bureaucrat left on the night shift was at a loss with what to do with me. He had to call downtown to find out what the right level of graft was to let an American lady into the country at night. He kept my passport, promising to have it returned the next day to my hotel, and let me through to meet my frantic Congolese compatriot, who had waited over five hours for me, and had heard rumors of bus plunges.

I guess some days it just pleases God to have everyone on their knees.

The People of the Bus

I was on the people's bus, again, traveling solo, despite the obvious handicaps. My first major handicap was the lack of language. On my journey, I would be in lands speaking Kirundi, Kinya-rwanda, Kiswahili, and the standard educated back up of French. I have at least a half a dozen words in each of those languages. Truly, not enough.

I had four border crossings to make, two each way. I had counsel on what to expect, but I am not knowledgeable enough to know when to pay up and when to have a nice African temper tantrum in response to the demands of petty despots and bureaucrats.

In Africa, border crossings – like everything else – are very real. You do them on foot. Your bus drops you on one side, and then you with all your luggage walk to the small building with the long line where you stand in the hot sun and wait for the exit visa stamp. Next, you pass by the men with guns guarding the actual border and show them your fine new stamp. Then you walk the ground that constitutes the no man's land until you get to the men with guns at the other gate, who look at you suspiciously and then condescend to let you stand in the long hot line where you hope to get the entrance visa to the next country. I do not know what happens if one country lets you leave and the other decides not to let you enter.

The no man's land between Burundi and Rwanda is especially spacious; there is a nice long walk and a river. I do not know who repairs the bridge. But there are poor children on that bridge begging. I do not think that they have stamps of any kind. I do not know which country claims them.

Traveling like this gets a person down to the basics. You carry enough water, and you rely on the kindness of strangers – a lot. Fortunately, I have found that African strangers are almost always extremely kind. I had a conversation many times that went something like this:

"Madame; blah, blah French blah?"

"I am so sorry, I have no French."

"Blah, blah Kirundi (Kinya-rwanda, Kiswahili) blah?"

"Oya, sorry, I really have no Kirundi, either. I have only English."

"Only English?"

"Yes."

"American?"

"Ego, yes"

"You go where?"

"Goma"

"Congo?" (Incredulous whistle.)

They always looked around for my handlers. Once a man asked me, "What? Does no one in the whole world love you?"

Often they took me by the hand, literally, and kept an eye on me. Nice folks; pity for the stupid and helpless.

The other thing you have going for you is the African cultural value of instant group identity. When you get on a bus, you enroll in the group of that bus. It is now *our* bus, and you are one of *us*. Our pale, foolish, little sister, but ours.

They try to educate you about thieves, as if you have no concept for larceny. They help you find food to eat. This can be challenging. Travelers often go hungry. But the bus drivers know the standard stopping places where roadside vendors sell fast food. This is usually a roasted cob of corn so tough that Illinois stockyard cows would send it back to the kitchen. The other choice is goat on a stick. On one of my buses, a kind old baba educated me like a child. "This is what Rwandan money looks like. Goat should cost this much. Here are two bills, go buy two goat sticks, one for you and one for me, and I will watch from here. It's okay – you can do it." Well, actually that was communicated with a couple of words of several languages and hand gestures – but it worked fine. Turns out that goat on a stick is delicious, and hurt me not at all. The baba also informed me that this roadside was famous for the sleeping potion in the Coke trick, where a planted thief on the bus cleans you out as you sleep. "Make sure you see them open your coke, sweetie." "Thanks, Baba."

Also like a small child, you need help finding the toilet. I tried to go from breakfast to dinner without, but some days I just couldn't make that twelve-hour wait. Toilets in Africa run the gamut from the fancy hotel equipment, with the lovely French bidet, to what the locals euphemistically call the "precision" toilet.

Now, you who have traveled may think you know about this phenomenon, but unless you have been to an up-country African precision toilet, you have not lived. The idea is a variation on the standard hole in the floor – try your best aim affair. At one of the borders, I was informed by my bus team members that this was a good place to go; you pay 100 francs to that man over there and he will escort you up the hill to the very nice facility run by his family for several generations now. I had hope. I paid my fare. I followed the man up the goat trail to an adobe outhouse. I was still hopeful. Because I didn't know any better. I entered the facility as the man stood guard for me immediately outside the door. He thoughtfully kept a hand on the latch. I felt so safe, because I could see him clearly through the many fingers-wide gaps in the door. I was grateful for the gaps, as they admitted the only light, allowing a good view of the target. The floor of the outhouse was constructed of sticks the size of broomsticks. The pit below was a refreshing two meters down. *Many* of the floor's sticks appeared sound. The broken ones were well-spaced. The essential gap in the floor was about a palm's width. Because the word "precision" is a serious euphemism, the sticks on either side of the hole were very slippery for a foot or so, and they turned nicely with this lubrication. Somehow, I did what I had come to do. I used one of my nice Kirundi words and thanked the attendant. He was also grateful, as he now had a story to tell his wife when she asked how his day went. My bus mates congratulated me on my courage.

After several long days of such travel, you think that you cannot be shocked. I considered myself to be seasoned beyond measure. Then life threw me a real curveball. On the last bus ride, we stopped at a roadside stand that was new to me. My bus mates informed me that this was a good place to use the toilet. I assessed my need and decided to be courageous. Behind the goat and coke stand was a very pretty yellow sign that said toilets. Hmm, a sign; did I dare hope? Naw. There was a man at the door, but he was wearing a white lab coat. Hmm. I opened the wooden door into a room with a sink, two standard porcelain urinals and two stalls labeled "Gents" and "Femmes". I pulled the door marked Femmes." And as I did, a cheery, obviously canned, Japanese voice, said in perfect English, "Hello! Welcome!" The toilet was the automatic flushing variety, and there was a sign stating that it was a gift to the people of Rwanda from the people of Japan. Those Japanese are so thoughtful! We should have them to dinner more often! I was a little disconcerted by the ghost voice of the Japanese girl; I kept looking around to see if she was holding the door for me, but I could not find her. I looked at the shiny receptacle. I knew if I missed, everybody including the Japanese girl would know it was me, because obviously everyone else had been very precise. Somehow I relaxed enough to do what I had come to do, but I jumped out of my skin a little when I exited and the invisible Japanese girl bid me good day. I bought a coke and some goat to calm my nerves. My bus mates congratulated me on my courage.

Student Teachers

Let me introduce you to my traumatology students.

I have 20 of them, about half and half men and women. Their ages range from the late twenties to the mid-sixties. Most have some education, but that ranges from primary to graduate school. They have been invited to this three-day workshop because they work in a helping field, or they are influential people in their communities. When we educate one of them, we educate whole communities and organizations. Several of them, like me, work for Trauma Healing and Reconciliation Services (THARS), but have been doing trauma listening with only the barest of preparation. A couple of them work in human rights organizations; there is a lawyer; there is one who works demobilizing child soldiers; several are teachers, from primary through high school; and there are a couple of university students.

Our job is to give them, in three days, the basics of psychological trauma and its effects, and a method of resolving trauma.

I have done this before, so I fully expect that a big piece of the intervention will be starting the resolution process for these students themselves. We send them home better than they came, and that is great advertising.

Now, changing the names, and with their permission, I will share a few of their stories.

Beatrice is a young woman who was married young and had three children. She was the recipient of a near-fatal beating. She experienced such a deep trauma response that she did not feel any of the pain of the beating until three months later, when the pain arrived, along with nightmares.

Patrice is a young man who was a soldier in the rebel army for several years. He was a teenager at the time; he attended school during the day and fought with the rebels in the bush at night. He saw a great deal of action and witnessed atrocities.

Maria is a young woman who was sexually assaulted by nighttime rebels.

During the war, Aaron was arrested because he was too highly educated. He was kept in a one-meter square cell for a long time. The prison was severely overcrowded. One evening, to relieve the overcrowding, the guards killed every prisoner in the jail except Aaron, who was spared because one of the guards was a friend of his.

Catharine's husband died. She was alone, and the situation was unstable, so she slept with his dead body for a week until she could get neighbors to help bury him.

Josephine is a grandmother. Her home was invaded by rebels who beat and tortured her and her family in an attempt to get money.

Angelique lost her son to illness. At the burial, government soldiers swept through shooting at anything that moved. The mourners fled, but Angelique stayed at the graveside because the grave had not been closed. The soldiers held a gun to her head, but then decided to leave her alive as she had experienced enough trouble that day.

Nine out of ten Burundians who are over the age of fifteen have experienced a trauma like this. Many of them have experienced many such traumas.

Hayo Daniella, age seventeen, daughter of my host and boss, has been my right hand this month. When she was six, she witnessed rebels coming into their house and holding her siblings and her mother at gunpoint. When they determined that the family had no money, they took the mother, in her nightclothes, gun to her head, children trailing behind, to the nearby household of some Mennonite missionaries who ransomed her for $60.00.

Dani helps me keep track of my stuff, minds my self-care, gives me spiritual counsel, prays for me, and gives me cultural information that I could get no other way. One of her jobs is to watch non-verbals, and listen to Kirundi side-comments when I am teaching and give me feedback as needed. This has proved invaluable. After our three days of teaching she told me this:

Day 1 "They are like people who have been working in a field with their hands, and we came carrying hoes, and they were happy because they know what the hoes are for, and they need them."

Day 2 "Now you have given them new food. They are like hungry lions, and you are the meat. If I tried to take you from them they would jump on me and tear me to pieces."

Day 3 "They are like soldiers ready to march. They are a little nervous, but they are ready to go try what you taught them."

I am grateful indeed.

A Rwandan Story

I was a single young man, alone in the refugee camp in the Congo during The Trouble. The Interahamwe were mixed in with the refugees. I was friends with a man who looked Tutsi, but was not. An armed group of Rwandese came at evening and took that man away. They took him into the bush and handed him a shovel and told him to dig his own grave.

The man's wife came to me, distraught, and asked me to help. I did not know what to do, and I did not think that there was much hope for the man. But the wife was in such anguish that I went to the Congolese Police who ran the camp. They were not too much interested, but I insisted that this was a good man, and that he was my friend and that I wanted to try and find him.

They asked me "Who has taken the man, and where have they taken him?" I did not know. "What is it that you want us to do then?" they asked.

I convinced them to come with me to see the wife and see if she knew the names of the men who had taken her husband.

It was late in the evening when we found her, gathered with some women, grieving loudly for a husband she presumed was lost. She did not know any names, but carefully described the leader of the gang who took her husband. One of the Congolese Police said, "I know that guy! – I know where he hides."

But it was very late and they did not want to go out into the bush. "He is surely dead." they said to me. "Then let us at least get this poor woman a body to bury" said I.

I convinced them to go out and take a look. We looked for a long time and finally at about dawn we came to a clearing. The killers were there. When they saw the police, they fled. At first, we saw no one else; then we saw the hole. Then we heard digging. And there at the bottom of a three-meter hole, still digging, was the man.

I called to him and he recognized my voice.

The man said, "My friend! I do not wish to die tonight."

"Then come out of your grave and live!"

"Do you also not accept for me to die?"

"I do not accept it – it is not your day."

And they brought the man up and he lives, even until now.

The Decision

The Kamenge Institute for Future Quaker Leadership, was a grand African name we gave to a three-week, English-intensive course covering Biblical theology, Quaker history, tolerance, and environmentalism. My students were young people who had twelve years of Education in French. French was going out of style and the University was now teaching in English: "You can adjust, right kid?"

In the Central African milieu, teachers are supposed to be strict – a variety of strict that Americans haven't seen in generations. They say it is "The Belgian style," but then, they blame a lot of things on the Belgians. In the lower grades, teachers manage up to a hundred students per class with corporal punishment that would make the CIA blush. (Force a rowdy eight-year-old boy to kneel for an hour on broken glass and bottle caps? Classroom management.) In the upper grades, they expel students for the slightest provocation. They discourage questions. Thinking for yourself is the last thing that they want you to do. They speak the truth and expect to see it back on the test. There are no textbooks, so students write their own comprehensive notes. They grade so tough that 50% is passing, and you are likely to be at the top of your class if you clear 70%.

I was famous at Kamenge Friends for being soft, and I intended to turn the teaching model on its head – I wanted them to *think*. I wanted all their questions, and I planned to present them with questions that had no answers. Everyone who attended would pass. But before doing that, I had to establish at least a modicum of respect. So with the help of a Kamenge elder named Joel I attempted to at least give the appearance of rigor. The Institute was announced at Kamenge for a month in advance. Student criteria were published. We made an application process. We gave an admission exam in English – I did want them to start with enough English to benefit from my teaching.

Thirty students sat for the exam. They were expecting grammar, spelling, and construction questions. They got three short essay questions asking them to imagine a better future for themselves, The Friends Church, and the country of Burundi. They were a little confused. Teachers did not usually care about their imaginings. I had to promise confidentiality before they would honestly assess their church and national leadership. I was already getting looks.

My students were attending on their only break of the year. Many of them were simultaneously studying for their national exams – the extremely difficult test that would determine if they were admitted to university. Some were already university students, and Bujumbura University had scheduled their own break intensives. I discovered that some of my students were planning to try to attend both – coming to my class one day and getting notes from the other class, and then reversing it on the next day. I was concerned about them jeopardizing their actual academic future for my enrichment opportunity. I counseled the most promising to prioritize their other work. They were not dissuaded. I felt the deep and sincere pressure to make what I brought them worth their sacrifice.

Twenty-seven of them passed the admissions exam. Their names were posted in the church yard on Saturday morning. On Sunday morning they were called up to the front of the church to be blessed along with their new, strange teacher. After church, Joel reported that quite a few young people had come up to him and asked if it was possible to be admitted at this late date.

Showing up late is pretty much standard operating procedure. Joel and I both hated to say no, but we had agreed that this was going to be our respect-earning strict point. The door was closed.

I fully expected to turn a few away on Monday morning. I steeled myself to the task. I told my Charge D'Affairs, Daniella, that I was going to be tough because equality required me to treat them all the same, and to respect those who had followed the process. Dani agreed that this was right. I was ready.

Only one extra showed up. His name was Victor. I prepared my best kind, but stern words. His supplicant attitude and posture were perfect. Dani whispered, "Be strong." The other students were watching as he approached me. Victor made his initial plea in English that was tentative. I reminded him of the process. He said he had been up-country and had not heard the announcements until yesterday. I told him that we were making no exceptions. He looked discouraged. He stared at the ground and then took a deep breath and looked up at me and made this speech, in perfect English:

"Teacher – I understand what you are saying, and I respect your rules. But teacher, when I heard about this class yesterday, my heart leapt within my chest, and I knew I had to be here. Elder Joel explained to me that this was not possible, but this morning when I got up for prayers my heart had not changed. So I have come. Teacher, you may chase me away, and I will go, but do you see that low wall there? If you send me away, I will go to the other side of that wall and sit and try to catch what you are saying. But teacher, I beg you, I know I do not deserve to sit with the class, but please, may I sit on this side of the wall?"

Three weeks later, we had a closing ceremony during morning worship. It was celebratory, but tough. Two levels of certificates were given. In the African milieu, certificates are extremely desirable. Those who had attended 90% of the class days were given a certificate of completion. Those who had split their time were given a certificate of participation. All were pleased.

After worship, I was invited to a special celebration with the Kamenge elders – reports, speeches, coke – *Kama Kawaide* (things are as they always have been). I praised these young people to the hilt, and asked that the elders consider adding a young voice to the elders' bench. My students were asked to send one representative.

They chose Victor.

Questions

It took me three days to get them to ask questions. I was starting to worry, but Dani told me to be patient. Partially, they still did not believe that I wanted to be questioned, and there was some reticence about forming questions in English. This was double-dip new territory for them.

When the dam broke, the flood was positively diluvian.

We talked race, we talked tribe. Yes, they asked about gays. Much more controversially, I took a positive stand on birth control. A few of the boys argued against it. The girls were eyes and ears wide open. We talked about female ministry and women's rights. We talked politics. Election season was in full swing, with concurrent "isolated grenade attacks." They talk about grenade attacks like weather. There had been some this summer, but they were not considered serious. They have rankings of grenade attacks there. We were having the localized and light variety. But still, talking about politics is dangerous business.

We carefully, but seriously, assessed the problems of corruption, not only in the government but in the Yearly Meeting. We talked about Burundian Quakers in politics, and about traveling with guns, and about the Peace Testimony. Their assessments were truthful and merciless.

We did all this in the context of studying the Sermon on the Mount, one verse at a time, with concurrent English language instruction. These students know their Bible – better than about 90% of American Christians. Their knowledge is largely oral tradition, just like their academic knowledge. They know their Bible from preaching, and they, like us, have some pretty wacky preachers. One of their greatest outrages is illiterate preachers. They believe that every pastor and evangelist needs college level Biblical education; I do not disagree. We often stumbled upon things that they had been told were in the Bible, which could not be found. For instance, they had been told that Jesus could not read and write. They had been told this by an illiterate preacher, of course. We found one verse in the New Testament that affirmed that Jesus was not a formal, life-long Rabbinical student like the Pharisees, but we found the verse where He read the scriptures in the Synagogue. They were offended on Jesus's behalf at the slander.

I spent a lot of time putting mortar into another gap. Despite their deep Biblical knowledge, this knowledge was rarely preached as applying to daily life situations. The Bible was preached unto repentance and then slowed way back. The Bible also preached righteous living, but this was that tired old list of evangelical don'ts that didn't go much past drinking, smoking, and sleeping around. If you carefully walk through the Sermon on the Mount, you can't stop there. We laid out every implication. You can't lie – ever. Hierarchy is un-Biblical. Tribes and genders matter not at all. Etc. etc. etc.

They took it about as well as the Disciples of old. On the third day, they screamed "We can't do it! – It can't be done!"

I broke our English-only rule, and replied "Et voila!" And then we all repented and tried to figure out what to do next.

Good Morning, Teacher

The THARS compound in Gitega had been blessed by an invasion of architects, ten of them. Hailing from Colorado Springs, they were the architectural equivalent of Doctors Without Borders. THARS had been given a land grant with strings: "Build on it or lose it." They had immediately put up one building on the high ground, but the rest of the land was sloped, with a ravine slicing the plot – challenging the builders. The architects and the surveyors they had brought with them were here to make a master plan for what was going to become a regional campus for training trauma healers and other helpers.

That morning, the surveyors were at work. I was one of their handlers. I had progressed enough in my functionality that I could be left to guide and see to the needs of the new kids. I felt cool. I learned a lot that day. I learned about soil drainage tests and carrying a bucket of water on my head over rough terrain without taking a bath. I learned how to chop Eucalyptus trees on command when they blocked the line of sight. And I learned that the surveyors needed a zone of safety around their tripods of at least six feet, because if the tripod got bumped before all the numbers were done – they were all bad. The challenge to this was the local community that had gathered to watch our work. Such an infestation of *wazungu* they had never seen. Such bizarre behavior – Men carrying great poles, who did nothing but stand. Men who poured water into a small hole they had dug and counted with their watches as the water drained away – What on earth did they think was going to happen to water poured into the ground? And then the great mother who looked into the machine which hopefully was not a gun. Looking afar and calling out words to a man who took notes for her – amazing!

Mostly the watchers were local women and children. The children were barely dressed, unless you counted mud as clothes, so I presumed they were too young to be in school or school uniforms. Some of the women had previously hired on for the ditch digging connected with the first building, and knew what we were up to. Our compound was in a Twa community; on the hill across the river and in the valley below us they farmed and raised goats. The Twa are the third ethnic group in Burundi. The Hutu and the Tutsi are much more numerous and well known. But the Twa are the aboriginal people. They are small of stature, traditionally makers of pots, they speak their own language. They are also the bottom of the social order.

I had literally drawn a line in the dirt around the tripod, and was both patrolling that line and playing with the numerous children in an attempt to keep them clear. The mothers were engaged in interested banter about us and our work; they sometimes helped me by calling the children back a bit.

The young Twa greeted me with the only English phrase they knew: "Good Morning, Teacher," to which the proper reply is "Good Morning, Class." They delighted in this exchange, which is inexplicably used at the beginning of every class day in Burundi, even though the rest of the day is taught in French. They clearly did not know what they were saying, which told me that they had learned it by hanging in the windows of the school that I assumed they were too young to attend. We repeated the phrases innumerable times, to their great delight.

They were not the only visitors we had that day. Up the road behind us was the local elementary school. Eventually, news of the great curiosity traveled, and soon a dignified young man came down to see what was going on. Teachers are highly respected in the community, and are expected to know what is going on. So, down came the young teacher. He was disappointed that I had no French. The mystery of an obviously uneducated *mzungu* was beyond him. He rolled his eyes and looked down his nose at my Kiswahili/French/Kirundi/English mash up, and walked back up the hill. Eventually, another teacher strolled down. He had a bit more English, and I was able to give him the basics of our work. He then went back up to the school. Finally, a dignified older man in a necktie came down – ah, the headmaster. His English was very good and he chatted quite happily with me and a couple of the architects. He knew about THARS and was very happy to see them working in the neighborhood. I took the opportunity to ask him something that I had been wondering all morning.

"Sir, I understand that the president has recently declared that all children in Burundi should be in school – that all school fees have been cancelled. Is this so?"

"This is correct; we have now enrolled every child in the vicinity."

"I understand that this has increased your class size and that some schools have split into morning and afternoon sessions."

"That is correct, our teachers are working very hard, but we have no desks or books for them. Only chalk for the board and the children write in the dirt with their fingers. Each of our classes has 100 students."

"Imagine! You are so dedicated – Truly it is amazing! – Then these children must be too young – or are they your afternoon class, not yet dressed for school?"

"What? Of whom do you speak?" he said, looking about at the road, completely ignoring the dozen or so children gathered around us.

"Why, these children here, the ones making our work so challenging this morning."

He looked down at the child upon whose head I had my hand. The child smiled up at him.

"Oh, *these*, but Madame, *these are not children*, these are Twa! If they are bothering you, just cut a switch and beat them off, they are no more bother than flies."

I was actually too stunned to speak.

The headmaster excused himself and walked back up the road, head held high, hands clasped behind his back. As he went, the Twa children called after him...

"Good Morning, Teacher!"

Le Flambeau School of Driving

I sail my Toyota Sprinter through Buja traffic. The seas are always rough.

I understand that there are some pretty hairy traffic situations elsewhere on this globe, but I would put the roads of Burundi up against any of them for the sheer diversity of the hazards.

Start with roads that are only sometimes paved. When they are paved, the potholes are carnivorous and camouflaged. Add a mix of vehicles that have been passed down from all the nations of the world. My little Toyota once lived in Kenya. I know this because the steering wheel is on the right side – fitted for the leftovers of the British Empire, where they drive on the wrong side of road. In theory, we drive on the right side of the road in Burundi. In my car, this makes passing interesting, since you cannot see around the vehicle in front of you. I station a child in my left seat to hang out the window and give me direction. They yell things like, "Go! It is good" or "Go! But use courage!" If they yelp and dive back in towards my lap, I know it is not a good time to pass. In actual practice, Burundian drivers drive anywhere that they please, in their own lane, in the lane of the oncoming traffic, or on what passes for a sidewalk. They pass you on the right or the left. On occasion, they will go right through you – well, it seems like they are trying. One day this week, the right side mirror of the Land Cruiser I was riding in shaved the cheek of a man on a bicycle. It was a nice close shave too – Aqua Velva required. There is a new infestation of Chinese 125cc motorcycles – mostly taxis. Niyonzima told me to stay off them – "They die like flies." I don't know – the flies seem to be doing all right in Burundi.

The rest of God's creation is also represented. Everywhere except downtown Buja you see long-horned cattle, cows and bulls together, moving through the traffic escorted solely by a boy with a stick. They are very well behaved. Texans would be impressed. There is always a nice sprinkling of goats and chickens, sometimes loose, sometimes tied – usually on their way to death. A new innovation in goat moving is to put each goat in a plastic grocery sack and then tie them individually to a bicycle. You can put six goats on a bicycle this way – their little heads sticking out into the flow. Goat marinated in diesel must be a delicacy here.

There is not a single lighted traffic control device in the whole country. There are maybe a dozen stop signs in this city of a million people. There are traffic cops. Peace has come to Burundi. They demobilized all the soldiers and have given them jobs as traffic cops. They have whistles now – the AK-47s are only upcountry. Burundians are not scared by the sight of AKs; whistles have absolutely no effect on them. I was told that if I felt like it, I could ignore the whistles because they have no vehicles to chase, and even if they wrote down my license number, the car is registered to some guy in Kenya.

When they run short of *beignet* money, the *gendarme* throw up a road block and shake drivers down for small infractions. The fee is paid on the spot and I do not think that much of it ends up downtown. The fee triples if you are *mzungu*. It is up to you to decide if you want to argue. It is all very straight forward; no Chicago-style subtleties here.

I have seen human road kill; there are neither paramedics nor ambulances. If you go down, you trust that strangers will drag you to the side and send someone to look for your relatives.

There is a driving school here. It is called "Le Flambeau School of Driving," and there is no irony intended in this. You see their battered cars with the terrified new drivers on the less traveled streets. I suspect that their teachers are heavy drinkers.

I wonder if the school teaches spiritual disciplines before they send their pupils out to the adventure. They should. Ask God for mercy, screw up your courage, pay attention, generously surrender the right of way, forgive the trespassers, have compassion on the pedestrians, release and retreat as necessary, be prepared for failure, and be grateful if you make it home alive. Only when you have mastered the interior can you hope to survive the streets.

You have to go deep before you can go far.

Even still, it may all go up in flames, because you are at the very edge of what is possible. But the edge is where God goes. It is where you find God at God's highest potency. God most incisive. God most creative.

I believe in continuing education for drivers – spiritual and otherwise. Myself included. I also think I am called to be a driver trainer – God help me. Pass the bottle.

I have been driving here in Burundi three weeks. I have been involved in two fender benders and been detained by the coppers twice – not for the accidents. I am doing really well. I duck, I weave, and I have learned to honk – liberally. This felt bad to me at first, what with the pregnant ladies, toddlers, and poor goats in bags. But one of my Burundian friends rode with me and told me that I was doing great, but needed to honk more.

"I don't really like to do that unless I need to."

"Peggy, truly, we are pacifists. It is better to honk than to kill."

Amen.

Safari Tatu

In 2010, I took my third African Journey. My itinerary started with a gathering of Quaker women in Kenya, followed by an overland journey of 1200 miles to Bujumbura where I was scheduled to teach Quaker youth. My international flight to Nairobi connected me to a puddle-jump flight to Mombasa on the Indian Ocean, close to the Tanzanian border (which was good, since the other border is Somalia). An after-dark taxi ride through Mombasa-town took almost an hour. Mombasa is a city of four million. It looked poor. When we got out, jet lag took me off to bed without much attention. When I woke up, I realized that I was not in Kansas anymore. I was at the Sun 'n Sand Resort. Seriously Five-Star, but African: which means you have a bidet, but the hot water only works sometimes. The property has a Disney-like Arabian Nights theme. The grounds were resplendent in tropical flowers of Edenesque variety. A series of outdoor salt-water pools were connected by flowing 'streams' and slides. There were poolside bars and in-the-pool bars. All with a view of the Indian Ocean.

I was here to take in the Friends United Meeting Women's Triennial. The site was chosen, by the Kenyan Committee, to give the 350 Kenyan women in attendance an experience as close as possible to an American Conference.

Oh sisters! America has nothing this wonderful!

I spent my first week sufferin' for Jesus.

The Mzee Baba Pastors

Gospel Ministry was never supposed to be all resorts, salt-water pools, and flowers, and so on the fifth of July I disembarked Mombasa for the trip across Kenya, then on through Uganda, Rwanda and down to my home base in Bujumbura, Burundi. Things got African fairly quickly, as I snagged the opportunity to hitch a ride cross-country with David Zarembka and his wife. (Dave started out American, but he has lived in Western Kenya with his Kenyan wife, Gladys, so long that he hardly counts as American anymore.) This ride meant the first 600 miles would be in the back of Dave's pickup, which is equipped with a secure canopy and bench seats. Sharing the back with me were four Mzee (seasoned) Baba (father) pastors from the Lugulu region. They were only going as far as Nairobi, – having, as they did, good sense – but they were good company. Bless the English Empire (long may she stay dead!) everyone who has been to school in Kenya speaks English.

You pack a truck bed thusly: the most senior goes closest to the cab, as the potholes are ferocious and sneaky, and the lift achieved is greater the farther back you go. So I was back by the tailgate, which gave me air from the windows and the ability to see forward – less puking that way. In there with the Babas, and their luggage, and my luggage, was some nursery stock one of them had acquired, and of course we stopped several times for road side produce. The Babas were amazed at my ability to snatch a tomato out of the air while myself airborne. When the road was smooth enough to permit conversation, we shared stories. We found common interests in obscure Biblical references and botany.

Neither Mama Gladys nor the pastors were drivers, and Zarembka had a bad leg, so when we were good and clear of Mombasa with at least a hundred miles to Nairobi, Friend Z stopped the truck for another round of the territorial marking of the countryside that old men seem so fond of, and announced "Your turn, Peg."

I said to the Babas, "What did the captain of Jonah's boat say to the crew and passengers?"

"Pray to whatever Gods you have!" Chorused the Babas.

"Good advice!" I said, "I'm going to drive!"

Much laughter and Booyah! The girl drives!

Gladys took a turn in the back and Zarembka coached me in driving at high speed on the wrong side of the road. I liked the outside edge of the road but he fueled my courage and insisted I take an inner line, as the worst of the potholes seem to be edgewise. After a few passes of petrol lorries within a foot without my screaming, we settled in, and I did my miles. On that stretch, I saw zebra, baboons, a lone giraffe, and many camels. On the far outskirts of Nairobi, I gave the wheel back and rejoined the Babas. They cheered my efforts and claimed that I was very good at sparing their spines. They asked if I had ever ridden a camel. I had not – neither had they – but I told them that I was an experienced horse woman. One of the Babas exclaimed "Truly – I love you!" And they all tried to convince me to delay my departure for Burundi with a tour of churches in the Lugulu region. This was mostly kindness, but I think they envisioned tomato juggling on horseback, followed by preaching, and it's true, you don't get that every day.

When they deplaned, half-way through a three-hour gridlocked Nairobi, I knew it was going to be lonely in the back without them.

The Last Homely House before the Mountains

After a three-hour crawl through Nairobi, well marinated in die-sel fumes, we started climbing. The entire road from the coast is a climb, of course, but it got obvious now. We reached the edge of the Great Rift Valley and then Lake Nakuru, where all the fla-mingos come from. From this spot on, until the shores of Lake Tanganyika, my path would traverse the Great Rift from one end to the other. It is old, and you feel it – seriously old. And beautiful.

About dusk it started to rain; we had a couple hundred miles to go. Zarembka and I conferred, and it did not seem like a good idea to give me another go at driving in the rain after dark, on unknown roads. The roads are *dark*. No lighting whatsoever, ex-cept for your headlights. There is usually a center line stripe, but no indicators for the sides of the road. Neither Gladys nor Dave could get excited about riding in the back again. So we found a hotel, and some supper at a Kenyan Truck stop. Nice cabbage stew, chapatti, and tea.

After a good sleep and breakfast, we continued up towards El-doret and then 40 miles beyond to the village where Dave and Gladys live. It is high on a rocky outcropping. Clearly volcanic, but ancient. We arrived just after I PM, and we were all glad that we had had the wisdom to split the trip.

Gladys' house is well ordered. We were greeted by their helper, Nancy, and some young relatives at loose ends, and tea was ready. The village water pump was out, but this was not a serious prob-lem, because the house has a water tank and solar panels with battery back-up to the electricity. Water, if we are not extrava-gant, and lights, but no water heating – it was enough. A good bed, good food and good company. I was happy to rest there be-fore the next leg.

African Relativity Theory

From Gladys' house, I would continue my journey on the people's bus. Everyone, including me, thought I would be tired at the end of the trip, but everyone, also including me, thought that it would progress without any real trouble, and that I might even enjoy parts of it. Dave had done it many times – he told me he would never do it again, but he blamed that on being an old man, and he had no doubts about the wisdom of my plan over flying back to Nairobi and then flying to Kigali. I have this travel allergy to retrograde motion – it has gotten me in trouble before, and will no doubt get me in trouble again.

What I was forgetting was the African Relativity Theory, which states that the difficulty of traversing any particular distance can be inversely proportional to the level of difficulty anticipated. Translation: "Whatever you thought? – It ain't gonna' be so!" This often combines with intermittent temporal anomalies, where time slows down or, rarely, speeds up in unpredictable ways. Also a factor is the African Amnesia effect – just because you really should have known better does not mean that you do.

Resting comfortably at Chez Zarembka, I was told that I would need to go back to Eldoret to catch the overnight through bus to Kigali. This, despite the fact that the through bus would pass right by the road to our town. But they knew the "Good" coach company, and it would be the big bus, not the *matatu* (bus of ten places.) Much better to be on the express than on the local line. The bus would leave at 5 PM and arrive in Kigali by breakfast time. Dave and Gladys needed to be about other business on my departure day, and this made Gladys a bit concerned – she wanted to see me onto the right bus – but Dave and I had spent a day swapping travel stories, he being a 40-year vet of the region, and he decided that any woman who had done the Congolese border crossing on her own could manage a bus in Eldoret. Being, as it was, Africa, where you just don't count on doing more than one task in a day, it was decided that I should get my ticket a day ahead. But being, as it was, Africa, I didn't actually need to do this myself, and there were several young relatives at loose ends who could be assigned the task. So two young nephews of Gladys, Pat and Mike, were sent to Eldoret with my money and a handwritten note from me requesting a ticket. They came back about dark, successful, with a ticket clearly marked for the next day, 5pm, through to Kigali with no layover in Kampala. Supposed to be sixteen hours.

Retrograde Motion

The morning was bright, and clear, and cool. I had packed for Mombasa and Buja and didn't really have much in the way of warm things, but *Hakuna Matata*, I was not staying very long. We saw the hosts off on their errand and started getting me ready for my trip. As a very last thought, Mama Gladys instructed Nancy to boil a few eggs and pack me some traveling food. Patrick had been assigned the task of accompanying me to the bus. He is a very good natured fellow. He and I had gotten acquainted when, at my request, he hiked with me up to the top of the rock out-cropping above the village the day before, and I liked him. Patrick said we needed two hours to get to Eldoret, and knowing the flexibility of bus schedules anywhere in the world – but especially here – I wanted to be at the station by 3:00 at the latest. So I figured we should leave by 1:00.

About 10:30, Gladys phoned Nancy. Someone she knew had called and told her that the through bus might not be running tonight, and that I should be prepared for changes. Having well-placed informants is part of the job of a well-run household, and I was grateful, but not terribly concerned. I finished loading my pack and told Patrick that I thought we should just go ahead and set off. Nancy wanted me to eat lunch before I left, but she hadn't started cooking it. I was not in a mood to wait. Nancy handed me two hard boiled eggs, a bread roll, and two crisp apples. Always good to start a trip with apples in your pocket.

It was about 11 AM when we went out through the gate, taking leave of Nancy and her helper. Housewives and children through-out the village wished me well, as if I had been there a month, not two days. Patrick shouldered my big pack, which at 35 lbs. I can carry comfortably, but I knew I would get weary of it soon enough and was glad of his help. We walked up to the village square and hired THREE *piki-piki* (small moto taxis) – one for me, one for Patrick and one for my pack.

Lumakunda sits about two miles above the main road, and when I say above, I mean that on a rainy day we could have sledded down. When we reached the tarmac of the main road, I looked right; the Uganda border was less than an hour away. Kampala was that way. Eldoret was left, slightly farther back towards Nairobi. My allergy set in, and I thought about just catching the next *matatu* to the border, but I had my ticket and my good sense, and I got ready to move to the rear.

We caught the next *matatu*, which, like all good *matatus*, had a name: "God is One." It is just good luck to have a name and most of them acknowledge God in some way. The ten seat Toyota vans frequently seat sixteen or more, plus baggage, produce, and livestock. They come equipped with a driver and a catcher/stuffer. In town, the catcher's job is to convince people to choose his bus over all the other obviously inferior buses, and to fill it to capacity as quickly as possible. He collects the fees and packs the sardines. The same job exists on the Tokyo subway, but those guys wear white gloves.

The bus looked full to me – ten seats, fifteen people and three chickens – but an old Baba was squeezed over and I was given a seat. Patrick stood, backside to the door, leaning over two seated people – which is usually the catcher's position. Our catcher left the door open and hung on the outside of the bus. We were off!

Matatus stop for everything. We stopped at least once a mile. At stops where we gain or lose a passenger, the catcher shuffled people. I was eventually shifted up to the seat of honor in the front, by the driver. Patrick got a seat with the chickens. He made no complaint. My bag was somewhere in the boot, although how the boot can have any space was beyond me. Two hours later, we were in Eldoret, at the lot which is home to all the buses. Patrick shouldered my bag and weaved off between the buses and people, cheerfully commanding me not to lose him. All the catchers tried to catch us, but we were set on bigger hooks. Away from Matatu-land and a block up the road, and we were at the small, tidy office of Kampala Coach, Ltd.

Our informant was correct. The ticket agent was apologetic but helpful. "The 5 PM through bus is not traveling today, ma'am, but since you are here in such good time, we can put you on the 2 or 3 PM bus to Kampala. – What? You prefer to go sooner, rather than later? Very well, Ma'am – the 2 PM bus it is."

Patrick was concerned about my transfer in Kampala. The agent was reassuring. "Do not worry a bit, Ma'am. You will arrive by 11:00 PM and almost immediately you will be put on the midnight bus going south to Kigali. It will be an easy and quick transfer. You will actually arrive earlier than you would have on the through bus. Our Agents in Kampala will help you with everything. Kampala Coach Ltd is the finest bus service in the region, we are known for our luxury and tender care." Patrick looked mildly concerned. The man was laying it on a bit thick – even by local standards of thickness. Stuff that thick is always a cause for concern.

But in fifteen minutes it was announced that the bus has arrived, "Behind the office," which turned out to be a block away on the next street. It was Greyhound-sized, and red, and shiny. I was impressed. Patrick saw my bag into the big boot and made sure I knew which locker it was in. He saw me all the way onto the bus, and conversed with the driver, who said that really, the transfer should be no problem. Patrick knew that Mama Gladys would quiz him on my status, and when it came to it, he seemed a little concerned about sending me off solo. I gave him my best "No worries, kid," and then prayed a blessing on him, gave him my spare Kenyan shillings that I now wouldn't need, and sent him off. He went as far as the street corner to wait and watch until the bus left. A woman who heard me pray changed seats and said, "I will sit by you." By 2:30, we were off.

My seatmate was a youngish widow with one young son. We discussed American TV preachers, which are syndicated and all the rage in Africa. Joyce Meyers is *huge*. The widow wanted to know what I thought about Joel Osteen. I explained my discomfort with his salary, but acknowledged that he is not likely a crook or faker like some of them. She thought that his wife looks "Proud – haughty – a woman can see this in another woman." I told her that this is indeed Victoria's rep. We agreed that John Hagee yells too much, and preaches fear. "I like hope – better" she said. I agree. She wanted to know what I think about life after death. "Where are the souls?" I gave her Jesus to the thief on the cross. She had seen spiritualists who charged money to talk to the dead. It turned out that she was worried about her husband. I encouraged her to communicate with him through Jesus – "He never loses track of anyone, and doesn't charge a fee." When she departed two hours later, just before the border, she thanked me for the conversation. "So nice to talk with someone about the things of God."

We made the Ugandan border about 5:30. A Kenyan exit stamp, then a good long walk – Then a Ugandan visa for $50. Same price for a night's transit or a month's stay. I was hoping that it will turn out to be about $10 an hour, but I ended up getting a lot more bang for my buck. We waited for our bus to arrive through the barriers. I turned down multiple chances to change some money into Ugandan shillings, but I couldn't see the need for it, and all I have is a stack of $100 bills – and I *know* I can't possibly spend $100 before morning. I was hungry. I ate an egg, an apple and the bread roll. A small boy was selling bananas. I wished I had some small money to increase my provisions – he would have happily taken my Kenyan shillings. But a Ben Franklin would buy a lot more than all the bananas this boy has for sale. I thought about using my wiles to get one of the nice businessmen on the bus to buy me some bananas, but I was just not that desperate – yet. I waved the boy off. "But really, Ma'am, they are *full* of potassium!" I complimented his marketing skills, and told him that they also had a lot of Vitamin B – he nodded, and filed this info away.

Our bus rolled through about 6 PM, and they gave it a final customs check. Our driver and conductor looked nervous. They asked me to bring my bag up from the boot, as the lockers would be sealed once they are checked. We waited. And then we waited some more. Finally, a full team of inspectors showed up, and gave our bus a body-cavity check from stem to stern. Then they went through the bus itself and looked at every passenger's luggage. They herded us all off the bus and checked it again. Everyone is nervous. Our conductor said this usually takes ten minutes. He denied knowing the reason for their concern. They held us for two hours. Then they let us go. It was 8 PM and dark. Off to Kampala.

Staying Alert

The roads in Uganda were significantly worse than those in Kenya, and our driver seemed to be determined to make up the time lost at the border. This is when I discovered that Kampala Coach Ltd. had been investing more in red paint than in shock absorbers. The potholes were bone-jarring, and the occasional sudden swerves attempting to avoid them had a tendency to put you in your neighbor's lap or on the floor of the aisle. After the first dumping into the aisle, I moved to the seat by the stairs, where I could wedge my pack and small bag between me and the barrier and the outer wall as pre-emptive "air-bags." This seat also provided great air flow from the door, which did not really shut. I pulled out my only long-sleeved shirt for warmth.

This seat also afforded me a view of our driver. Our driver was taking regular sips from a flask.

"Our driver appears to be drinking," I said to the man next to me.

"Oh, yes, they all do that – they need to stay awake, you know."

"No, I mean he seems to be drinking alcohol."

"Yes, a little whiskey to stay sharp."

"Wouldn't you want to take tea or coffee to stay awake?"

"No! Tea makes a person ready for bed!"

I encountered this idea several other times in East Africa – the belief that alcohol keeps you sharp and tea makes you sleepy. (Ironically, in the region that invented coffee, most locals don't drink it.) Sometimes I would forget my place as a guest and try to explain stimulants and depressants, but this is rude. I asked around, and found that *drunk* driving (emphasis on severely drunk) is discouraged. But drinking and driving is not illegal in most of the countries I was in.

Many of my fellow passengers had the gift of "sleeping in any circumstance." I tried, and failed. We flew through small towns, and I watched as roadside shops stayed open for late business.

Eventually all closed but the drinking houses. In between towns, it was truly dark. Our driver was making liberal use of the entire road, as evidenced by the occasional sudden headlights appearing around what I presumed from the centripetal forces to be blind curves, with the attendant blaring horns and cursing.

Dante's Bus Station

I am sure that Kampala is a lovely city. I am sure that it is first-rate in many ways. I am sure that Uganda has much to offer – I hear that it has 600 varieties of birds. But I saw none of that. Whenever you enter a city by bus, you see a different city than you see as a tourist flying in for your vacation. We reached the far outskirts of the city at about 10 PM. Not much was open. As we entered the city itself, everything was barred and gated, like you would see in the bad parts of New York. Also like New York, the homeless were out; but there are no city ordinances against garbage fires, so that is what they were using for heat. Heat was needed, as it was probably in the low sixties and dropping. The miserable humans dressed in layers of rags around the fires lent a discernible air of Gehenna to the place. Dante would have been at home.

We reach the bus station about 11:30. It has huge arched iron gates, topped with replica spear-head decorations and coils of razor wire. Inside the gates, a row of buses is parked; above them, a dimly lit area. Our conductor says that there was no room for us inside the gates, and that we will be parking here in the street. Transfer passengers are told to make their way up to the office and check in. Our driver opens his door and drains out into the dark. We all start to gather our things. The conductor is about to take off when a passenger near me shouts,

"Man! You aren't letting this Mzungu walk up there by herself, are you?"

"Oh, Kiswahili-curse-word, okay – stay where you are, lady, I will go get some help."

I am mildly concerned that he thinks that he needs reinforcements, but I thank the other passenger, who just shakes his head.

I am alone on the bus for a couple of minutes. There are men at the door calling for me, having marked my presence. When the conductor comes back with two other guys, he gives me my instructions: "Okay – in and up – don't stop – stay right behind me!" Off of the bus, my small phalanx of bus employees shout and slap and push their way through a crowd of what I presume are mostly taxi drivers, sure that I am a potential fare to the nearest hotel.

Some of you have experienced the African airport taxi crush. Bus station taxi drivers are several magnitudes more desperate and aggressive than that. Taxi drivers attempt to get hold of your bag, because they know if they get your bag – they will get you. Many arms are reaching and tugging at my bag and my clothes. Men are shouting for me to join them. Other, more ragged, arms are also attempting to reach me. I presume these are a sprinkling of thieves, pickpockets and beggars – because that is just standard. I manage to keep my footing on very uneven ground in almost no light, with my top heavy pack being yanked left and right. My tucked-down head still identifies the smells of burning garbage, human waste, goat Barbecue, stale beer, and unwashed and unwell humans. Not quite Reavers, but close. (Sorry – *Firefly* reference.)

When we get through the gates, my phalanx reverses and pushes me up a small flight of stairs, to what I presume is safety.

Ships in the Night

I enter the bus station a bit rattled, but actually encouraged. All I have to do is identify the correct bus, get on it, and then I can sleep, rolling or not. I am getting tired enough that I am sure sleeping will not be a problem.

The bus station consists of two areas: an outer courtyard, above the buses and open to the night air, and an inner semi-enclosed room. The courtyard is a concrete pad with two walls and some benches: it also has a food kiosk, and, to let you know that you were really in a bus station, a TV anchored up in the corner. The inner room has a desk with an employee behind it, an area for parcels, and an area marked "sleeping space," with reed mats on the concrete floor and sections marked for men and women. A dozen people are making use of it, despite the bright fluorescent lights – really, some people do have the gift of sleep. I see no evidence of restrooms.

I make my way through the crush at the desk and display my ticket to the agent. I ask if the midnight bus has left for Kigali.

"No, it has not gone."

"Good, I want to get on that bus."

"I am sorry – That bus is full – you will have to go on the 2 AM bus."

"Sir, I was supposed to be on the through bus, please see my ticket here, and it was promised in Eldoret that I would be put on the first bus out of here – that would be the midnight bus."

"Actually, Ma'am, your ticket is for travel on the 8th of July and in fifteen minutes it will be the 9th, so you are going to have to buy a new ticket for the 2 AM bus."

"Now see here, Sir, I was sold a *through* ticket to *start* on the 8th, it is not my fault that I am not right now on my way to Kigali. You will send me on my way as quickly as possible! – and I am not giving you another shilling!"

He silently writes "2 AM" on a piece of scrap paper and hands it to me as if we were not both conversing in the Queen's English. I take his paper and just as silently crush it in my hand, drop it on the floor and stomp on it while giving him my best steely gaze. I lean in.

"Get me on that next bus – or you are going to wish you had!"

He gives me a wry smile and says, "We shall see what we can do."

Deciding when to be patient and when to have a fiery temper display is an African finesse point. Guess right, and way opens magically. Guess wrong, and you will back-burner yourself into the previous century. After twelve hours of uncomfortable travel,

I am getting beyond finesse. But I think that I just might have guessed right. He writes me a scrap of paper that says "Next bus."

I decide to do a little recon. I go out to the courtyard and start pleasantly polling any passengers who are awake about their destinations. There are two directions to go that night: south to Kigali, Rwanda, or north to Juba, Sudan. I am very clear that I do not want to accidentally get on the wrong bus, fall asleep, and wake up in the Sudan. I identify a young girl traveling with her old father. They are Burundians going through Kigali to Buja. The girl has English. They are waiting for the midnight bus and have been there for a couple of hours. I tell her, that if she doesn't mind, I am going to attach myself to their party and that when she gets on a bus I am going to get on that bus. "I'll just tell them I am your mama." She laughs. She is glad to have the company. I lean my pack against the concrete wall, put my small bag under my knees, and pretend it is a recliner. I sit and practice relaxation.

I don't know where bus stations all over the globe buy speakers, but they are universally bad, and here the messages are completely in Kiswahili, of which I get about one word in ten. I ask my new friend Chantelle if she is catching them. She is. God bless multi-lingual children. I ask her if she has found any bathrooms. She says they are there, down by the gate, "But they are not nice." Burundian girls are tough; if she is turning her nose up at it, it has to be bad, and I do not want to get within ten meters of that gate. I decide to tough it out. She and her Baba have plates of food – potatoes and beans and greens. Apparently the kiosk is feeding transfer passengers. But you have to get a voucher from the man at the desk. Hmmm. There are also cokes and fried bread for sale, but I have no shillings. I eat my second apple.

We wait. Midnight comes and goes. I keep checking my pocket watch. Chantelle says, "You need to work on your patience." I am quite accustomed to being eldered by African teenage girls, and I tell her that she is right. I settle in to watch the movie. It is The Karate Kid – the new one – with Jackie Chan. Dubbed into Kiswahili. The layers of surreal are not actually calculable. But the plot is so predictable that I follow it with ease. Baba Chantelle dozes with his head in his hands. Then the movie is over, Chantelle looks at me, and I say to Chantelle "I would look at my watch, but I am practicing patience." She laughs and says, "I will investigate."

She comes back with the report that the midnight bus has its engine compartment open, with several men inside. She is obviously peeved. It is 1:30. I refrain from counseling Chantelle about patience.

At 2 AM, the 1 AM bus from Juba arrives, and is re-designated the midnight bus to Kigali. When they announce this, Chantelle pops up like toast, rouses the Baba, and says to me – "Tu Gende (Let's move.)" I am in complete agreement. We make the bus, which is thankfully inside the barrier, just as the last of the Sudanese passengers get off. We choose seats, Chantelle and Baba across the aisle, me trying the Southwest Airlines Jedi Mind trick of "You really don't want to sit with me," to get the extra seat. I say to Chantelle, "There is no Earthly power that can get me off this bus now." and she smiles. I am hearing a lot of Kirundi/Kinyarwanda, which is a great comfort. I almost manage the extra seat, but the last passenger to board joins me. He is about 25, at least six feet tall, and chatty. I decide not to care. I will ride next to Shaquille O'Neal in a foul mood if this bus will just go south. I wish I knew which way was south.

At 2:30 the midnight bus rolls out. Surely nothing can go wrong, now.

Fifteen and a half hours into a supposed sixteen hour trip, and not half-way there.

Dawn of the Dead Travelers

My relief gives way to annoyance when we pull into a petrol station at the edge of town, but really, I can't be opposed to the notion of being fueled up. It takes 30 minutes to fill the big bus. Then, to my enormous dismay, the bus turns around and goes back to the bus station. What sort of velocity do you need to escape this place? We apparently lack a conductor, and had simply been allowed to ride along for the fill up. A fresh conductor joins us. It is three-thirty. Perhaps now?

And then the young fellow seated next to me speaks up.

"Say, Conductor, do you have our complimentary water? Our tickets say that we will be provided bottled water on this trip."

"No – do you want me to go get water?" asks the conductor.

"I do." says my seatmate, oblivious to the hissing and growling and wall of hatred radiating from his fellow passengers.

"You have got to be kidding!" I say. "We are working on four hours late, and you want to slow us down!?" I haven't seen a toilet since the Kenyan border, eight hours ago, and drinking water is the last thing on my mind.

"We paid for the luxury bus, and I mean to get what I paid for." he says.

An entire busload of Christians ignore the Sermon on the Mount and commit the sin of murder in their heads.

The conductor goes back up into the station and eventually comes back with a case of bottled water. It is 4 AM, and we appear to be leaving Kampala, but I am not convinced.

The roads are bad, but I don't care. Our driver drinks, but I don't care. I wedge my pack between me and the seat in front of me so that I physically cannot be thrown out of my seat when the brakes slam on, I put my small bag between me and the wall so that when I am hurled outward I have something to cushion the impact, and I turn my back on my seatmate and try to sleep. My dozing is intermittent, due to the flailing arms and knees of the boy next door. He is not wedged in, and occasionally gravity attempts to put him in my seat. Despite this, he stretches out and snores peacefully.

About 6 AM, the darkness starts to lift. I give up on sleep and watch the Ugandan countryside fly by at warp speed. Uganda looks poor – you can tell this when the roofing is rusted, but there are enormous white cranes in the marshes. I decide to take out my final hard-boiled egg and call it breakfast. I find it nestled intact in my bag. I hold it up and try to compose a prayer of gratitude. At that moment a pothole gets us and my egg is airborne and crashes to the floor, cracks and rolls towards the back of the bus. Somehow this manages to disturb my seatmate and he sits up and says "What was that?" "My last bit of sanity breaking – not to worry."

At 7 AM, the bus pulls off at a petrol station and the conductor announces that this will be our only morning rest stop. I look across at Chantelle, "Toilets?" "Of some sort." she says. Everyone gets off. I follow the parade. Behind the station is a Ugandan people's relief station. This means that, behind a low wall, there is a three meter by three-meter concave concrete structure with a hole at the low center. It is not only unisex, but is used by eight people at a time, two to a side. The surface is slippery and sticky at the same time. The men have the obvious natural advantage of distance, and don't actually have to step onto the concrete. African ladies step up onto it, raise skirts, and squat. Gentlemen are very careful in their attempts to not splatter the ladies. If you must do something other than make water, you squat with your back to the hole, and there is a garden hose to wash solids into the abyss. Not everyone had been so thoughtful. Like most western ladies, I prefer trousers for travel. I take in this entire scene and scan the area for friendly bushes. I ask Chantelle if she thinks anyone would care if I went off into the brush. She looks shocked, and mildly disgusted. "You can't do that when there is a toilet here." she says.

The social rules seem to be urban elevator. Do not converse, do not make eye contact, do not look at others. Unless, of course, a white lady is about to drop trou, in which case anyone could be forgiven for taking a good look, because God knows, she might have a tail or something in those trousers, and this may be your only chance in this life to see such a sight. I hope they were satisfied.

Blessings

We make the Rwandan border about 10 AM. Again the routine with the exit stamp, the separation from bus and bags for the walk across no man's land, and the entry stamp. I love the Rwandans. The US and a number of other countries are listed as "Friends of Rwanda," and no visa is required and no fee is charged. But you still fill out a form and get a nice stamp. I always put "pastor" as my occupation on the forms, and it does buy me some respect. I am through immigration in record time.

Since I expect to stay in Rwanda for the best part of a week, I change some money. $100.00 USD gets me 5,500 Rwandan francs. I feel like Melinda Gates, except I am sure that Melinda smells better than I do. I head to the bathroom. Yes, a real building! It is still unisex, but you enter a room with shiny sinks and urinals and stalls marked Ladies, Gents, and Staff. The stalls have doors that go to the floor! The actual toilet is still a keyhole in the floor affair, but it is porcelain and flanked by grippy foot positioners. And best of all, a young man stands ready and throws in a bucket full of soapy water between each patron. When you emerge, a smaller boy stands ready at the sink to hand you a bar of soap and pour water over your hands from a jerry can. (You didn't think the faucets worked, did you? silly reader!) I am tempted to strip and scrub, but I settle for up to the elbows, and my face and neck. I laugh in delight, and the boy laughs with me as I splash him. As in all African public toilets, you pay for this privilege, but I tip big in Rwanda, God bless them!

Next I buy a coke. First caffeine in 24 hours. I am still hungry, but renewed. I go and join the people of my bus, because we are about to be treated to the Rwandan plastic bag search. Rwanda is a proud country. Their president openly states that he wishes Rwanda to become the Singapore of Central Africa. They have recently made plastic shopping bags illegal in the entire country. This is a good thing. Plastic bag trash is the new paving material in most of Africa. The open burning of plastic material is a toxic smell you become accustomed to. Rwanda has done away with at least some of this. Every bus, every person, and every piece of luggage is checked at every border for contraband plastic shopping bags. At first I am told that they did this with the military and guns, but it has now been privatized. Our inspector is about twenty years old and wears a t-shirt emblazoned with G-Man, but he takes his job very seriously. It is serious work. If they find a bag, it is confiscated, and you are forced to buy a paper sack at a very inflated price to hold your goods. Then there is a great scolding – and then they throw the plastic bag on the ground, and it blows off in the wind. It is very clear that it would not be a good idea to question the environmental wisdom of the bag disposal method. They don't like plastic in Rwanda, and they don't like questions. They are very fond of soap, obedience, and respect. Our bus passes the inspection, and as soon as the driver comes back with the customs paperwork, we will go. Everyone is encouraged.

I am finishing my coke and wondering what to do with the plastic bottle when our conductor approaches me. He and I are alone on the far side of the bus. He graces me with a big grin – the first I have seen from him.

"May I ask you a question?"

I am feeling better, too. "Sure – go ahead."

"Are you married yet?"

(Important note: many Africans I have met have a terrible time guessing the ages of *wazungu*. As best I can tell, they are gauging by shape, size, hair color and style, and how you move. I am not traditionally built; my hair was not gray, I wear it long and often loose, and I do not move like an old woman. They guess my age anywhere from 25 to 40, never the 52 that I was on this trip. I am no better at gauging their ages. The human software for this seems to have limits.)

I laugh at the conductor. He is tall, large, round, and I would guess him at 30 – could be anywhere from 25 to 50. Certainly old enough that he has a wife and kids someplace back up the road.

He misinterprets my laughter, and leans in, and backs me against the bus.

"Because I have always wanted to have a sweet white baby doll like you..."

His breath is sour and hot. Things just got serious.

I put a hand squarely on his sternum and give him a gentle push back. I pull myself to my full height and give him my very best withering glare – eye to eye.

"Sir! You are extremely mistaken. I am a mother. (I push – he gives.) I am a grandmother. (I put a finger in his face as he steps back again.) And I am the pastor of a church, on my way to teach Bible in Burundi." He stops breathing and stares at me, eyes wide open. He looks as though he wants to melt into the ground. He is saved by the driver showing up and shouting, "Tu Gende!" Passengers materialize, and we all climb back on the bus.

The conductor gets on the bus last, looking like a whipped dog. He tries to avoid me, but this is made difficult by my having the aisle seat at the top of the stairs right across from his perch. For effect, I pull out my Bible and my reading glasses and read from the story of Boaz the Good and his treatment of Ruth, sharing with Chantelle the fine points of the story. Several rows participate in the impromptu Bible study. The conductor is very quiet. After about 50 kilometers, I put the Bible away. We all close our eyes in prayerful rest.

After a bit the conductor comes and sits on the filthy step below me. Quietly he pleads his case. "Ma'am, Pastor, I am very sorry for what I said to you. I beg you to forgive me. I am not a bad man, really. Please do not curse me." They take the power to bless and curse literally and seriously. This man is extremely worried. I give him some quiet counsel on his duty to protect his passengers, especially women traveling alone. Then I tell him that I will forgive him, and that in fact I will give him a blessing. He beams up at me. A reprieved man.

"In the Name of Jesus – Whatever you sow, you will reap ten-fold. If you give peace, peace will come to you, if kindness, – kindness, if trouble – TROUBLE."

His smile freezes.

"I advise you to be a very good man."

Welcome Home

It was almost noon. The Rwandan border crossing had eaten another hour and a half. I was now twenty-five hours into a sixteen hour trip. But we were rolling! Sadly, we were rolling on the wrong side of the road. At the Uganda/Rwanda border, the road goes from British influenced – drive on left – to French influenced – drive on right. Our Ugandan driver seemed determined to be true to his country's ways. Several passengers kindly reminded him of the switch, but he continued to drive on the left unless actually facing down another vehicle. When this occurred, he swerved violently to the right and cursed them; taking offense at their blaring horns and counter-curses. We proceeded the better part of two hours in this manner, until we reached the outskirts of Kigali and the traffic became thick enough to force our driver to assume the obviously flawed and counter-intuitive position.

Just as there is a refreshing vigor in fresh roads, there is a special sweetness in coming from the unknown into space that you know. One glimpse of the Kigali Hills, and I knew where I was. I could have driven from there, and it might have been a good idea. Even before reaching that spot, the flora had become familiar, the people customary, and the sights comprehensible. Not home, but close enough.

In due course, 27.5 hours in, we arrived at the section of Kigali where the buses live. It was blue with diesel smoke. Kigali lies in a bowl, and the buses live at the lowest point. I knew the name of the hotel I wanted – the Okapi – but I had not stayed there in three years, so I was hoping it was there, open, still respectable, and had a room for me. If not, I was ready to say the magic word "Intercontinental" and blow 200 bucks on clean-and-fed. In Kigali, "Mille Collines" will also work – if you have to ask how much, you can't stay there. I wonder what happens if you come in on the people's bus, get into a taxi, and say, "Mille Collines." The cognitive dissonance might damage the taxi driver.

Getting off the bus in daylight was merely purgatorial rather than hellacious. The crush of taxi drivers was the same. They were shouting and ready to grab my bag, but daylight and known territory makes a gal bold. So from the top of the bus steps I chose my man – a small, Congolese looking fellow with an open face and a clean shirt. I pointed at him, shouted "Wewe!" (You!), and launched my bag at him. It caused him to take two steps back, but he was grinning. Tu Gende, Madame! The Francophone title felt so comfy. He turned and I followed. His taxi was parked nearly a block away, but we made it. I swatted thieves like flies.

I had to pay my man half up-front, because the cab had no gas. He put in two liters. But he knew the Okapi, and I knew where it was and approved of his efficient route. You have to be efficient when you only have two liters of gas in your cab. Fortunately, the Okapi is mid-way up one of the Kigali hills. He could easily coast back down to the bus-yard. I am sure he did.

The lady at the desk of the Okapi was coiffed beautifully, dressed smartly, and smelled delicious. She looked at me as if a leprous alley cat had just walked in. Not far off. If my skin had not looked sort of white, I would have gotten no further.

I quietly pleaded my case. "Bonjour, Madame, I am Peggy Senger. I have no reservation, but I have stayed with you before, and I am sincerely hoping that you have a room available for me."

"It is a bit early; check-in is not until 3 PM."

Oh, how the Rwandan people love rules.

"Madame, I am just off Kampala Coach from *Kenya* – I am a desperate woman."

"Ah! So sorry, Madame – that is a terrible journey."

"I can wait if I need to – I could order food in the dining room – I have not eaten today..."

The thought of sending me to the dining room clearly appalled her. She was likely married to the maître d'.

"No, no, the dining room may not be ready for you either – I shall find you a room. Gervais will carry your bag."

A room was found. It came with unlimited hot water, free soap, a shiny private flush toilet, and a bed. What else could the Mille Collines possibly have?

Scrubbed pink, coiffed, made up, and in a dress and heels, I entered the dining room at 3 PM. The maître d' greeted me by name.

"Ah, Madame Peggy, so good to have you at the Okapi again. Your table is ready. I have made coffee, as I think you prefer. Crème, non? Chef will be happy to make you anything you desire. Welcome home."

What was unusual about my transit?

The answer is... nothing. This is standard middle class African travel. There is a whole level of travel below this for the poorer class.

Middle Class travel means:

- Unpredictable schedules – Standard
- 27 hours for a 16 hour trip – Standard
- Filthy toilets – Standard
- Eating once in a day while traveling – Standard
- Sexual Harassment for unaccompanied women – Standard
- At risk for theft – Standard
- Cold, tired, no place to wait comfortably – Standard
- Drunk and dangerous drivers – Standard
- Terrible road conditions – Standard
- Dangerous equipment used for public transport – Standard
- Oppressive and illogical bureaucracies – Standard

During one of the legs of the trip, an African business man inquired about my mission. When I informed him, he puzzled, "Why aren't you on an airplane?" It was a good question. Upper middle class Africans take the plane these days. David Niyonzima takes a plane if he has to go from Buja to Kigali. My desire to see the country, and to experience at least once, the way in which my friends live, was a privileged whim. I was "slumming," knowing that I could leave the rugged path at nearly any time. None of the other people on my bus had that option in reserve.

Getting yourself killed while slumming would be an ignoble death.

I am glad I did it once. It was an education.

I don't think I will do it again.

Loving Las Vegas

I was passing through McCarran International Airport with three hours to blow. The State of Nevada is, at times, difficult for me to enjoy. As a mental health professional and a volunteer fire-of-addictions fighter, the "Addictions R Us" atmosphere creeps me out a bit. I suspect that the blessing of Las Vegas is the feeling of normalcy for folks who may not always feel so normal at home in Des Moines. There are people there who will cheerfully help you hock your wedding ring to continue playing games, and do it as if this were perfectly normal behavior. There are people who will help you get married to someone you met yesterday, and act like this makes perfect sense. Women on stage wear enormous hats and not much else – no problem. Night and day have no differentiation. The party is endless – of course it is.

I did not intend to join the party. But I told myself that I would self-pamper by using the break to buy a good, relaxed meal. So, I walked the concourse with anticipation, scoping out my choices. Alcohol – slots – slots – chocolate – greasy burgers – alcohol – slots – alcohol – Subway – slots: those were the choices. Subway appeared to be the top of the food chain. The most wholesome option was a flavored oxygen bar. Now, while I might wish that I could survive on peach flavored oxygen, I had been on one four-hour no food flight, and I had another one ahead of me. "Six-inch turkey, please."

With two and a half hours yet to blow and still in the mood to be nice to myself, I looked for an opportunity. I am a collector of novel experiences, and when I spied a bored-looking shoeshine man, I realized that warming one of those shoe thrones would add to my collection. My boots agreed.

The gentleman attending to my iguana skins was from Kenya. I had been to his homeland recently and we had a nice chat about Africa. Then I asked him how he felt about Las Vegas. He looked up at me, clearly deciding whether to give me the tourist bureau answer or the truth.

"The truth, please."

"I have a daughter in college at home, and she is precious to me. So I am forced to love Las Vegas because I love my daughter."

I told him it was the best reason I had ever heard for loving Las Vegas.

Bus Karma

All I wanted to do was get home. I knew that the weather was dicey, and more than dicey, up in the Northwest. I had reports from Alivia about two treacherous Seattle drives. But my travel day was supposed to be a break between storms. I was in Albuquerque, and it was three days before Christmas.

My daughter looked online and said that they were landing planes at PDX, and took me to the Sunport. (That's what they call the airport down there.) Things looked good. But then the man who took my baggage said,

"They've cancelled the first flight, but we are going to try and get the next three planes in."

He looked me earnestly in the eye and added, "Good Luck, Ma'am"

"Bonne Chance, Madame" is one of my code words with God. It usually means "Heads up Peg – this may get rough." With no great leading on the line, I should have taken my bag back, called my daughter, and gone back to her house for another week of baby snuggling. But one of my character flaws is a severe allergy to anything that feels like going backwards. And one of my consistent delusions is that the normal rules of the universe don't apply to me. The combo gets me in trouble all the time.

So I let him take my bag and I went up to the gate. Then I watched as they cancelled the next flight and the line of people trying to re-ticket became a hundred strong.

Everyone who flies much knows this scenario. They don't just cancel all the flights at once, they put out the false hope that maybe the next one will get through. While adding incrementally to the host of the distressed and desperate.

My flight was supposed to go to Phoenix, and there I would change planes to Portland. Phoenix was no problem. I would get there, and get stuck there. For who knows how long. Phoenix is nothing and no one to me.

I wanted a little insider info. I saw a Southwest employee at a gate where there were no planes or people. I sidled up.

"What do you know about Portland tonight?"

He shook his head. "Come around on this side."

He showed me a screen on the computer of all flights in or out of PDX. All red – cancelled. Dead planes taxi-ing.

My flight was one of two that had not yet got the hatchet.

"Do you have any powers at this terminal?"

"I can't write you a new ticket. I can print you a new boarding pass – maybe keep you on that plane in Phoenix. It ends up in Oakland. Is that any better for you?"

"Much better! – drop me there, please."

And he did. And then he used his walkie-talkie to find a man on the tarmac to find my bag, and he used his magic marker to mark it OAK instead of PDX, which would have got it pulled at Phoenix.

Having made a Luddite vow of low tech for the trip, I had no phone. I asked a young random stranger if I could use her phone. She handed me her blackberry. I had to ask her to punch in the numbers to Liv. The tiny keyboard confounded me.

"Liv – Can't talk long – gonna get stuck – call Pam and Helen and see if they are in Oakland, and if they can swoop me up, tell them I will be on a flight coming from Phoenix."

Fly by faith, not by sight.

The trip to Oakland was uneventful.

I was about ready to ask another friendly stranger for a phone when I saw Pam at the bottom of the escalator. Ahhh.... a port in the storm. Before we left the airport, I checked with another Southwest employee. All flights cancelled to PDX. The next available seat four days hence, on Boxing Day. I took a reservation for it.

After a good meal and a glass of wine with good friends, I settled in for the night. Not home, but within striking distance, I felt. If not home for Christmas, then at home with people who love me. I had no complaints.

In the morning, I felt peaceful. But after coffee I broke my techno fast and used Pam's computer to check out the situation. No planes going north. No seats on any trains. Buses selling seats, but not driving over the Siskiyou Mountains into Oregon. I called home. They told me that the Christmas Eve service was on, as the weather was breaking in Salem. Christmas Eve Service in 36 hours, weather permitting.

I love the Christmas Eve Service at Freedom Friends. We have candles, we have Scripture, and we have sweet music. (Some Friends do.) I had not missed leading a Quaker Christmas Eve Service since 1995. It is my favorite moment of the year. But this looked like the year. Being a good Quaker, I was going to be okay. I called home and told them so. Liv thought it sounded like I was trying to convince myself. My daughter said it sounded like I was lying. The former, most likely. But I settled in and took a walk about Oakland. Palm trees and hoodlums, so festive.

At the grocery I had another funny omen. They had Rwandan Coffee – an extremely rare find. From the Gorilla Mountains, on the road to Goma. I laughed and bought some. I told myself, "At least you aren't taking *that* bus ride today..." (Sometimes I don't listen to myself very well)

I went back to Pam and Helen's and decided to read my e-mails – about 375 of them. The Greyhound site popped up, because I had hibernated without closing. They now said that they were going north. I called in telephonically and asked them if this was for real. They assured me it was. They had seats, on a bus that would go overnight and have me in Salem for breakfast a full twelve hours before the Christmas Eve Service. I bought a ticket.

Pam and Helen were only a little disappointed that I was bugging out so soon. Pam, a wise traveler, said that she had good experience of Greyhound in a pinch, but explained to me that a bus ticket was not a guaranteed seat, just a promise to take you that way whenever they could. You get in a line, and when the bus comes in, if eight people get off then eight people get to climb on. The rest of the line waits for the next bus. Hmm. I would have to change buses in Sacramento. Sounded like a likely place to get stuck. Pam kindly allowed that while she wasn't driving to the State Capitol to get me tonight, she did know Quakers there, and would call them if need be.

I proceeded.

Greyhound is the people's bus. I noticed immediately some groups of people who choose it. The nicotine addicted were the most obvious. They stop nearly every hour or so, and almost the whole bus gets off to smoke. Also aboard were those who smoke other plants and who do not want to go through any kind of personal security check. Several passengers had a personal space zone that was pretty spacey. You thought about whom you wanted to sit next to, and whether you wanted to have a second-hand stimulant or relaxant. We also had people who might not want their weapons confiscated. They did a cursory check of the bags. They might have noticed a bomb, or an AK, but small arms and drugs on your person – no problemo. We don't see them – you don't have trouble. Oh yes, and the elderly who only speak Spanish. And single moms with kids. These were the people of our bus.

On the trip to Sacramento I sat by a Hispanic man who looked for all the world like Admiral Adama on Battlestar Gallactica. Turned out he was a professional boxer and Nam Vet, now doing medical administration, who had just taken a course in disaster relief and trauma. He was looking towards a new career in counseling. We had a lot to talk about. I encouraged him to think about getting into trauma work with vets. His last words to me:

"Thanks for the talk, Peg. I think you did a little work here tonight. Now rest and get home safe."

At Sacramento, there were twice as many people wanting to go north as there were bus seats. People were nervous, edgy. They guarded the line from people cutting with a ferocity that the "A" group on Southwest never has to muster. We formed tightly knit bands for the purpose of watching luggage during toilet breaks. We stayed in line a couple of hours. We watched over the very young and the very old. Tweakers from the street tried to cage food from travelers. Young hoodlums bantered and cussed. Even young hoodlums sometimes try to go home for Christmas.

I made the bus. They had an empty one for us. It looked a little old. It was "Restroom equipped for your convenience." Turns out that means an open-drop-latrine sloshing about in the back compartment. Nice, I thought – almost African.

Our driver, handing out boarding stubs, seemed peeved. She told us that she thought we would have to change to another bus at Redding (the last stop in California) because she didn't think they had her scheduled any farther. She drove like Jehu through heavy rain to Redding, getting us there about midnight. She said it would be a ten-minute stop.

I watched her have a heated discussion with the station master and a driver who had just got in from the north. They had her scheduled through to Eugene. She did not want to go. She had enough hours, said the master. The other driver was on mandated six hour rest. Our driver jumped ship. She said in a loud voice, "I declare myself fatigued – I am unsafe to drive," and she picked up her bags and walked off the premises. We were marooned.

The other driver popped his head in. "Don't worry folks – they are going to get you another driver, and then you will be on your way." An hour later, the station master boarded. "We are trying to get you another driver – they are putting one on the next bus from Sac – it will be about two more hours." Then they closed up the station with the vending machines and decent toilets. They turned out the lights. They left us there in an idling bus (so we had heat) with not one employee to watch us. We could have driven the thing off – it occurred to some of us.

At seven hours, they opened the station back up and the driver from the north came back, just as a bus finally got in from Sacramento. He was supposed to be their driver. He looked in on us. "You aren't the people from last night? – O, God – You are! I guess I'd better drive you." We approved of his initiative.

Before we left, they allowed people from the bus behind us to fill any seats we had left. The more elderly and lame joined us. And, sitting across the aisle from me, an enormous black man who seemed extremely agitated. But we were off, thirteen hours into what was supposed to be a thirteen hour trip and not even out of the valley.

We then discovered why our previous bus driver had bailed. In the next seven hours our driver got us over the two sets of mountains, the foothills of Shasta, and then the Siskiyous. But not without having to stop the bus four times to chain up. A little man, but hardy, he was not allowed to accept help from any of the strong young men on the bus, as this was against regs. We did have the old school bus. He told us it was an M-12, no automatic chains or toilets, but dependable. He didn't grumble a bit about dragging chains out of storage and wrapping the many wheels, then unwrapping them whenever we hit clear pavement. When the chains are on, you can only drive 35 mph.

Our previous driver would have been doing that in the pitch black of a 3 AM night. I would have bailed too.

We made Central Point, Oregon (outside Medford) about noon. Still six hours from home, but still possible to make church. If we hurried. The large man next to me got off the bus – he was still aggravated. I observed him have a couple of words with some young men from another bus. I watched him wave his arms and storm off to the truck stop. I went in and tried to find a phone. The man was ahead of me. Shouting into a pay phone. Having what I immediately recognized as a full-blown African temper tantrum. By this I mean that I recognized his accent as clearly African, and that he was whipped into a frenzy at some offense.

I made my call home and went back to the bus. Several members of the Central Point Police Department were getting off our bus. The African was talking heatedly with our driver. Then the officers were talking to the people of the other bus. I got on the bus.

I asked a nearby passenger "What is the deal with our African friend?"

He said, "Heck if I know, he don't speak a lick of English, I tried ta talk to him and couldn't understand a word he said."

I sat down. I watched out the window. I tried to stay out of it, physically and mentally. But I kept wondering if he was West African or Central African. Central Point is serious Yokelville. This guy could get himself hauled off to the pokey without much effort. Offering a perfectly normal African bribe would do it. Shouting at police officers in a perfectly normal African tone of voice might do it. Sheesh. I got off the bus.

I walked over to the man, who was now fuming alone.

"Bad travel day?"

"Bad? It is Terrible! Terrible! A nightmare," he said, in the Queen's English with a very thick, north-central African accent. Kenya or Uganda, I thought. Ugandan by the look of him.

"Could be worse." said I.

"How? How could it be worse than this – You do not know any-thing!"

"It could be Addis Ababa at midnight."

He stopped, stared at me.

"What did you say?"

"You know, when they take your passport and you stand in line for hours to try and get a bed in a hotel ten miles from the airport, and they only have one visa clerk for 600 people."

"YOU – YOU have BEEN there!" I had his attention now.

And I asked him what was so bad today. Turns out that on the other bus were some young hoodlums he had seen at Sacramento. They had attempted to cut into his line. They had tried some cul-turally appropriate California young black guy banter. He had not let them cut. They had cussed him out. Called him a homosexual. Said something that implied that gays should be killed. He had thought he had avoided them, and then here they were in Oregon, and they said something to him again.

Turns out he *was* Ugandan. Survived the Lord's Resistance Army as a boy. Working now for a British petrol outfit. He had been flying to Alaska via Seattle and got dropped in Oakland. His com-pany, in its wisdom, put him on the bus.

Of course, he believed that these young men were planning to murder him – why else would they say so? They hurled the worst insults known to man. And he believed that they were armed and he was not. He had walked into the Truck Stop and called 911 and reported attempted murder in progress on the Greyhound bus. The police seemed corrupt because they acted as if they could not understand what he was saying in perfect English, although they themselves talked very funny. And he did not know where he was, and did not know what to do.

He agreed to accept my help. So I translated, African Queen's En-glish to Oregon Yokel English. And it was agreed that the officers would check the young men for weapons, and that we would get on our bus and that our driver would not allow them on our bus or park next to them again, and that we would all be peaceable and go on our way.

The Central Point PD was glad to declare it an internal Greyhound matter. Our driver was relieved to go on. The Ugandan felt listened to and accepted my assurances that we would be safe. And when we were all on, I changed places and sat with him, and said,

"Can I tell you a story?"

He agreed, and I continued,

"Let me tell you the tale of my bus trip from Buja to Goma."

And he laughed at all the right places, and was amazed at all the right places, and eventually took a nice nap.

When I got off at Salem with fifteen minutes to spare until Christmas Eve service, I said,

"May you reach successfully"

And he said "Salama" which is, in the Kiswahili – "Peace" – and the name of my home town.

In the Hands of the TSA

I was at Midway, coming home from a great ministry gig. I had been in the land of my mother's people, and it had been a time of deep personal connection as well as good work. I was heading home happy.

I prefer the lesser of the two Chicago airfields. I usually get in and out quickly and can take back streets to my brother's house. It was a Sunday morning, and everything was light and smooth. The rental car and the big bag had checked in easily, and I was early going through TSA.

Because of the emotional tethers of the week, I had more family heirlooms on my person than I would normally carry. In my little shoulder bag I had my Grandfather Hubbell's preaching Bible. It is seven decades old now, and the onionskin pages are loose from their binding, but the worn leather feels like unction in my hands. It goes out rarely, and only for good reasons. I wrap it loosely in fabric to travel, and I never let it out of my sight. I also had my Grandmother Hubbell's diamond lavalier. It was the only diamond the woman ever owned; it is tiny, and the setting is fragile. I had worn one and carried the other on a visit to their graves, and to ground me while preaching.

Just for balance, I had the silver and mother-of-pearl cross that my grandmother Senger was given on her honeymoon in 1905 – she was a Chicagoan for much of her life. I usually wear it, but not when going through TSA.

To add to the breakables, there was a brand new coffee cup that I had found while God was telling me a joke during my stay. And there was an antique Japanese fan that delighted me. I am no dummy, so the mother-of-pearl pocketknife that was my father's last gift to me was in the big bag with my liquids. I was personally metal-free, and I expected to breeze through the checkpoint. I am an expert at hopping in and out of my cowboy boots.

I carefully positioned my little bag on the conveyor, de-shoed, and made the "I surrender" gesture for the back-scatter device. I came through and reached for my boots and bag. Then I noticed the confab at the X-ray screen. The screener had called in a second. They conferred and looked me over – I smiled a cheerful smile. The older man with the blue gloves picked up my bag and waved me over to the special look-see table. He was wearing the TSA regulation frowny face. Wordlessly, he started to go through the bag. I had the regulation case of sudden nerves, and babbled.

"So, I can't imagine what looks hinkey in there. I'm a seasoned traveler. Put all the metals and liquids in the checked bag. I know I'm not allowed to help with this, but if you could tell me what you were looking for, maybe I can give you a clue..."

He pulled out the make-up bag and opened it with a bit of disdain, seeming to say, "I don't really like pawing through ladies' personal things." He looked at me. He acted like he thought we were wasting our time. He found some bobby pins – he sighed. "Probably these pins here..." he began.

Then his eyebrows went up, and he gave me a look. With two pincher fingers he lifted out the knife. Daddy's knife. The one I was sure was in the big bag.

"Oh, rats! That's not supposed to be in there..."

"No, ma'am, it's not."

"Crud, that's precious to me. That is the last thing that my late daddy gave to me. – Aw, man, what are my options here?"

"You surrender the knife and go on. Or you have me put the knife back in the bag and I walk you back to the airline and the bag gets checked."

"Can I take some things out and carry them in my in hands?"

"Nope – the bag is mine, or the knife is mine. You watch me carry it out, but it doesn't go back in your hands."

"This is scary! You're asking me to give up that precious thing or risk a bunch of other precious, fragile things to the handlers. I don't think I have the courage to check that bag." I was thinking about the destruction of the preaching Bible, and I was about to let the knife go. Grandparents before parents. My heart was pounding. I'll bet my eyes were a little wild.

And then Mr. TSA lowered his voice, leaned closer, looked me in the eye, and said, in a sudden baritone profundo:

"Daughter, the opposite of fear is not courage. It is trust. How much trust do you have today?" And the whole area got kinda fuzzy in my peripheral vision, and I froze as those words echoed in my soul.

The opposite of fear is not courage – it is trust.

I said, "That's not a regulation TSA bulletin, is it?"

He smiled at me.

"Trust" I said, "I'll go with Trust."

"Good Choice." And he put my knife back carefully in my makeup bag and walked me back to the airline, and he got to go to the front of that line and give the bag to the agent, who checked it in.

Myths

If you could see the Earth illuminated when you were in a place as dark as night, it would look to you more splendid than the Moon.

—Galileo Galilei, *Dialogue Concerning the Two Chief World Systems*, 1632

If somebody'd said before the flight, "Are you going to get carried away looking at the Earth from the Moon?" I would have said, "No, no way." But yet when I first looked back at the Earth, standing on the Moon, I cried.

—Alan Shepard

Five hundred and thirty-three people have been in Earth orbit. Twenty-four have gone beyond Earth orbit. Twelve have walked on the moon. Turns out old Galileo was right: the earth is round, and she is a beauty. Also, it turns out that the moon is not made out of green cheese and that the dark side is just like the light. One of the most important tasks of far explorers is to refute some commonly held notions. The Earth's atmosphere, the vast heavens above our heads, is fragile and wafer-thin, and it scares everyone who looks at it to see how alone and vulnerable we are. Boundaries of countries can't be seen from space. Every human who has gone up there has come home with a new attitude.

The scenery was very beautiful. But I did not see the Great Wall.

—Yang Liwei, China's first astronaut, 15 October 2003

You develop an instant global consciousness, a people orientation, an intense dissatisfaction with the state of the world, and a compulsion to do something about it. From out there on the Moon, international politics look so petty. You want to grab a politician by the scruff of the neck and drag him a quarter of a million miles out and say, "Look at that, you son of a bitch."

— Edgar Mitchell, Apollo 14 astronaut,
People magazine, 8 April 1974

Mapping out the extremities of God's love, seeing things as they are, and could be, makes a person impassioned. Your patience for lies and stupidities evaporates. You want to shout things. You want to shake people. Because you have been shaken.

The Myth of Isolation

Lying in my childhood bed, listening to the sound of silence, I was terrified. I awoke with the sense that something was very, very wrong. The light was wrong. It was way too late in the morning for me to be in bed on a school day. The normal sounds of our household were absent. The teakettle had not whistled: that was the sound that usually ended my dreams. The sound of my parents sitting at the kitchen table reading the scripture and praying for each of us children by name had not occurred – that was my normal, ten-minute warning for getting up. I listened carefully; there was not a sound in the house. Then I listened for the sounds of the city. I was, after all, in Chicago – there were millions of people out there. But the whole world had gone silent. There were no cars or trucks rumbling down Harlem Avenue, a block away. There were no sounds from the neighbors. There were no airplanes in the sky. A city of millions was still.

I came swiftly to the only conclusion that a child of Evangelical dispensationalists could come to. Jesus had come like a thief in the night and had taken away every good person from the world, and I was alone in my family, un-raptured. I was scared but not really surprised. I wasn't all that good of a kid. But then I thought about it some more and wondered if my little brother might not still be sleeping in his bed. He was kind of a pain in the neck; he might still be here. I thought about how a couple of kids might try to survive the Apocalypse. I knew we were in for at least seven years of tribulation. I wondered if I could forge a note that would let me get the folks' money out of the bank before it was too late. I wondered if we could get to our cousins – those people were Elvis worshippers and had just found out how wrong they were – but it seemed like taking up with heathens might be a bad idea just at the moment. I eventually decided to go and see if my brother was present. I left my room and saw the silent, empty kitchen. The clock confirmed that it was past time to leave for school. No doubt now. I crept into the living room and, to my utter shock and amazement, there sat my dad. He was looking out the window at the two feet of snow that had fallen unexpectedly in the night. No work, no school today. No trucks, no airplanes. A city silenced by God, but not robbed by God. I crawled into my dad's lap and breathed in the relief of the pardoned sinner. I was not alone.

The fear of being alone, temporarily or permanently, is not just an irrational fear of religious children. The fear of being alone is one of the most pervasive and destructive fears in our world. It touches almost everyone, eventually. It causes suicides. It fuels addictions. It provokes people into crazy behaviors that increase rather than decrease their chances of loneliness. And it is a groundless fear. Because true isolation is a myth, an urban legend, an impossibility.

Every major religion teaches this. Christendom in its right mind teaches this. Jesus said, "I will never leave you or forsake you, not until the end of time." The Apostle told us that we are surrounded by a host of witnesses cheering us on to finish our footrace. Angels manifest at the oddest moments, speaking the inevitable "Fear not."

Science teaches this. We really are all connected. The wings of a butterfly can start a hurricane. There are resonances between particles at a distance.

The mistake comes when we try to use feelings to predict fact. Now, I am all for feelings. Get the full 96-crayon box of them and use them as often as you can; but as predictors of fact, they are notoriously fallible. Sometimes we feel lonely. This is the feeling that defines a craving for more or better relationships. It hurts. It is supposed to. But if we sit in the lonely feeling and use it to predict an isolated future, and let that fear escalate, we will do nutty things. We will forsake our integrity. We will medicate our loneliness. We will attempt to latch onto anything that seems to offer relief.

Loneliness is a feeling given to us by God to cause us to seek community. You may be unlucky in love, but community does not rely on luck. It relies on initiative. You have to get outside of yourself and your feelings and do something to connect. You have to give, and be vulnerable enough to let others give to you. It is hard work, but it works every time.

You commune with the past by living up to the investment that those who have loved you have made in you, and listening for their cheers from the stands. You commune with the future by investing in others, and by tilling the soil and planting the seeds that will feed and shade those who will come after you. You live in anticipation of their gratitude, knowing that you will take your place in the spiritual mezzanine to watch their performances. You choose, by will, to live in the truth that you are a valued piece of a great company of saints. You take responsibility for your feelings and your life.

The fear-mongers of this world and of the spiritual realm would like you to live in the fear of isolation. They want you to predict, and then live in, the lie that you are likely to end up alone and scared. This will prevent you from making those healthy connections with the past, present, and future that foil the fear-based plans they have for controlling your present.

Let us reject this lie. We are not alone. We were not born alone. We were not alone before we were born, we will not be alone in our lives or our deaths, and we will not be alone after our deaths. God is as close as your breath. The saints are as close as the ear of your soul. Community is as close as your outstretched hand.

The Myth of Centrality

Who am I to judge?

—Pope Francis

If there was ever a job description that included judginess as a core competency, I would think that Pope would be it. The founding principle of the job is, *I'm outta here – I'm leaving you the keys – what you keep will be kept, and what you let go of won't matter, in this world or the next – try not to blow it.* Sure, Supreme Court Justice might be similar – but they only get to be judgy about one country in one world. Small potatoes compared to the Pope.

Pope Francis may be just another old, white privileged guy in privileged white clothes in a privileged town, but we love him for the things he gets right. Like the fact that it is not all just about him. I loved it when the quizzer tried to trap him with a question about an obvious sinner. They tried to trap his boss with the same question a couple of millennia ago. Neither of them took the bait. Shortly thereafter, Pope Frankie started firing people. Loved that, too. The job description does include the occasional table tipping and swinging of whips.

I think the real wisdom here is not the part where you judge or don't judge; the wisdom is in the first part, in the *Who am I?* You may be the ace up God's sleeve, but any shark has four aces, and God has as many suits as the stars. God is not running out of Popes any time soon. Quakers like to say that we didn't get rid of the clergy; we got rid of the laity. Everyone a priest – nobody a Pope. Anyone can give the holy food. Anyone can absolve a sin and make it disappear forever. Couples can marry themselves to each other, and baptism can happen in the car during a bad commute – all it takes is the willingness to surrender and drown in God's love.

Frances Albert Sinatra liked to sing, "It had to be you..." That is one of those great dysfunctional mopey love songs, the premise of which is that there is only one love out there for you and you have to find that love or be lost. I think that I am standing on really safe ground to say that God never has, and does not now, sing from Frankie's songbook – and not just because of the Mob thing and the "My Way" nonsense.

When I was a kid, I was taught that I had to be ready to talk to anyone about God at any moment. They loved to say, "You may be the only Christ they ever meet." So, basically, if I didn't do my job and the person landed in H E double-hockey-sticks, then it was my fault. They told me this from about third grade on. This is Sinatra Gospel, not Jesus Gospel. (Ironically, my people hated Sinatra.) Fortunately, that was also a serious lie, or at least a stupid mistake. No human is ever the only Christ anywhere. They forgot their own book which says, "The Light – which is Christ – is in everyone who ever came into the world." (John, the groovy disciple – the first words.)

So when I figured out that lie, I decided that what I was really supposed to do was to be the hands and feet of Jesus all the time. Christ in me, recognizing, serving, and encouraging the Christ in you. Helping, feeding, clothing, opening the church doors, cleaning the church toilets, whatever, whenever. Man, did that get exhausting.

Then I found out it was okay to say no, or not right now, to God. Because when I walk around the world awake to need, seeing with God's eyes, all I see is need. And sometimes it is really needy need. Occasionally, the pull to do something is strong, and I am strong, and I am the best thing God has going at that moment at that place, and I can do something. But I am never the only thing that God has going, and rarely the best. If sometimes the need is great, but I am not carrying what I need to give what is needed, it's all right if I step aside for a moment. The Presence says, "S'okay. I got this."

Today I saw a very drunken man trying to cross five lanes of crazy traffic in a major wind storm. He was staggering before the gusts started. I thought he was gonna die. Part of me wanted to stop traffic and get him across the road, and I probably could have done it. But I didn't. I made sure I didn't hit him, and then I drove on, saying a prayer for drunks everywhere.

Because it didn't have to be me.

The Myth of the Emo-Link

Sometimes I invite attack. Before me was a group of teenagers. Kids who had been expelled or had dropped out from the local high school. Tough boys, a few pregnant girls. I was the guest speaker at a mandatory lecture at the alternative school.

My job was to leave them some tools to deal with abusive relationships. I have done this a hundred times in the last dozen years. It was a topic these kids knew as well as I did – probably better. They just hadn't found any solutions yet.

I always start with prediction and choices. If you can see what is coming next, you can sometimes step out of the way. This works, and it is usually where they are at. Victims or perps – and I always have both in the room – know what happens, but they lack models for dealing with it. They think victim and perp are the only two choices. So I give them other choices.

However, making new choices is still a form of reaction, not pro-action or prevention, so that is why, if I have time, I always do a little exercise that spins their heads. I demonstrate, and so expose them to, the virus of invincibility.

It goes like this.

I start at the place in the talk where I explain that one of the predictors of an abuser is that they blame other people for their feelings and behaviors. And then I appear to take a little tangent.

"You know kids, nobody can 'make you' feel anything. You do know that, right?" (They look confused.)

"No, seriously," I say, "You can be, if you choose, in control of your feelings. Nobody can make you angry; nobody can make you sad, unless you want to be."

They scoff, and without fail, one of them says, "My parents make me angry," or even better, "I can make people angry" Oh, how I love that one.

"Really, son? You have that power – you can make people angry – just with your words?"

"Yep"

"Okay," I say, acting surprised. "Let's try a little experiment."

I make an amnesty deal where the young man will be allowed to use any words he likes, even the ones that get you detention, even the ones that get you expelled, for the length of the experiment. The room fills with tension. I have their undivided attention now – and they are rooting for their peer.

"Okay, son. The feeling is 'angry.' You have one minute to say anything you like to me – *anything* – and try to make me feel the feeling 'angry.' I promise to be entirely truthful about what I feel. Go."

Now we find out how much nerve the young man really has. Some just bail right there. But many make a valiant effort. This boy did. He took a moment for observation and then went for what he thought was the weak spot of every female – looks. He detailed my physical imperfections. Not as brutally as he might, because I was standing as he sat, and slowly moving in closer, and staring him straight in the eyes with a smile on my face, and this was starting to unnerve him. But oh, how he tried.

"One minute up."

I reported on my feelings.

"I am feeling slightly amused, and proud of you, young man. You showed courage, you gave it a good try. You didn't flinch. I respect that. I like you. I am not, however, in the least bit angry."

Then I ask the class if they can figure out why he failed. They are smart. They begin with things like, "You had time to get ready," "You knew what was coming," "You set the thing up," but they eventually come around to, "You didn't want to be angry. You made up your mind that you weren't going to get angry."

"Bingo!" – It is one of the things that separates you and me from the critters. Kick the dog, and he is going to snarl or cower – perp or victim. But you and I have other choices. I have been practicing, and I have gotten pretty good at picking what I am going to feel. At least when I am ready for it. At that point, about two out of ten think an entirely new thought – and the virus has taken.

I call this problem the Myth of Emotional Cause and Effect – or Emo-Link. It is the mistaken idea that there is a mechanical linkage between other people's words and behaviors and our feelings, and then our own words and behaviors.

The tyranny of this myth is all around us. It is the thinking behind the notion of a 'crime of passion.' It ends relationships. It enslaves people. It starts wars. The applications are legion:

I cannot control my lust, so you Madame, need to cover up better.

I was afraid, so of course I had to lie.

He hurt me, so I had to hurt him back. I had no choice.

He cheated – I was so devastated, I just had to drink.

He/She/They were asking for it.

The lie is that there is a hard connection between the external world and your feelings. The truth is that there are default settings, and something like emotional cruise control, but that we can take our emotions off cruise anytime we want. This set up is necessary, it is smart, and it is God-designed. I mean really, it would be too much work to have to think it out every time. "Now, hmmm, what feeling shall I use here? – I have so many to choose from." It is efficient to have some default settings where certain feelings pop up in certain settings.

But default settings are set in childhood, and so many of our childhoods were severely faulty. The people who raised us didn't have much range, so we fall back on some pretty simple, often reptilian responses. Or they had all their wires crossed and then so do we. Or they had no governors on their motors and every little thing was *huge*. So we over-react.

If we are lucky, as adults we get the chance to learn how to reset our buttons. This is called healthy detachment. Buddhists tend to be much better at it than most Christians. We really should invite those folks over more often. They have this notion that you can do pain without suffering. The idea is that you can notice your pain, be honest about it, treat it if need be, but not make a federal case out of it. Spare the angst. Disengage the drama clutch and leave it in neutral for a minute while you decide what to do. Just because people are offensive does not mean that I have to be offended. What a time-saver – that one is.

Booker T. Washington got it; he said, "I permit no man to narrow and degrade my soul by making me hate him."

It is Yoda, not the Three Stooges.
It works. It is efficient. It is anything but boring.

I recommend it to your attention.

The Myth of Irrelevancy

She killed herself at the time of our usual Wednesday appointment. After a year's hard work. She killed herself because I took a week off for my daughter's wedding. Apparently I didn't love her enough. At least that is what the note said.

He came for Spiritual Direction. I was thinking I would impart God's grace. After some honest questions and honest responses, I ended up midwife to the birth of his atheism.

"You, I had hopes for..." the old woman said, tears in her eyes. As I walked away from her church, her project, her mentoring, her hopes for me.

I was once, briefly, the mother of a nation and the hero of a revolution. There were courageous, grown men who would have followed me into battle without a second thought. We made peace instead. One severely bad actor was removed.... Three sprung up in his place.

The little church, my best effort, my greatest contribution to the conversation, may not survive my lack of energy to sustain it. It is Christ's very own commanded project. They will say that it was mine, and that I failed.

There are so many more. They line up at night at the foot of my bed to wish me goodnight with a litany of failure. They say I made no difference. They say I made things worse. I cannot call them liars. Like the grass, I sprang up lively, and grew, and dried, and burned. Ashes to ashes, dust to dust.

But – picking at the boils that each accusation has laid upon my skin – I whisper one thing: "I know that my Redeemer lives." And this is what THAT ONE says:

> When my words come out of MY mouth, and when MY words come out of your mouth, when I act through you, nothing is wasted. The ground we work will prosper. When you leave you will leave happy, and your heart will be at peace, for you shall see things as they are. The mountains are singing back-up and the forests are giving you a standing ovation. What looks like seas of blackberry brambles will turn out to be as solid as old-growth fir. I will take your work and words as MY NAME, and it will last forever, impossible to cut off or destroy. (Isaiah 55)

THAT ONE will take my words and my work (and your words and your work) as a HOLY NAME. For all the filth and blood that we as Christians have heaped upon the name of Christ, it turns out that the naming goes the both ways. And that HOLY NAME will be a long one, for it will contain every true act and every true word and every true love ever embodied with hand or breath by a human creature. Indeed, it will be the filth and blood that turn out to be ephemeral, temporal, unsustainable, and the Love that appeared to fail will turn out to be a metal with no half-life at all.

How dare we think ourselves irrelevant? How dare we, while we can still whisper faith, and breathe love, and put our hand out to do the simplest kindness? How dare we accept the Devil's own picture frame of time and numbers and resumes? Why do even look at the critics' reviews in the morning papers? Why do we let them steal the truth and glory of the stage?

And even if we become the critics, and line up at the foot of one another's beds to refute and refuse – or if we sew our mouths shut and shackle our hands and put out our own eyes – are we not still relevant? For our silence and our absence is as eternal as our work. Do we not then shorten the NAME OF GOD?

Not necessarily. Blind and shackled and dumb, we are still Samson. And we can pull down the drinking hall of Babylon.

The Myth of Scarcity

Thirty years ago, I was great with child. I was awaiting the birth of my second, and what would turn out to be my last, child. I was 28, and we had an almost five-year-old daughter named Emily. Five years of undiluted parental devotion had allowed this child to become confident, precocious, and fun to be around. We were confident of our parenting skills. I was not worried about birthing this new life. My husband had gotten a decent job with health benefits just in the nick of time. It seemed that all was well.

Nevertheless, I was terrified. It was a fear that I did not think I could say out loud. I did not know that anyone else had ever had this fear.

I was afraid that it was impossible to love another child as much as I loved Emily.

Then Laura Joy Parsons arrived. I took one look at her and my maternal love instantaneously and miraculously doubled – just like that. Emily suffered no loss of love. Laura received all that a baby needed.

I have since found out that this is a very common fear of second-time parents, but rarely a fear of third-time parents. It is a miracle that sticks.

However, I think that it is an example of a larger and more pervasive fear-based belief system – the myth of scarcity. This myth says that there is never enough of anything to go around, and you'd better get yours while you can and hoard it as long as you are able. This toxic belief creeps into every area of human existence and relationship. It shapes government policy, haunts people's dreams, and fuels competition in every arena. It says, "There is not enough love, money, happiness, fame, health, time, space, work ... for everybody – so protect what you have and watch out for those other guys." It is the absolute proximate cause of all jealousy, envy, and most strife. It is the ranchers vs. the farmers. It is old immigrants vs. new immigrants. And it is absolutely, refutably, experientially *false*.

Three examples: resources, time, and love.

There are enough resources in this world. Sure, we will run out of oil at some point. But until old Sol quits on us eons and eons from now, there will be sources of energy; sun, wind, tides, hydrogen, fusion, etc. We will figure it out. There is enough food in this world – there is no excuse for a hungry child anywhere. There is enough work to do in this world. The reason that some do not have enough, and hear me – children in much of the world are truly deprived – is not because there is not enough to go around, it is because what there is has been criminally distributed and shamefully wasted. Communism is an attempt to address this criminal distribution. It has failed, not because it is a bad idea, but because the implementers – time after time – have been seduced by criminal greed. Capitalism says that if you rely on individual initiative and a free market, the distribution will be corrected by opportunity and philanthropy. Capitalism has also failed because its implementers have been seduced by criminal greed. And criminal greed is almost always based in the myth of scarcity.

We hoard because we fear.

Hoarding is not God's way. The Hebrew children in the desert were given one day's manna in the desert each morning – the stuff rotted if you tried to keep it overnight (except on the Sabbath when you could keep two days worth.) Jesus prayed for "daily bread," reinforcing this concept again and again. Don't worry about next week's bread: trust, and work, and it will come. God's way is to use what you need and share anything extra with someone else. There is enough.

One of the most nefarious incursions of the myth of scarcity into most of our lives is the belief that there is not enough time. That life itself is too short. We run at a frenetic pace and wail at the lack of the 25th hour and the eighth day. This belief rules many a life and ruins the quality of life. It is impossible to simultaneously savor and rush something.

The truth is that time is darn near infinite, at least from our perspective. Almost every faith teaches that you, or at least some part of you, *is* infinite, immortal. There is something else after this. We don't know or agree on what that something is, but most of us believe in it. And since this life includes the possibility of quality and meaning, there is no reason to believe that the something out there will not be at least as productive and meaningful. Our sensation of rushing time comes from bodies that age, and our propensity to chop time up into tiny bits, so that they seem to fly by.

What we do not have is the ability to do two things at once in any really qualitative fashion – this from a woman who can multi-task with the best of them. The truth is, I don't drive as well when using the phone, and drinking coffee, and listening to music. I don't pay as close attention to my loved ones when I am preoccupied. I do not have infinite choices. I have many choices, but I must choose how to spend my time. The responsibility flipside to the freedom of this choice is that I need to relax about the things that I do not choose and trust that the universe will take care of them. When I do this – when I concentrate on one good choice at a time, when I trust – then time slows down. I savor things, enjoy them, and remember them better too. There is enough time to do everything that I really need to do – because I do not need to do everything. I'm just not that important.

The most relationship-wrecking, and hence human-wrecking, application of the myth of scarcity is that there is not enough love to go around. We believe that if the object of our desire does not love us that no one ever will, so we get pathetic or controlling. We believe that our friend shouldn't really have other friends because that will in some way impoverish us. We believe that God is a worse parent than we are, and cannot love all of us equally. We buy into the lie that God has favorites – us, if we are arrogant in our fear – or them, if we are victimized in our fear.

The truth is that love is the most obviously infinite resource in this reality. It is renewable. It is multiplicative. It easily trumps death. People who lose a loved one grieve, but do not lose their capacity to love. Mothers and fathers love each of their children completely without robbing the others. If we believe that love is unlimited and time is unlimited, then there is no reason for jealousy. We are given these miracles to teach us about the truth of God's love. God's love is infinite, and so is ours if we let it be. There is enough.

The Myth of the Narrow Will of God

It was a perfectly curved road. It was a beautiful morning somewhere in upper eastern Oregon. I was riding with a good friend. Walt was riding sweep on his Beemer; Rosie and I were up front, slicing the curves. I was singing. It could not have been more perfect. And then the road straightened out, and at a wide spot, Walt put on his blinkers and signaled me to pull off.

I executed the stop and wondered what was wrong. Beemers don't really have problems, and Walt could usually ride me into the pavement. He stopped and whipped his helmet off and sort of charged me. I could see that he was white-hot mad. I had no idea why.

"You've got two choices here, Peg, and one minute to choose. Either you cut a safer line through the curves, or I am turning around and you can find your own way home. Because there is no way that I am going to follow you around one of these blind curves and watch you go splat on the front of a log truck. There is no way I am going to call your people at home and tell them that you are road kill. You can ride right, or you can ride alone!"

Walt is a gentle man, and I had never seen or heard him angry before. He was my daughter's guitar teacher, and he had been investing in her weekly for years. He darn near raised her with me. He was my safest long-haul riding buddy. We liked to do a longest day of the year – longest ride of the year run. I thought about what he has just said. I thought about arguing, or excusing, or joking, but I didn't think for long.

"God, Walt. I'm sorry. I wasn't thinking about the risk, and I was risking everything. You are right. I will do better."

Because on motorcycles, there is a correct line. And it is narrow. If you can see clearly through the curve, you can slice it and cross the yellow to make the way straight. If you cannot see through the curve you stay away from the yellow, and you take the right-hand way and watch for that log truck coming around, because he may be slicing into your lane. We had been riding blind curves, and my tires had touched way too much yellow.

Some people think that the will of God is like a motorcycle line. It is narrow, it is discernable, and if you slide off of it to the right or the left you are doomed. Much prayer and fasting and waiting is done to discern the 'just right' choice. What college should I go to? Should I marry him? Should I take this job, go on this mission, have another child? So much anxiety, so much fear. And when the answer doesn't seem clear, often there is paralysis, or terror of making the wrong choice.

I took a 15-year-old African girl shopping at Macy's once. I told her she could have any dress she wanted. She could not choose. She eventually broke down in tears, because it seemed such a momentous choice to her. It seemed to her that she would never again be given such an opportunity, and she was afraid she might choose the wrong dress; she feared regret. It was cruel of me. I should have chosen a dress or two and presented them to her. She would have loved any one of them; all of them were better than any she had ever owned. But I wanted her to feel the power, the thrill of choosing. Which is great – if there is no consequence to the choice. Which is great, if you believe there will be other choices. But if you believe that God is watching as you choose, and that the wrong choice leads to misery now and perdition later, then the choice is torture.

God does not work this way. God is not a Mack truck coming around the bend if you slip a little off course. God is not a giver of gifts who gives only once. Opportunity does not come knocking only once at your door. Opportunity is there right outside your doorstep every single morning of the week. This is what God said to a guy named Micah, who was all wrapped in knots.

"This is the only thing I ask; be fair, cut people slack and love doing it, and then bring an open heart and come walk with me."

God's only will is that you walk in an awareness of God. God will go with you to any college, any job, any calling. God will love who you love and try to help you love them better. When you mess up, God will be with you in that and walk you out of it. When you sin, God will be very close, whispering to you about better choices. God wants to dance with you. You can let God lead, but then you have to be finely attuned to the gentle nudges of direction. God is also happy to let you lead. God likes being Fred Astaire, and also gets a kick from being Ginger Rogers – backwards in high heels. And if that is just a little too close for you, God will do-si-do, or clog somewhere in your vicinity. God wants to have any relationship you are willing to have. God's mercy and resources renew every morning.

God doesn't worry about you like my friend Walt worried about me, and God doesn't get mad. Because God knows there is no truck around the bend.

The Myth of the Apocalypse

Dear Lord Jesus, preacher said you are coming real soon.
Now would be a good time.

—The pre-math test prayer of all Evangelical children

Like all children raised under the apocalyptic cloud of Dispensationalism, I spent a great deal of my childhood alternately fearing and hoping for the end of the world. I was a bad child raised by good parents, so the Rapture was particularly troubling, as I knew they would go and I would not.

Later in life, I turned the fear into a standard Chicago-based joke. "People say that no one can predict when the Lord will return. This is not quite true: I know exactly the place and quite a bit about the timing. It will be at Wrigley Field. The Cubbies will be about to win it all – top of the ninth, two outs, two strikes against the batter. Then the trump will sound, and Jesus Christ will land on second base. Because the Universe cannot allow the Cubs to win the World Series."

Further on in my career as a semi-pro religionist, I discovered the Apocalypse rooters. These folks bill themselves as proponents of glory. In my experience, they are often a bitter and shrinking remnant of a narrow theology of judgment. When they see that the world is not only failing to embrace their world-view but rapidly leaving it in the dust, they hunker down into an attitude:

"Just you wait and see. Jesus is going to return, and *then* you will find out how wrong you are!" Sometimes they pine so much for Armageddon that they actually do things to try to make it come. They say "Come Lord Jesus!" but what they mean is, "Come and prove me right!"

Then I discovered that Christians do not have a lock on Apocalypse-rooting. I have met environmentalists so frustrated that they were rooting for Peak Oil or Global Warming or some other enormous disaster to prove them right, to the dismay and destruction of the deniers. Their Fundamental judgment and ire can match any fire-and-brimstone preacher. They predict and pray for a new heaven and a new Earth, where the remnant will survive and return to the imagined peaceful, joyful, agrarian ways of a past that never existed.

What the world-enders all miss is the fact that apocalypses are as common as dirt. When Jesus wept over Jerusalem and predicted its doom, He wasn't even being especially prophetic. Anyone with eyes could see *that* Roman train wreck coming. Foreseeing the apocalypse of Jerusalem wasn't exactly hard.

Homo sapiens seem to be good at wiping things out. Met a Neanderthal recently? A Javan tiger? A West African black rhino? A member the Yuki Tribe in California? We have seen the Rwandan apocalypse; our parents saw the Nazi apocalypse. Maybe we learned this from Mother Nature – she did a pretty good job on the dinosaurs. Name an epoch, century, or continent that is apocalypse-free. Can't.

The other thing that the doom-sayers miss is that life so often finds a way through. Have you ever witnessed a personal apocalypse – that of a serious addict who completely flames out, then finds recovery, sobriety, and life? I have; it is a glorious thing. Flattened cities build on the rubble. Ozzy Osbourne is walking around today with Neanderthal DNA. We are told that the birds we feed in the park are descendants of dinosaurs. Destroyed matter turns to energy and back again. Stars and planets die and are born again. On some cosmic level, nothing is lost. God built this into the universe so we would understand, and have hope. Hope even beyond death.

Existence is hard. It is so tempting when facing the apocalyptic to pray for escape, to pray for the judgment of the stupid and mean. We all do it. But this isn't Life's way. Life works through the stupid and the mean (including you and I) to find a way forward. There is no escape from the tribulations of the hard work of progress.

Quakers have made a theological suggestion about this: the idea of Christ, come and coming. I believe that Jesus of Nazareth was The Christ. But you do not have to believe that to see the Christ spirit in Him. The Christ spirit is simply Love, given place and breath. This Spirit pops up everywhere, often in the most unlikely places. It is most crystalline and transcendent in the ugliest of surroundings. This Spirit is so strong that it cannot be put down. It is so pervasive that it permeates all that is. The Anti-Christ is the futile attempt to kill Love. We all have the choice to express Christ or anti-Christ with every breath and every deed. When we cooperate with Christ and express that Spirit, we incarnate it. Again. Perpetual Christmas Day. There is and will be no second coming of Christ. What there is and will be are the infinite comings of Christ.

I hear the dread hoof beats of horsemen as often as I am tempted to sin. I find Jesus at my side, sliding off his white charger as often as I need Him. Together we root out the anti-Christ in my soul and then move the lines forward. I find Christ everywhere. I take the process of Christ-finding as far afield as I can, to the places and people that the fear-peddlers judge. I hear the trumpet sound a dozen times a day. Daring me to explore the depths of the Divine. Challenging me to make God real to the very edges of my world.

Calling me to glory.

Epilogue

I'm coming back in... and it's the saddest moment of my life.

—Ed White expresses his sorrow at the conclusion of the first American spacewalk during the Gemini 4 mission, June 3, 1965.

Gratitudes

Every explorer needs backers. It amazes me how many people have invested in me: time, energy, expertise, belief and love. My whole life, blood relations and total strangers have encouraged me, made space for me, and asked how they could help. It can't be about me – can't be.

It isn't possible to name them all. But a good crew had something to do with this particular work. Larry Moffitt did the first edits on the UPI columns. Against his better judgment he let me know that my procrastination was sometimes a sign of unction. William Ashworth believed in this book from the get go. When a great writer likes your book, it helps. When a great writer offers to edit you; you say yes, please. Working with him on the organization was a Spirit-greased delight.

Marge Abbott and Pam Calvert believe in some version of me that I keep trying to live up to – do other people have bffs they almost never see? William Zuelke is my soul's resort; he named my charism and gave this book a theme – Matteo Ricci is standing in this book for him. Eric Gentry made me a trauma healer, David Niyonzima gave me a place to do my practicum – not many girls get to do finishing school in a war zone.

Brandon Buerkle has brought beauty and form to my voice. Audrey caught the flaws. They both worked so very hard on this.

My daughters keep me grounded. My grand-daughter makes me aim for the stars.

Alivia is my living, breathing, unforgettable proof that God knows me, loves me, and knows what I need even when I have no clue.

I am abundantly supplied.

PSM
Salem, Oregon 2016

About the Author

Peggy Senger Morrison is a freelance provocateur of grace. She is a recorded Friends minister and was the founding pastor of Freedom Friends Church, Salem Oregon. A counselor for over 20 years, her major focus was trauma healing. Peggy is the author of Miracle Motors: A Pert Near True Story, a motorcycle theology. Peggy is presently ministering and working off her Karma in higher education, running community-college based, high school completion programs for super-marginalized youth. Twice a mother, once a grandmother, she is delighted to be married to the beautiful and talented Alivia Biko.

You may contact Peggy through Unction Press at unction.org

Also By Peggy Senger Morrison

Peggy was known as a storyteller from an early age – sometimes "a bit of a prevaricator" – so it stands to reason that a hooligan God set her on a path so full of the improbable that few would believe it. From a Holiness Women's Clergy convention in Texas, to an African war zone, this motorcycle-riding, Gospel-preaching, trauma healing Quaker in high heels and leathers takes you on a wild ride as she learns to navigate life on God's terms.

—Katharine Hyzy, editor,
Miracle Motors

The world is full of people who can write well but have nothing to say. Conversely, there are those who see what goes on but can't articulate it worth diddly. Peggy observes and describes life with clear eloquence. Unforced wisdom, useful and harvestable, abounds throughout. She comes with a few quirks acquired from having an extraordinary ability to really see people and the flaw of giving a crap about what happens to them.

—Lawrence Moffitt, Peggy's editor at Spirituality.com,
United Press International

Peggy calls it the Summa Theologica Motorcyclia of a Bisexual, Quaker, Motorcycling Preacher.

The text of this book is set in Grad, produced by Mark Simonson Studio. The headlines are set in Franklin Gothic URW Condensed, from URW++. Both typefaces are licensed through Adobe Typekit.

CPSIA information can be obtained
at www.ICGtesting.com
Printed in the USA
FSHW010745281018
53363FS